CW00557518

THE REFORM OF LOCAL GOVERNMENT FINANCE IN BRITAIN

The Reform of Local Government Finance in Britain

EDITED BY S.J. BAILEY AND R. PADDISON

ROUTLEDGE
London and New York

First published 1988
by Routledge
11 New Fetter Lane, London EC4P 4EE
29 West 35th Street, New York, NY 10001

Printed in Great Britain by
Billing & Sons Ltd, Worcester

British Library Cataloguing in Publication Data

The Reform of local government finance in
    Britain.
    1. Great Britain. Local government. Finance
    I. Bailey, S.J. (Stephen James), *1951–*
    II. Paddison, Ronan
    336'.014'41
    ISBN 0-415-00530-2

Library of Congress Cataloging-in-Publication Data
    ISBN 0-415-00530-2

CONTENTS

CONTRIBUTORS

Ken Young Institute of Local Government Studies, University of Birmingham, J.G. Smith Building, P.O. Box 363, Birmingham B15 2TT

Professor Peter G. Richards Red Lodge, Hadrian Way, Chilworth, Southampton SO1 7HZ

John Berridge Dept of Political Science and Social Policy, The University, Dundee DD1 4HN

Christopher Himsworth Faculty of Law, University of Edinburgh, Old College, South Bridge, Edinburgh EH8 9YL

Professor Tom Wilson Flat 1, Chatford House, The Promenade, Clifton Down, Bristol BS8 3NG

Clive Martlew Training and Development Manager, Glasgow District Council, 48 Albion Street, Glasgow

Professor Gordon Hughes Department of Economics, University of Edinburgh, William Robertson Building, 50 George Square, Edinburgh EH8 9JY

Professor Robert J. Bennett Department of Geography, London School of Economics and Political Science, Houghton Street, London WC2A 2AE

Richard Jackman Department of Economics, London School of Economics and Political Science, Houghton Street, London WC2A 2AE

Dr David King Department of Economics, University of Stirling, Stirling KF9 4LA

Steve Bailey Department of Economics, Glasgow College, Cowcaddens Road, Glasgow G4 0BA

Ronan Paddison Department of Geography, University of Glasgow, Glasgow G12 8QQ

PREFACE

This book of readings was compiled during the period between publication of the Green Paper 'Paying for Local Government' (Cmnd 9714) in January 1986 and the passage of the English and Welsh Community Charge (Poll Tax) Bill through Parliament during the first half of 1988. The Scottish Bill reached the statute book in May 1987.

Whilst the Scottish Bill had a fairly easy passage through Parliament that for England and Wales generated a particularly contentious debate centred on the lack of account taken of the ability to pay the tax. Despite a three-line whip, the Government's Commons majority of 101 was cut to 25 when the vote was taken on the Bill. It then received an equally rough ride through the House of Lords, where it secured a majority of 134 only after the Government secured an unusually high turnout of Tory Peers. (It was only the second time since 1831 that 500 Peers had turned out to vote).

The main parliamentary issue has now been resolved in the Government's favour and the community charge should be on the statute book before the end of July 1988. This book provides the reader with a balanced and comprehensive examination of the British Poll Tax system.

INTRODUCTION

During recent years the financing of local government has become a key policy issue in most developed countries. In general the problem is seen as one of ever-rising local expenditures creating intolerable fiscal pressures on the local tax base. This ultimately leads to fiscal crisis, often through a local taxpayer revolt. The widening resource gap is exacerbated by the simultaneous cuts in the real levels of intergovernmental transfers, namely grants paid by the upper tier of government to the lower tier of local government.

Such cuts are deemed necessary by the perceived needs of central government to reduce, or at least constrain the increases in, public expenditure. According to the broad 'supply-side' school of economic thought, it is held that excessive levels of public expenditure can impair the productive potential of the economy. This could occur, for example, whereby the growing public sector deprives the private sector of scarce productive resources and, in necessitating higher levels of taxation to pay for those resources, makes productive effort less rewarding. Hence growth of the economy is inhibited, ultimately to the disadvantage of society as a whole.

In tandem with this more narrow economic rationale for constraining public expenditure in general and local government spending in particular, the value of such expenditure has also been brought into question. For example, it is increasingly argued that central and local governments provide goods and services which are simply not highly valued by the recipients of those outputs. In part, this is of economic origin in that anything that is free at the point of use or consumption will be consumed until the value of the last unit received is zero. Hence it is argued there will be an inbuilt tendency to overproduce goods and services which are financed out of general tax revenues rather than from charges to consumers. Bureaucrats and politicians also have a vested interest in service expansion. More generally, it is also argued that individuals should be free to spend their own income as they wish rather than have it taxed and spent by supposedly profligate central and local governments.

Although still a matter open to dispute, the present British Government has accepted that the bulk of local government expenditures will continue to have to be financed from local taxation rather than from local user charges. This decision rests upon the conventional wisdom that local government services usually provide community-wide benefits which justify community financing or, alternatively, it would be grossly inequitable or inefficient to charge for those services which provide more exclusive benefits to recipients.

The inherent expansionary tendency of local government expenditure, the expectations of ever-rising spending on social service functions, the rising demands on service provision caused by demographic trends, the rising costs of producing public services and so on, all occurring simultaneously, increasingly bring into question the adequacy of the local resource base. Formerly, such adequacy was seen in terms of whether or not sufficient revenues would be forthcoming to finance expenditures and so ameliorate the looming local fiscal crisis. The local property tax has generally been seen as insufficiently elastic since it does not bring about an automatic increase in revenue in line with rising expenditures. The tax base (assessed value of properties) is usually fixed for years on end so that a purposive decision has to be made to increase the tax rate (called the rate poundage or mill rate). Increases in tax rates are politically unpopular and so there is an inbuilt tendency towards resource constraint.

It is these simultaneous and mutually reinforcing tendencies towards service expansion and fiscal starvation that create the revenue imbalance for local governments which depend, solely or primarily, on the local property tax. In the past, the solution in most developed countries has been to increase intergovernmental aid, widen the local resource base and, sometimes, to reduce the expenditure responsibilities of local governments by transferring functions to higher tiers. Currently in Britain, as elsewhere, the first of these three solutions is no longer seen as a long term primary solution to the current fiscal problem. The British Government has also decided, for the time being at least, not to reduce the present array of local service responsibilities. Hence the third solution is excluded. The policy emphasis therefore rests on the second of these solutions, namely the local resource base.

Whilst formerly the adequacy of the local rate was judged in terms of the revenues generated, the current nuance of 'adequacy' is no longer restricted simply to fiscal potential. In Britain such adequacy is now also judged in terms of the accountability of the local tax and expenditure decision process. The current British Conservative Government argues that the large discrepancy between the right to vote in local elections and the requirement to pay local taxes means that many people can vote for higher expenditure levels without having to bear the financial consequences. Hence the local property tax is inadequate in that there is no close match between ownership of property (and therefore liability to pay property tax) and eligibility to vote.

There are two mutually exclusive solutions to this mismatch. The first solution is to restrict the franchise to payers of the property tax. The second solution is to make eligibility to vote conditional upon payment of a local poll tax. Both solutions would be decried as anti-democratic and a reversal of the historic progression towards a fully democratic state. The solution adopted by the current British Conservative Government is a crude variation of the second alternative, namely the introduction of a per capita tax paid by all adult residents and which will completely replace the domestic property tax.

Since not all resident adults are eligible to vote in local elections (e.g. temporary foreign residents) the Government argues that the per capita tax is not a poll tax. In practice, however, the two are almost completely synonymous. Furthermore, the scale of tax relief for low income and other groups will be so limited as to match closely legal liability for and actual payment of the per capita tax. To all intents and purposes Britain will have a poll tax in operation during the 1990s.

Again, because the adequacy of local taxation is judged in terms of accountability, the British Government has ruled out supplementing the property tax (or even the per capita tax) with other local taxes such as local sales tax or local income tax. Britain will continue to have only one local tax, unlike almost all other developed countries. However, it will be even more unlike them in that whilst the property tax is widely adopted, a per capita or poll tax is almost completely unheard of and nowhere serves as the sole local tax. Hence it remains to be seen whether this novel proposed solution to the fiscal problems of local government is a long term one, rather than simply a short lived and essentially unsuccessful experiment at local tax reform.

The succeeding chapters in this book provide the context from which this local tax reform arose and into which it must fit. That context is multidisciplinary in its broadest sense and the property tax issue is an excellent case study of how superficially discrete academic disciplines are highly enmeshed in practical policy terms, ranging from the more narrow tax and accountancy issues through legal, political, economic and administrative issues to broader considerations of equity, civil liberties and ultimately of constitutional reform. All of these issues are addressed by the individual chapters.

This book should be essential reading for all persons with an interest in local government in terms of its topicality and wide coverage. It is written in laymen's terms, blends practice with theory, and avoids use of jargon so that discussion is intelligible to the non-specialist. It will also be of use to students of public administration, economics, politics, finance, law and urban issues. A companion volume 'Local Government Finance: International Perspectives' by the same editors, looks at local fiscal issues of current concern in other countries. Both books arose from a day seminar held at the University of Glasgow's Centre for Urban and Regional Research in 1986.

Whilst no definitive conclusion is drawn about the viability of the current reform it is clear that the problems and implications raised by that reform are considerable and may be sufficient to undermine its value. The following chapters make a wide range of observations and the concluding chapter attempts a synthesis of them. Some of the main points are as follows: the reform of local taxation is not a new issue in Britain; the current proposals are narrow rather than comprehensive in nature; the rationale for reform is open to question; it is not clear that reform will achieve what is intended; the consequences of reform have not been fully considered; there has been inadequate consideration of experience in other countries; there is no clear reason why introduction of a per capita tax necessarily precludes other local taxes, particularly the property tax; whilst the per capita tax is a new idea in the current debate it is not necessarily a long term solution simply because of that; local government in general and its financing in particular will always be a source of argument; there is no once-for-all panacea to the current problems; it is open to question whether a problem really exists as perceived or even exists at all.

Chapter One

LOCAL GOVERNMENT IN BRITAIN: RATIONALE, STRUCTURE AND FINANCE

Ken Young

INTRODUCTION

A century ago, the question of local government occupied the attention and energies of statesmen, the press and intelligentsia to a degree which today's debates only faintly echo. Popular emancipation through the extension of the franchise brought to the forefront the need for some form of elective institutions below the level of the state, building upon and making universal the model of the reformed borough council of the 1835 Municipal Corporations Act. Views differed as to the precise purpose of these local councils. Radicals saw local government as a vehicle of popular mobilisation. Some Conservatives saw the need to resist the extension of reform for that reason. Others saw the possibility of local democracy as a counterbalance to the administrative state, the coming of which seemed the natural corollary of popular politics. The settlement of the question of local government through the 'county councils act' of 1888 and the 'parish councils act' of 1894 (followed five years later by the completion of London government reform) satisfied most of these aspirations. In the following decade the moderate politics of the provincial cities and the aristocratic dominance of the counties laid to rest many of the more lurid fears.

Footnote: This chapter is a revised version of an article by the author appearing in M. Goldsmith 'Essays on the Future of Local Government' University of Salford, March 1986.

It was a robust settlement, capable of withstanding the strains of a century of social, political and demographic change with periodic adaptations and adjustments to structure, functions and finance. That the settlement has now collapsed is due not to any inappropriateness of structure (so easily revised) nor to the atrophy of local autonomy (so often exaggerated) nor even to any special deficiencies in its financial underpinnings (so long thought tolerable). It has collapsed because we have lost sight of the underlying rationale - the why of local government - a rationale that any Victorian politician understood intuitively and which has been embedded in the implicit political education of succeeding generations.

That loss points up a failure in the political education of the governing classes, whose grasp of the intimations of the British political experience has never been less sure. For no counter-rationale has been offered. No political party argues that the time for local government is past, that central determination of local issues is proper or more appropriate. Rather, specific interventions to achieve national purposes at the sub-national level are pursued, for reasons for expediency, at the expense of local authorities. This is to make no judgment about the propriety of the purposes themselves nor of the likely efficacy of the means by which they are to be sought. It is possible to be agnostic on a range of issues from metropolitan government and inner city regeneration to school governors and the business rate while recognising that their cumulative impact is to change the nature of the polity.

It is of course necessary to recognise that governments will assume the responsibility for the public welfare in a wide range of senses, from promoting educational achievement to fostering competitiveness. Indeed, we give too little critical attention to the question of how governments can pursue their legitimate national aims when these must be achieved largely through local actions (Young 1983). But these responsibilities are not exhausted by the pursuit of programmes; the maintenance of the polity itself - what in another regime might be termed 'upholding the constitution' - is fundamental. And when we lose sight of the rationale for local government the way is open for an unconsidered, insidious and cumulative process whereby the substance of local democracy can be unintentionally quashed. It is in this sense that a programme of governmental actions towards local authorities may be described without paradox by a great public lawyer as 'politically unconstitutional' (Griffith, 1985).

The root of this 'unconstitutionality' lies not in particular actions but in the assumptions which underlie them. Thus, the Government's rejection in the 1986 Green Paper <u>Paying for Local Government</u> (Cmnd 9714) of structural changes (understandable) and of increased Whitehall control (laudable) in favour of the abolition of domestic rates and the substitution of the community charge is in itself no more than a controversial and perhaps ill-considered move, the merits of which will be fully explored by the other contributors to this volume. My concern is with the underlying assumption, with the lack of political understanding revealed in the Green Paper's claim that the principal rationale for local government is the provision of services to local people. 'What is the role of government in this country?' asks the Green Paper. The answer - 'the main role of local government is to provide services in a way which properly reflects differences in local circumstances and local choice' (Cmnd 9714, p. vii).

This innocuous and apparently self-evident claim must be challenged. True, the popular support for local government is probably shaped more directly by the experience of service delivery than by any other factor. True, many influential and well intentioned people expect local government to fight its corner on the basis of its record on local services. But to found the existence of local authorities on service provision alone is to provide an inadequate rationale. Other agencies may do particular jobs more effectively. The boundaries between public provision and market provision are a matter of historical accident and are not immutable. The public good can be equated neither with municipal imperialism nor with minimal local government. Service issues can be settled from time to time on their merits. The danger lies in a sequence of pragmatically adverse judgements about the competitive advantages of local authorities as providers of particular services being taken to imply the redundancy of local government as a political institution. It implies that local government is to be viewed in terms of convenience and, if that convenience is exhausted, as something expendable.

Local government is first of all a <u>political</u> institution and a vital part of the framework of democracy in Britain. The secure foundation of a system of local government therefore requires a wider rationale than that provided by the Green Paper. The wider rationale is to be found in large measure in the report of that other inquiry (The Widdicombe Report) - announced in tandem with the finance studies which culminated in the Green Paper - 'The Inquiry into the Conduct of Local Authority Business' (Cmnd 9797). Widdicombe's analysis, unlike that of the Green Paper, is based on the view that the case for local government must rest on three distinct, but practically inseparable bases. I shall call these the arguments of pluralism, participation, and public choice. Taken together, they constitute a rationale for local government that can be as robust and relevant in the twenty-first century as in the nineteenth and twentieth. However, a rehearsal of these arguments - political arguments within each of which there are many different positions to be taken - is a vital but neglected preliminary to any consideration of the essentially subordinate issues of structure, functions and finance.

(1) PLURALISM

The first line of argument in defence of local government derives from a concern with political liberty which predates democracy and yet is recognisable to us. It can be located in the rise of the modern European state in the 16th and 17th centuries. At that time it became necessary to redefine the relationship between state and citizen in terms of intermediary corporations which, by protecting existing privileges or liberties restrained the power of the would-be autocrat. The fear of absolutism and the dispossession of lands and wealth was sufficient to support the rise of pluralist doctrines as rhetorical counterweight to the growth of the state.

Those who claim to find little relevance in the general propositions about local government and political liberty focus too narrowly upon the freedom of the individual and the direct significance for him or her of central or local government power. This preoccupation with a polar tension between the individual and the state is part of the heritage of J.S. Mill. It reflects the sense that the mediating institutions of the medieval world would have been swept away, leaving only Law to mediate between the individual and the state in an otherwise face-to-face encounter.

Yet the fundamental point about the significance of local government for political pluralism rests on no such bald polarity. Rather, it concerns the need to moderate a tendency or temptation towards autocracy which is itself destructive of good government.

Intermediary bodies, as corporations in their own right, interpose themselves between the individual and the central power. Historically, a good deal of early pluralist thinking derived from the controversies over the relations between city and monarch (Lustgarten, 1983; Nicholls, 1975). Those relations demonstrate that governments generally find such intermediaries inconvenient, even as forces to be reckoned with. But this is proper. Their role is to mediate and temper the exercise of political power.

It must be recognised that there is no challenge to sovereignty itself here. No rival mandate need be invoked. While some distinctively American arguments about local government presuppose a divided sovereignty or 'a real division of power' (Maas, 1959) they are, however widely quoted, of little relevance to Great Britain. The theory of the intermediary corporation subsists quite happily with the notion of sovereignty and no particular difficulty arises in the case of the unitary state in which local authorities draw their status from Parliament. For John Milton, writing in 1660, every county in the land should ideally be 'a kind of subordinate Commonaltie or Commonwealth ... so it be not supreme but subordinate to the general power and union of the whole Republic' providing thereby 'not many Sovranties united in one Commonwealth, but many Commonwealths under one united and trusted Sovrantie' (Wickwar, 1970).

This I take to be the classic statement of the proper relationship between centre and locality in Great Britain. It makes no claim that would not be readily conceded by the British public, who appear to combine belief in the value of independent local government with a recognition of the superordinate nature of the centre. It is, after all, no accident that the heyday of local government was also the heyday of the symbols of monarchy and indeed of its inflation into the Imperial ideal. The celebration of the centre and the celebration of the periphery went hand in hand in Victorian England. They can and should do so today.

Again, this view has little to do with democracy as such. Modernisation and change lead to both an extension of the scope of government and to an increase in popular expectations of government. Over time, government's capacity to satisfy those demands increases, but eventually at a diminishing rate, while expectations continue to increase. The governmental crisis of modernisation can be tackled only by further extending the capacity of government, or by lowering expectations, or by a mix of both measures. Local government has an important part to play in this particular school of statecraft by helping to maintain a sense of the possible and by ensuring that government's own reach does not outrun its grasp too far. This is what I would term the underside of the intermediary theory. Local authorities, as intermediaries, buffer the central power from the ultimately unmeetable pressures of a mass democracy. Pluralism is good for governments too.

The rise of the European autocracies between the wars quickened interest in the longstanding pluralist arguments (Anderson, 1967) and encouraged not a return to the phoney historiography of the Anti-Centralization Union but to the idea of the intermediary corporation. The young Harold Laski wrote that the implication of what he called the 'monastic state' in a modern complex society was 'the transfer of freedom from ordinary men to their rulers' (Laski, 1925). Douglas Cole, another committed interpreter of the pluralist tradition, commented that democracy can work at the scale of the modern nation-state 'only if each state is made up of a host of little democracies' (Cole, 1960). And it was this relationship between local government and what we might term the culture of liberal democracy that William Robson had in mind when he wrote that:

> there can be no such thing as local government ... under a dictatorship. Freedom in the localities implies freedom at the centre. Dictatorship at the centre inevitably involves the arbitrary suppression of local freedom and initiative, the curtailment of local responsibility and opportunity (Robson, 1935)

These were arguments put in time of political crisis, and it is perhaps only in such times (the leap in the dark of franchise extension, the rise of the dictators) that thoughts turn to the justification of a plural society (Young, 1985a). It should be no surprise, then, that the last few years should have seen a ferment of intellectual activity in which the democratic left have returned to the pluralistic strand in English socialist thought. Earlier in the century Guild Socialists argued for the autonomous organisation of the workplace in their gentle and so-English version of European

11

socialism. Today, this same impulse to both mobilise and defend working people at the smaller scale manifests itself in Local Socialism (Gyford, 1985; Boddy and Fudge, 1983). The practice of this new municipal pluralism, with its emphasis on local self-determination and experiment, are at the forefront of the campaign to defend local government against the centre. It places considerable importance upon the advocacy role of the local authority, speaking for an area against the central power as the Greater London Council and Metropolitan County Councils have done with such vigour. It is decentralist and participatory. It concedes the validity of many of the criticisms of local government as both autocratic and inefficient. Above all it argues that a new social order cannot be achieved by wrestling control of the state, but must be built from the bottom. Whether or not the new pluralists convince in their assertion that recent developments in local democracy are 'prefigurative' of a socialist society, their practical effect has been to instill a new vibrancy and, despite the weight of central constraint, a new confidence in the significance of local government for the maintenance of a diverse and plural society. I have dealt so far with men of the left. But the political traditions of pluralism are not exclusive. They run in the mainstream of the British political tradition. Conservatives too address themselves to just these issues, even if they express themselves in different terms. Concern for diversity and the moderation of central power is a recognisable strand in the Conservative inclination.

'Nothing could be more abhorrent,' remarked Tory historian Sir Keith Feiling, 'than a copy-book bungaloid state of amiable mediocrity, a centralised system to destroy local government ... or the congealing of the vital force of property in the dead hand of an entail ... diverse quality, and not gross volume, are the Conservative criteria of well-being' (Feiling, 1930). Centralism is antithetical to the Conservative tradition, with its emphasis on 'established constitutions, local rights, sharp vigilance against centralisation and uniformity, strict preservation of individual liberties' (Kirk, 1954). Localism was celebrated as quintessentially English by Hilaire Belloc and G.K. Chesterton, largely in opposition to the technocratic centralism of H.G. Wells, who dismissed them as 'local, local up to the ears' (Wells, 1906).

We see then that the pluralist argument for local government is more varied and subtle than it is often portrayed. It belongs to no party and to all. Furthermore, it is in no way dependent of federalist forms, it cannot be dismissed by ministers citing the obvious fact that we live here in a unitary state. Rather, it is because we live in such a state that local government, as a means of symbolising the importance of the periphery, becomes important. The magic of centrality is all too compelling and insidious.

Against the symbolic supremacy of the centre (Geertz, 1977), custom happily dictates a healthy suspicion of the powers of ministers and central bureaucracies, the more so the more overtly they invoke the symbols of statehood. We live with a tension between the forces of centralisation and the political irritation they cause, irritation that from time to time expresses itself in mild cautionary revolt. But negativism of this sort is not enough. We should be as capable as were the Victorians of celebrating both the centre and the periphery. At the end of the day, the pluralist argument is an allegory of good government.

(2) PARTICIPATION

The central argument here is that local government is a school in which democratic habits are acquired and practised and the infrastructure of democracy laid down. The British political experience - and its exportation of democratic institutions - has consistently reflected these assumptions about the nature of political education. The argument centres on building what might be termed political capacity. For example, underpinning immediate post-war thinking, particularly within the Fabian Society (Hinden, 1950) was an explicit connection between local democratic institutions and the processes of individual and community development - social, economic and political. Lady Hicks above all argued this case, that through the extension of local government the energies of people would be channelled into a process of 'government from below'.

It was a clear analogy with the assumptions about political education and development that also characterised the debate in Victorian England. The extension of the franchise prompted that enormously creative political generation to consider ways in which a democratic society could be groomed - against the clock, as it seemed - for self-government. Tocqueville, who we tend to see today as the prophet of mass society, emphasised the educative value of local institutions. John Stuart Mill too, saw the principal value of local government as raising the political capacities of a people.

The educative value of local government has as a result been largely taken for granted in Britain. Assumptions taken for granted are not commonly examined, and the most cursory glance will show that there are indeed several distinct strands here. A number of them were confronted in the well-known debate on 'local self-government as a basis for democracy' which entertained the readers of the journal Public Administration during 1953-4, and from which we still tend to take our bearings.

The first point concerned the viability of local government in a democratic society. Professor Georges Langrod contended that the extension of democracy through local government leads, through the mobilisation of the people, inevitably to the achievement of a centralist democracy and the suppression of local government itself. Local government thus contains within itself 'the seed of its own death' (Langrod, 1953, p. 33). This development was not seen as a matter for much regret. For Langrod, and for his supporter Leo Moulin, local government was in many respects parochial, anti-democratic, 'weak and outmoded', an obstacle, in short to the higher democratic will of the nation (Moulin, 1954, p. 437). Hostile as they were, however, these two commentators were urging the educative value of local government in dialectical terms.

A separate issue was raised when Moulin disputed the contention that local government was an effective training ground for national politicians. There was little evidence that national politicians were so recruited, nor could Moulin see much value in that transition from local to national politics. Both of these arguments missed the point about the development of political capacity in a society. Keith Panter-Brick's reply to these European critics of local democracy remains relevant to our concerns today:

> True, not many local mayors are capable of being great statesmen: but they are both politicians. As such, they have to learn the art of winning consent if they are to remain democratic in their ways, the statesman as much as the mayor. Otherwise they lose office. Now to win consent it is not necessary to give way to every demand: it is sufficient to distinguish rightful claims from unjust demands and to persuade others, even those

whose demands will not be satisfied, that one's cause or policy is a just one ... Within any locality, however small, there are always conflicting demands to be satisfied, and are these not settled on the same basis as at any other level? (Panter-Brick, 1954, pp. 438-9)

This is surely a clinching argument. The case for local government as a training ground for democracy (as it is usually expressed) does not rest on the extent to which national politicians are recruited from the ranks of the local (although no-one can deny the value of such an apprenticeship) but on the extent to which the political art is learned among that inevitably small proportion of the population who will hold office at any one time. The quality of local democracy is in their hands.

The third point is that the practice of politics by elected representatives may be said to have an educative function for the electorate at large. There are always hard choices to be made and it is for local councillors to explain why they are hard, to attribute and claim responsibility as appropriate, and to appeal for support. That responsibility is avoided when the constraints and choices that obtain in reality are misrepresented. A reasonable level of public knowledge and trust is an integral aspect of local democracy, and one that must be nurtured by the free flow of information and publicity. So too must those skills of free discussion not easily conjured into existence overnight.

The briefest review of the last two volumes of British Social Attitudes (Jowell and Airey, 1984; Jowell and Witherspoon, 1985) casts a good deal of light on how these arguments for local participation stand up in practice. First, there is a strong desire to keep local government local. Hostility to central encroachment is deep-seated, and central determination of rate levels finds few supporters even among 'partisan' Conservatives. People also have a clear view of what qualities they think are important in a local councillor, and these differ notably from the qualities expected of an MP; local knowledge and connection and accessibility are paramount. Finally, when faced with decisions by government which people think are 'unjust and harmful', people are far more confident of their ability to have an impact on that decision at the local than at central level. They are also far more likely to express themselves politically, either as individuals or in association with others, at the local level.

Even the introduction of strong party affinities into local government can be seen as inherently subversive of the local.

> It is not self-government or democracy if the policy of local councils is dictated by Whitehall in the name of that foreign myth 'the State', or by the central office in the name of the Conservative or Labour parties. I cannot imagine a better trio to sit together on a committee of a district or borough council than a diehard Colonel Blimp, a practical housewife who neither knows or cares about politics, and a keen young trade unionist. But the advantage of such a trio's wide range of understanding is lost immediately they begin to think of themselves as members of a party than as human beings and neighbours (Lord Howard de Walden, quoted in Young 1975)

On this version, party identification is inherently subversive of local autonomy and risks the submission of local government to 'that foreign myth, the State'.

In actuality, at least in most authorities outside the larger cities, the sense of local commonality among councillors is at least as impressive as the cross-cutting allegiance of party. But this sense of representativeness, of speaking for a place, was diminished by the 1974 re-organisation. The political significance of the sense of place awaits rediscovery. It is an important foundation of the pluralist case and is central to the larger rationale for local government.

This last point, the question of citizen assertiveness and efficacy, comprises the fourth and determining point in respect of the values of local political participation. There is an important argument about the existence and persistence of what has been termed 'the civic culture' in local affairs. That 'spirit', to which Hugh Whalen referred, has been often derided for its inherent conservatism. But I make no apologies for resurrecting the issue or for being unimpressed by arguments that we have moved from a law-abiding culture of civility to a rough and noisy participatory struggle (Young, 1985b). All the evidence suggests that while there is much that can be done to open up the decision processes, local government works sufficiently well to constitute an important channel for participation in the democratic processes for most people. More local it could

Table 1.1: Attitudes to local democracy, 1965 and 1985

	1965 agree %	1966 agree %
'So many other people vote in local elections that it's not important whether I vote or not'	10	16
'The people you vote for say they'll do things for you but once they're in they forget what they've said'	56	66
'The way people vote at council elections is the main thing that decides how things are run in this locality'	77	60
'Local council elections are sometimes so complicated that I really don't know who to vote for'	29	24

Source: Cmnd 9797 (1986) Research Volume 3 'The Local Government Elector'.

be, but that vital civic culture would be poorer, and dangerously so, without it.

In this context it is also worth pondering some of the findings of the Widdicombe Committee's survey of public attitudes to British local government, carried out for the Committee in 1985 by NOP Market Research. The survey revealed fairly high levels of public understanding of local government and quite extensive reported contacts between voters and local councillors and officers. Satisfaction levels were high and there was also strong support for the existing range of local authority powers. Local authorities were seen as rightly acting as the 'voice of the community' in representations to central government and there was a strong preference for elected councils over appointed boards. But on the question of confidence in the local democratic processes, comparisons with responses to the Maud committee survey of twenty years earlier are more ambiguous (Table 1.1).

Too much weight should not perhaps be put upon these answers, but they remain the only time series data on the question of public confidence. And it must be a matter of some surprise that positive scores on these questions have declined over the twenty-year period, not least because some of the factors most closely associated with high scores on indicators of political confidence - membership of the middle class, voting in local elections and owner occupation for example - have so changed over the period as to promote an expectation of higher, not lower, scores in 1985.

It seems, then, that although there are strong participatory elements in British local government there are also signs that these elements are weaker than might be expected. Political education and the habits of politics remain one of the foundations of the overall rationale for local government but here, as with the pluralist case, there is much room for further development to translate potential into reality.

(3) PUBLIC CHOICE

The third set of arguments concerning local government refers to the necessity for local needs being locally defined, in order that appropriate services can be provided. However, the requirements of efficient, economical and effective services are infinitely varied. The right area of provision for one service will be sub-optimal for another. All jurisdictions for service delivery purposes involve compromises. In theory a network of single-purpose agencies would achieve a closer relationship between need and provision, service by service, than a conventional multi-purpose local authority. The multi-purpose authority is not then just a matter of convenience, for it is the principal mechanism through which local choice can be expressed. Choice, that is, not merely about desirable service levels in respect of particular functions, but about balance and relative needs. These inter-service choices are the essence of political life, for it is only in respect of them that the qualities that Panter-Brick rightly invokes are actually exercised. Different client groups, different interests, competing claims have to be confronted and settled.

On this reckoning, the long slow movement through the nineteenth century from ad hoc administration to the high tide of multi-purpose local government in the inter-war years was indeed A Century of Municipal Progress (Laski, Jennings and Robson, 1935). Equally, the steady retreat from that ideal towards the fragmentation of local government, the loss of services and the creation of new ad hoc agencies may be seen as Half a Century of Municipal Decline (Loughlin, Gelfand and Young, 1985). Behind these most recent detractions from multi-purpose local government lie the new willingness of those at the centre to bypass local authorities, rather than to work with them, whenever they deem a national - or merely a supra-local - interest to be at stake. Hence the appointment of single purpose agencies whose rationale is not to strike a balance between competing priorities but to pursue a single remit with single-mindedness. The criteria of 'success' are clear cut and such an agency as the London Docklands Development Corporations has every chance of succeeding in its own terms. But it amounts to an abrogation of the political process and there can be no real claim to the exercise of local choice; it is administration and nothing else.

So far the arguments for locally-elected bodies as service providers have turned on the need to provide for political choices as between competing local priorities. But further arguments about responsiveness may be invoked. One, which has received considerable political attention in recent years, is the argument that local government has an inherent capacity to innovate. Paradoxically, this argument leads one to qualify the picture of a relentless centralism serving to diminish the scope of local government. Local government is seen as having a domain of operation with changing frontiers. At any point in time, a few authorities will be experimenting at the frontiers of public service, using (originally) private act powers, or imaginative interpretations of their existing powers, or (latterly) their limited general powers under S.137 of the 1972 Local Government Act.

Two thirds of Section 137 expenditure in 1984-5 went on economic development activities and a further 14 per cent on advisory and welfare related schemes. Many of these reflect imaginative schemes which, developed in one area, are soon emulated elsewhere. In Great Britain as a whole, only one third of the possible expenditure under S.137 (S.83 in Scotland) has been incurred; much scope remains, at least for authorities outside the metropolitan areas (Ramsden and Capon, 1986).

Large areas of 'invisible' discretion exist in the choices to be made as to the balance between mainstream services. Any service-based analysis is likely simply to focus on variations in provision as departures from the assumed good of a standard level of service. But multi-purpose authorities make their own trade-offs, often in response to local needs or preoccupations, both between alternative modes and levels of provision within a service area, and between service areas themselves. The tighter the overall financial constraints, the greater the ingenuity displayed in the search for ways of providing a locally favoured scheme.

New practices are quickly imitated, the innovation diffused and the frontiers populated. Thereafter come pressures for more specific enabling powers or the closer attentions of central government. Eventually, public general legislation may transform a service originally developed in this way and even take it out of local government altogether (Young, 1986). Against such domain contractions must be set the expansion which is likely to be taking place elsewhere as local policy-makers continue to respond creatively to the continuous manifestation of local needs. Only bodies with broad general powers and, more important, with a generalised remit to secure the well-being of the locality, can be expected to operate in this fashion.

Finally, the mistaken search for the optimum size of authority which characterised the late 1960s stems from the impulse to minimise the effects of local choice. Such arguments have been based in equal part upon assumptions about costs and assumptions about competence, although the evidence that either is systematically related to particular population sizes or their associated scale of operations is extremely flimsy. Local authorities are having to realise the scope for providing their services in a range of different ways from contracting out (thus opening up some additional areas of local choice as to providers) to joint or delegated provision. As a result, the future pattern of service provision looks as if it might become more variegated than in the past, thereby underpinning more firmly the notion that local government is a major vehicle for the exercise of public choice.

This last argument about the optimum size of authority derives from the economic theory of 'public goods'. Its origins can be found in Mill's proposition that local government could be justified in terms of groups of local residents sharing common concerns which are the business of nobody else. Economists from Hayek to Buchanan have been struck by the extent to which the provision of variable services for specific territories by local government units provided a close analogy for the market place. Local authorities could offer varying taxing and expenditure packages, and citizens would reveal their individual preferences through their residential choices.

On this view, the various levels of government would have assigned to them functions 'in accordance with the spatial properties of public goods externalities embodied in the carrying out of those functions' (Brennan and Buchanan, 1980). Thus the political economists provide a set of justifications for a system of government in which local institutions have an important part, the so-called 'theory of fiscal federalism' (Buchanan, 1960; Tiebout, 1956; Hirsch, 1970).

But fiscal federalism is often misunderstood as an argument for keeping local government local. All it actually offers is a means of identifying what is, on efficiency grounds, the smallest feasible scale of provision. It is entirely compatible with centralised responsibility and decentralised administration. Second, it does not in itself establish a case for multi-level government; for, as the liberal economist James Buchanan confesses, there is in the conventional theory of fiscal federalism 'no analysis that demonstrates the superiority of a genuinely federal structure over a unitary structure' (Brennan and Buchanan, 1980, p. 174). The economists find that they are forced to make what we would regard as political assumptions in order to justify local government. And so we are led back to the arguments for pluralism, participation and public choice.

CONCLUSION

In this paper I have advanced three complementary lines of argument as justifications for local government. In doing so I have sought to mark out issues which the debate on the future of local government, so evidently now beginning, must address. It is for others to develop those arguments, choosing their own emphases according to the dictates of their political predispositions. But I do believe it to be true that any valid theory of local government must be a political theory, drawing from arguments about pluralism and participation, and from arguments about the ability of local government to generate innovation and to maximise public choice. The currently fashionable concern to regard local government as simply nothing more than a convenient mechanism for the delivery of public service is, in the long run, the most dangerous to its continued survival and vitality. These three kinds of argument, while distinguishable, are in practice inseparable. How far we emphasise one against the others is a matter of personal and political inclination. But we can afford to overlook no one of them if we are to reconstruct, as I believe we must, that commitment to local government which distinguished the late nineteenth century and represented the best of Victorian values.

REFERENCES

Anderson, O. (1967) A Liberal State at War (Macmillan, London)

Boddy, M. and Fudge, C. (1983) Local Socialism (Macmillan, London)

Brennan, G. and Buchanan, J.M. (1980) The Power to Tax: Analytical Foundations of a Fiscal Constitution (CUP, Cambridge)

Buchanan, J.M. (1960) Fiscal Theory and Political Economy (Chapel Hill, N.C. University of N.C. Press)

Cmnd 9714 (1986) Paying for Local Government HMSO

Cmnd 9797 (1986) The Conduct of Local Authority Business: Report of the Committee of Inquiry into the Conduct of Local Authority Business (The Widdicombe Report) HMSO

Cole, G.D.H. (1960) Essays in Social Theory (Macmillan, London)

Feiling, K. (1930) What is Conservatism? (Faber and Faber, London)

Geertz, G. (1977) 'Centres, Kings and Charisma: Reflections on the Symbolics of Power' in J. Ben-David and T.N. Clark (eds) Culture and its Creators (Chicago University Press, Chicago)

Griffith, J.A.G. (1985) 'Foreword' in Loughlin et al (1985)

Gyford, J. (1985) The Politics of Local Socialism (Allen and Unwin, London)

Hinden, R. (1950) Local Government and the Colonies (Allen and Unwin, London)

Hirsch, W.Z. (1970) The Economics of State and Local Government (McGraw Hill, New York)

Jowell, R. and Airey, C. (1984) (eds) British Social Attitudes: the 1984 Report (Gower, Farnborough)

Jowell, R. and Witherspoon, S. (1985) (eds) British Social

Attitudes: the 1985 Report (Gower, Farnborough)
Kirk, R. (1954) The Conservative Mind (Faber, London)
Langrod, G. (1953) 'Local Government and Democracy' Public Administration, Spring
Laski, H.J. (1925) 'The Pluralistic State' Philosophical Review 28
Laski, H.J., Jennings, W.I. and Robson, W.A. (1935) A Century of Municipal Progress (Allen and Unwin, London)
Loughlin, M., Gefland, D. and Young, K. (1985) Half a Century of Municipal Decline (Allen and Unwin, London)
Lustgarten, L.S. (1983) 'Liberty in a Culturally Plural Society' in A.P. Griffiths (ed.) Of Liberty (CUP, Cambridge)
Maas, A. (1959) Area and Power (Free Press, New York)
Moulin, L. (1954) 'Local Self-government as a Basis for Democracy: A Further Comment' Public Administration Winter
Nicholls, D. (1975) The Pluralist State (Macmillan, London)
Panter-Brick, K. (1953) 'Local Government and Democracy: A Rejoinder' Public Administration Winter
------ (1954b) 'Local Self-government as a Basis for Democracy: A Rejoinder' Public Administration Winter
Ramsden, P. and Capon, S. (1986) 'An Analysis of Local Authority Discretionary Expenditure in 1984-85' in Cmnd 9797 (1986) Research Volume 4 'Aspects of Local Democracy'
Robson, W.A. (1935) 'The Outlook' in H.J. Laski, W.I. Jennings and W.A. Robson (eds) A Century of Municipal Progress (Allen and Unwin, London)
Salisbury, Marquess of (1885) Conservative Policy A Speech to the Electorate, Newport, Mons, Oct 7, 1885 (Hartford)
Tiebout, C. (1956) 'A Pure Theory of Local Expenditure' Journal of Political Economy, Oct
Wells, H.G. (1906) Mankind in the Making (Chapman and Hall, London)
Wickwar, H. (1970) The Political Theory of Local Government (Columbia, S.C., University of S.C. Press)
Young, K. (1975) Local Politics the Rise of the Party (Leicester University Press, Leicester)
------ (1983) 'Introduction: Beyond Centralism' in K. Young (ed.) National Interests and Local Government (Policy Studies Institute, London)

------ (1985a) 'Re-reading the Municipal Progress: A Crisis Revisited' in Loughlin et al (1985)

------ (1985b) 'Shades of Opinion' in R. Jowell and S. Witherspoon (eds) <u>British Social Attitudes: the 1985 Report</u> (Gower, Farnborough)

------ (1986) 'Local Economic Development: A Vacuum in Central-Local Relations' <u>Government and Policy</u> Autumn

Chapter Two

THE RECENT HISTORY OF LOCAL FISCAL REFORM

Peter G. Richards

INTRODUCTION

It is important to look at contemporary events in the
context of the experience of the past in order to ensure that
judgement is not sacrificed to the problems or passions of
the day. Nowhere is this principle more relevant than in the
matter of local rates. Over the last 150 years there have
been many, many attempts to alter the local rating system
in response to a variety of pressures. The fate of these
reforms should help any appraisal of current proposals. In
what follows the main emphasis is on England and Wales but
the lessons are also applicable to Scotland.

No tax has been more unpopular than the local rate.
Complaints against it have been legion. Now as in the past it
is claimed that the burden is higher in some areas than in
others; that some categories of ratepayers are unjustly
treated; that assessments are unfair as between properties;
that rates are regressive so that the poor pay
proportionately more than the rich. Above all, a recurring
complaint has been that the level of the rate poundage is
too high. The recent culmination of political pressure
against the rate is to argue that the whole system should be
ended and be replaced by some other form of taxation.

The reasons for hostility to the rate are not hard to
find. The rate is a very visible tax; you are painfully aware
it is being paid. Many national taxes are lost in the price of
a commodity or service. Alternatively, an automatic PAYE
deduction makes less impact than a personal payment.
National taxes have traditionally been related to income,
personal circumstances and the range of goods an individual

chooses to buy. None of these factors have ever applied to the local rate. Nor has rate liability been related to the extent of the use made of local authority services. Faced with such a plethora of criticism, it is remarkable that the local rate has survived.

The longevity is due essentially to its flexibility. The administration of the rating system has been continually modified particularly with regard to assessments. There have also been changes in the distribution of the rate burden between various categories of ratepayer by full or partial derating of particular forms of property. Finally, there has been a history of constant pressure on central government to provide financial aid to ease the rate burden. Of course, given a desire for an ever wider and better range of local services, only the last alternative provides any real prospect of curtailing local taxation.

THE PROBLEM OF VALUATION

The system of central grants grew slowly through the Victorian period and rather more rapidly since 1918. Throughout the nineteenth century local communities were expected, with some limited exceptions, to pay for the services they provided. Thus the reform of the Poor Law in 1834 was a response to middle class concern at the burden of the poor rate and is the prime example of a major change in social policy being stimulated by resistance to taxation.

But the reform of the Poor Law also had an effect on the administration of the rating system. By forcing parishes into unions so that they could jointly build workhouses, the Poor Law Amendment Act created a necessity to achieve greater uniformity in local administration of the rating system. When a parish or a borough was a completely separate financial entity, it did not matter whether the level of local assessments was high or low provided that individual properties were assessed fairly in relation to each other. If all assessments were high, rate poundage would be low: if assessments were low, rate poundage would be high. However, once parishes were forced to act together in a union and the union levied a rate of so many pence in the pound, then the level of assessments became crucial. A parish that was under-assessed in relation to its neighbours had an unfair advantage.

The Parochial Assessment Act, 1836, was the start of a

series of attempts to impose uniformity on local valuation. In the twentieth century, as the county councils became more and more important, the same problem arose in relation to boroughs and districts in the same county. The Rating and Valuation Act, 1925, sought to deal with the problem by creating larger areas for the administration of assessments: some 600 Poor Law Union valuation committees were replaced by 343 area assessment authorities. But the Act was not successful in achieving uniformity. Valuation is a very subjective process and was subject to local traditions and pressures. The Departmental Committee on Local Taxation had recommended in 1914 that all assessments in England and Wales should be made by the Land Valuation section of the Inland Revenue, but this degree of centralisation proved unacceptable until 1948. Today there is still concern in Scotland about the inequities caused by differing methods of valuation of properties as compared with England and Wales.

The failure of the 1925 Act to solve the problem led to the appointment of a further official committee of enquiry in 1938 but, due to the outbreak of war, the report, Valuation for Rates (Ministry of Health), was delayed until 1944. However the research material collected by this committee was made available to Professor Hicks and his book The Problem of Valuation for Rating (Hicks, Hicks and Leser, 1944) drew fresh attention to the problem. In the post-war period the Labour Government decided to extend the central grant system to help poorer areas by allocating funds so as to compensate for lower than average rateable values per head. This arrangement, although justified in terms of economic egalitarianism, produced an immediate inducement to local under-valuation. The lower the level of assessments, the more grant would be attracted. Uniform valuation was vital if this scheme was to work fairly. Centralisation of valuation machinery became inevitable and was duly authorised by the Local Government Act, 1948.

Since 1948 the problem has not been who should be responsible for valuation but how the process should be carried out. The traditional means of fixing the annual value of a property for the purpose of rating was to enquire what rent it could command in a free market. However, the introduction of controlled rents for smaller houses during the 1914-18 war and the continuation of this policy in peace-time greatly restricted information about rental values. Council house rents were reduced by subsidy. To try to meet this situation, the Local Government Act, 1948, decreed that properties built since 1918 should be assessed with reference to building costs while older properties should still be valued on the rental basis. This scheme produced great administrative difficulties, not least because building costs varied considerably in different parts of the country. When the Conservatives returned to office the scheme was abandoned and a fresh valuation list based on traditional methods appeared in 1956.

The law required that a new set of assessments be produced every five years. However, because of political and administrative difficulties, this timetable has been regularly set aside. Since the end of the war in 1945 only three reassessments have been made in England and Wales - in 1956, 1963 and 1973. Each has aroused a storm of protest as particular groups of ratepayers have claimed they have suffered harsh treatment. In particular, pensioners complained. Perhaps this was because they had more time to complain; perhaps their budgets were tighter than those of people in employment. It is also the case that the assessments of modern bungalows often increased rather more in proportion to the assessments of other properties. In Scotland the timing of revaluation has been different: the latest revaluation in 1985 produced such a flood of protest that the Government started a basic re-examination of local taxation.

The lack of information about rents has persisted and the valuers have generally failed to take full account of the inflation in property values. Changes in price levels in England and Wales since 1973 are unrecorded. It is commonly suggested that assessments should be based on capital values rather than rental values. As things stand, the assessment of a property in the valuation list is frequently around 0.5% of its capital value so that any reassessment on the annual value basis would involve multiplication of the present figure by a factor of about 200. It may be a coincidence that the publication of the last two new valuation lists in England and Wales was followed shortly afterwards by a narrow defeat of a Conservative Government at a general election. So it is perhaps not surprising that there is to be no further revaluation of domestic property. New properties are assessed 'in accordance with the spirit of the list'. Extensions are ignored: all pretence at equity has gone.

Derating

Resistance to having to pay the local rate has been so strong as to stimulate group activity to try to reduce the burden on particular sections of society. This political pressure has not infrequently forced the central government to take action either by derating property or granting rebates to needy individuals.

The farming lobby was very vigorous. Agricultural depression at the end of the nineteenth century led to farmers obtaining substantial relief. The farmers argued that their land was not a measure of their wealth but was essential to them as a means of production as raw materials would be to a manufacturer. In 1896 agricultural land was derated by 50% in respect of the poor rate and by 75% for the urban sanitary rate. (The poor rate covered all expenditure in rural areas. The task of amalgamating the two rating systems in urban areas was lengthy and not completed until 1925.) In 1923 agricultural land was derated by 75% for all purposes and in 1928 was declared free from rate liability altogether. On each occasion rate aid for farmers was provided by a Conservative government.

1928 saw the extension of the derating process to industry and the railways both of which were relieved of three-quarters of their liability. The purpose was to lower industrial costs so the British manufacturers could compete on more favourable terms with industry abroad. It was hoped that this policy would reduce unemployment, help the balance of payments and strengthen sterling. Not all the Conservative Ministers were convinced of the virtues of this semi-concealed subsidy (Keith-Lucas and Richards, 1978, pp. 139-40). However, the consequence was that local government suffered from the application of national economic policy. Local authorities were compensated for the loss of rateable value by a government grant. The local tax base was eroded and local finances were propped up by a national subvention which clearly could become a reason for greater state intervention in local affairs.

It was common for local valuers to make 'sympathetic' assessments on properties used for charitable and educational purposes. Once valuation was nationalised in 1948 such sympathy was no longer possible: servants of the national government had to apply the law uniformly and without particular favours. Two Rating and Valuation Acts passed in 1955 and 1961 were needed to meet this problem.

As a result, almshouses and properties used mainly for charitable purposes enjoy 50% derating. Local authorities can agree to remit their rates entirely and also offer a 50% reduction to a wide range of properties, not conducted for profit, which are concerned with education, charity, social welfare, literature, the arts or religion.

As noted above, the first post-war valuation list appeared in 1956. Because of the inflation of property values, the assessment on the existing lists had become absurdly low and it was realised that up-to-date figures would involve large increases. To cushion the blow for domestic ratepayers and minimise the political consequences, it was decided that residential property should be assessed at 1939 values. This policy introduced a new form of derating - derating through time. Since agriculture was free of rates and industry was derated by 75%, it followed that only shops and offices were paying rates on current values. Not surprisingly the organisations representing these interests complained of unfair treatment. To mollify them, shops and offices were derated by 20% in 1957. By now it was widely accepted that the operation of the rating system was becoming grotesque. Either it had to be strengthened or it must break down completely.

The tide turned temporarily. The Local Government Act, 1958, reduced the derating of industry from 75% to 50%. In a period of full employment the arguments used thirty years before about the need to use the rates as a means to reduce unemployment no longer had any force. But the valuation lists still failed to reflect current values of residential property. In 1961 the government grasped the nettle and agreed that the next valuation list should be based on current values. Partial derating of industry, shops and offices also came to an end. Except for agriculture, education and charitable concerns, it seemed as if the rating system was restored. Industrial derating in Scotland continued initially at 50 per cent (later reduced to 40 per cent) reflecting differences in valuation practices.

Rate rebates

The political storm caused by the 1963 valuation list produced an orthodox response from the Conservative government of the day - an official committee of enquiry was established. However, the terms of reference were unusual in that the committee, under the chairmanship of Professor Allen, was required 'to assess the impact of rates on households ... with special regard to any circumstances likely to give rise to hardship'. So the committee was not asked to propose changes in policy. In fact, this limitation may well have increased the impact of their report. The central factual message was not obscured by controversy over policy recommendations. And the factual message was that the burden of the local rate fell much more harshly on the poor than upon the rich. Rates amounted to about 8% of the very lowest incomes but less than 2% of the highest incomes (Cmnd 2582, 1964-5, p. 141). So the local rate was highly regressive. This was no surprise to informed opinion but the Allen Report gave official recognition to the situation and placed rate reform high on the immediate political agenda (Ilersic, 1965, p. 59).

By the time the Allen Report appeared, the Conservative government had been replaced by a Labour administration. The timing and content of the report made it doubly sensitive. With its tiny parliamentary majority Labour ministers were desperately keen to improve their popularity. And the central purpose of the Labour movement has always been to improve the lot of the poor. Faced with an official report that stressed that the poor were being harshly treated - how could a Labour Cabinet stand aside? The responsible minister, Richard Crossman, had some difficulties with the Treasury but ultimately the Cabinet accepted the need for national subsidies to help the domestic ratepayer (Crossman, 1975, pp. 349 and 419). Two schemes for rate rebates were adopted.

The effect of a rate rebate is similar to derating in that less money has to be paid to the local authority. Yet the legal form is different. Derating involves a change in the law which reduces the rate liability of an occupier. A rebate does not affect the formal mechanism of rating but provides a subsidy which cancels the whole or part of a rate bill. Rebates are more flexible in that changes in benefit can be effected by statutory instrument while to alter derating provisions requires a fresh act of parliament.

One type of rebate applied to all domestic ratepayers; the other was restricted to those with low incomes. The Local Government Act, 1966, reorganised the system of central grants to local authorities and a fresh element, the domestic element, was introduced into the general grant which paid for a fivepenny reduction (approximately 2.1 new

31

Table 2.1: Rate and grant income of Local Authorities in England and Wales

(Rates + Grants = 100%)

Year	Rates Income £m	Rates Income %	Rates Income Quinquennial % Increases	Government Grants £m	Government Grants %	Government Grants Quinquennial % Increases	Retail Prices Index
1913-14	71	76		23	24		10
1920-21	152	71	114	63	29	173	159
1925-26	149	64	-2	85	36	35	74
1930-31	150	54	1	126	46	48	54
1935-36	165	55	10	135	45	7	44
1940-41	203	46	23	240	54	78	86
1945-46	223	48	10	238	52	-1	100
1950-51	292	48	31	313	52	32	115
1955-56	403	44	38	508	56	62	152
1960-61	697	47	73	774	53	52	170
1965-66	1,132	47	62	1,294	53	67	204
1970-71	1,640	41	45	2,395	59	85	258
1975-76	3,795	33	131	7,857	67	228	564
1980-81	7,847	35	107	14,309	65	82	937

Sources: Annual Abstract of Statistics (HMSO). Retail Prices Indices (HMSO 1986).

pence) in the rate charged to residential occupiers. By stages the size of this remission was greatly increased and now stands at 18.5p in England and Wales and 7p in Scotland (again reflecting differences in valuations).

The second form of rebate arose from the Rating Act, 1966, designed to help those with low incomes. It permitted collection of rates by instalments and provided for total or partial remission of rates for low income households. The scale of assistance is adjusted from time to time to take account of changes in the value of money and each applicant for remission is subjected to a means test. As a result rates are no longer regressive at the lowest levels of income (Cmnd 6453, 1975-6, p. 431 and Cmnd 8449, 1981-2, p. 13).

Government grants and central influence

The development of government grants to local authorities is, in theory, a separate topic to rate reform. In practice, the two are closely related. The greatly increased amounts of financial aid from the Exchequer eased the burden of the local rate. Had this assistance not been forthcoming, there would have been pressure either to transfer some local services to become a national charge or to find other sources of local taxation. Thus grants have cushioned local finances against demands for more drastic change.

Table 2.1 shows the growth of rate income and of government grants for local authorities in England and Wales. Two features are notable. One is the astronomic increase in the figures which outstrips the rate of inflation and demonstrates a real increase in the range and quality of local services. The second is that grants have formed an increasing proportion of the total amount. Figures for the next year in the quinquennial series, 1985-6, are not yet available but it is certain that they will show a reversal of this trend as the Conservative Government has restricted increases in the Rate Support Grant and has required local ratepayers to make a bigger contribution towards local expenditure. However, this change merely brought into sharper focus the very problems of the rating system that increased grants had sought to ameliorate.

Inevitably, the growth of national financial aid increased ministerial concern with levels of local expenditure. And this concern became more acute in periods of economic difficulty. In the 1970s this country suffered

33

from the rise in oil prices which led to high inflation, difficulties with the balance of payments and ultimately the need for help from the International Monetary Fund in 1976. In 1973 the Conservative Government initiated a process of rate monitoring in which local authorities were requested to inform Whitehall of their proposed rate poundages for the coming financial year. The idea seemed to be that if the Government thought a rate increase was too high, it would ask a local council to think again and cut its expenditure. There was no statutory basis for this process. It caused much resentment in local government circles and was not repeated. But it was a harbinger for other sterner controls that were to come.

In 1975 the Labour Government established the Consultative Council on Local Government Finance (CCLGF). Initially the idea was to create a consultative body in which Ministers, civil servants and representatives of the local authority associations could talk together about problems of local finance. It soon became a forum for pronouncements of national policy about grants combined with exhortations to curb local expenditure and thereby reduce rate increases (Rhodes, 1986, Chap. 4). The Conservative Party is keener to curb public expenditure than the Labour Party but there is no difference between them in believing that local expenditure is now so important that it must be subject to central influence in the pursuit of unified government control over economic policy.

The Thatcher Government imposed financial curbs on local government of increasing severity. The Local Government Planning and Land Act, 1980, changed the basis of the grant system so that if a local authority spent in excess of a figure fixed by Whitehall, the ratio of grant to its expenditure was reduced. In subsequent years the scale of these penalties was sharply increased.

Next came an attack on the freedom of local councillors to decide the level of the rate. The first move was to try to control local expenditure through referenda. In 1981 the Labour-controlled council at Coventry held a referendum which offered a choice between higher standards of service or a lower rate: the result was a handsome victory for a lower rate. Mr Heseltine, Secretary of State for the Environment, was encouraged to produce a plan that gave electors a general power to control rate poundage. The scheme envisaged that the Government would decide the maximum rate which each county and district could levy in April. If councillors thought the permitted rate insufficient, they could raise a limited supplementary rate in July. If councillors wanted still more revenue, authority for a further rate was to be obtained by a local referendum held in October. This complex and bureaucratic scheme was roundly condemned in local government circles. It constituted a fundamental challenge to the principle of local representative democracy and implied that councillors were not to be trusted. Opposition to rate referenda extended to many Conservative supporters and the plan was dropped.

Instead, the Local Government Finance Act, 1982, prohibited the raising of any supplementary rate. This provision may have increased local rates slightly by encouraging councils to increase balances to meet unforeseen contingencies.

Nor did the penalties imposed through the grant system always work as the Thatcher Government hoped, especially where, as in the case of the Greater London Council, an authority lost all its grant through the penalty system. The 1983 Conservative election manifesto promised 'to provide a general scheme for the limitation of rate increases'. So the Rates Act, 1984, empowered ministers to limit the rate poundage to be levied by particular local authorities whose expenditure levels had exceeded limits fixed by the government. This measure totally reversed conventional wisdom about local finance. In the past it has been held that the unrestricted right of local authorities to levy a rate or impose a precept was an essential guarantee for the security of loans made to them: this right is now seen as less necessary than the need to control local expenditure.

Other sources of local revenue

In the closing stages of the last war and the early days of the post-war Labour government, there was considerable public debate about the future of local government. But this discussion concentrated on boundaries and the distribution of functions between tiers of authorities. The emphasis was geographical. Finance was ignored. The common assumption was that the rating system was adequate.

However, the 1950s saw some growth of discontent. Rate increases were unpopular and there was increasing awareness of the regressive effect of the local rate. One idea for reform was that a site should be valued for rating purposes rather than the value of property. The proposal attracted little support and was rejected by the Simes Committee (HMSO, 1952). Much more important was the work of a study group established by the Royal Institute of Public Administration. Its report (RIPA, 1956) recognised the limitations of relying on rates and grants and urged strongly the need for fresh forms of local taxation to be made available to ensure the independence of local government from central control. It proposed a local income tax on personal incomes limited to a maximum of threepence (1.25 new pence) in the pound; entertainments tax was to be transferred from the Exchequer to local authorities again subject to a maximum level fixed by statute; motor vehicle duties and driving licence fees should also be transferred to local authorities.

Richard Crossman, Minister for Housing and Local Government 1964-6, made speeches critical of the rating system (Crossman, 1975, p. 402). A White Paper, Local Government Finance in England and Wales (Cmnd 2923, 1965-66, para. 6) referred to the prospect that a reorganisation of local government structure, due to follow from the work of the Royal Commission established at that time, 'should provide a more promising context for drastic reform of local government finance'. Yet the terms of reference of the Royal Commission concentrated on areas and functions. The subsequent Report (Cmnd 4040, 1968-69) accepted that wider powers of local taxation were needed to sustain the vigour and freedom of local government but had nothing to say on the merits and demerits of specific proposals. Meanwhile the RIPA issued another publication on the subject (Hildersley and Nottage, 1968) and the Institute of Municipal Treasurers and Accountants produced pamphlets on Sales Tax, Local Charges, Local Income Tax and Rates. The Local Government Act, 1972, ignored all these suggestions. The structure of local government was reorganised but the basis of local taxation was unaltered.

By 1974 there was a new outburst of irritation against the rates. Rate demands had greatly increased due to a unique combination of factors. The increase in oil prices and falling exchange rate produced high inflation; the 1973 valuation list had a severe effect upon many properties; the creation of the new English and Welsh water authorities also in 1973 increased water and sewerage rates; getting the new structure of local authorities to work increased administrative costs; the lack of base budgets in many new authorities also helped to increase expenditure (Richards, 1975, pp. 161-6). The discontent led to a pledge in the Conservative manifesto for the general election of October 1974 that 'within the normal lifetime of a Parliament we shall abolish the domestic rating system and replace it by taxes more broadly based and related to people's ability to pay'. The Labour Party were more cautious: after they had won the election, a committee was established to review the problem.

The Layfield Committee on Local Government Finance produced the most comprehensive review of the subject ever to appear in an official publication. Its Report (Cmnd 6453, 1975-6) stressed the link between central grants and central influence. The position of local authorities was undermined by their lack of taxing capacity. The report also expressed concern about public confusion over accountability for local expenditure, a confusion that arises because most local spending stems directly from a legal obligation placed upon local authorities by central government. So councillors do not have full control over how much money they spend or what they spend it on. The Layfield Committee stressed the need for clear accountability. Those who cause expenditure should also have the onus of raising the revenue to meet the cost. It argued that if present trends continued, this principle would require Ministers to find almost all the revenue needed to cover local expenditure. Central government would provide grants and also indicate the rate poundage needed to pay for an acceptable uniform standard of local services. As a prediction of the situation ten years later, the Layfield Report proved remarkably accurate.

The Layfield Committee disliked the prospect it foresaw. It wanted local councils to be able to make their own decisions about spending and taxing. Even so, the Committee accepted that Whitehall would want to supervise the sum total of local expenditure in the pursuit of national economic management. It also stressed that greater local autonomy depended on fresh powers to tax. Accordingly, the report reviewed a number of alternatives for extra taxing capacity.

Many of the conclusions reached were negative. Assigned revenues, the transfer of particular national taxes to local authorities, was felt to have no advantages over the existing grant system. A sales tax, the level of which could be fixed locally, was not acceptable on grounds of accountability and perceptibility. Because the tax would be lost in the price of a commodity, people would not realise they were paying tax and so purchasers would not feel that the local authority should be in any way responsible to them. (Surely this was a highly idealistic objection which could certainly be applied to the collection of all indirect taxes by the national government.) The Layfield Committee also argued that the same obstacle applied to a local takeover of motor fuel duties. Further, if local levels of sales tax or fuel duty varied significantly, there would be a tendency to buy in cheaper areas.

However, the Committee did support the introduction of local income tax (LIT) on personal incomes as a supplement to the existing rate. The burden would vary with the ability of the individual to pay. The tax would be unconcealed and would enhance the accountability of local authorities to the electorate. It was admitted that the operation would be expensive to administer: the cost was estimated at £100 million a year. The Committee also accepted that LIT would require simplifications to be made within the system of national taxation and that it would affect the use of income tax as a tool of economic management by the Treasury.

The present author submitted a memorandum of evidence to the Layfield Committee which argued against LIT not on the basis of principle, or of cost, or practicability, but because it would be politically unacceptable to a Cabinet either Labour or Conservative. Income tax was regarded as the main weapon for control of the economy and Ministers would never surrender any part of it. And so it proved. The Green Paper (Cmnd 6813, 1976-77) issued in response to the Layfield Report noted the 'local freedom to vary LIT would have to be closely constrained so that it did not unduly complicate central government economic and financial management'. Further if LIT were absorbed in PAYE deductions, its visibility would be decreased; accountability, heavily emphasised by Layfield, would be lost. LIT was rejected. By ignoring political realities and through an exaggerated idealistic concern with public accountability, the Layfield Committee had driven into a cul-de-sac.

The Conservative election manifesto for 1979 was hesitant about rate reform. It stated 'cutting income tax must take priority for the time being over the abolition of the domestic rating system'. But memories of the 1974 pledge remained. It was said that the Prime Minister was particularly sensitive on the subject. Another Green Paper, Alternatives to Domestic Rates (Cmnd 8449, 1981-2), was published in December, 1981. The intention was to promote public discussion. Yet the style of the document was not stimulating and repeated many of the objections made by Layfield to alternative taxing methods. One fresh idea appeared - a poll tax. Everyone on the electoral register would have to pay a flat rate tax. However, it was recognised that there would be difficulty in stopping evasion. Public reaction was mixed but largely hostile. Such a system would be more regressive than the rates had ever been.

In 1983 it seemed that the Government were resigned to little change in the pattern of local finance. During August a White Paper appeared (Cmnd 9018) Valuation and Rating in Scotland: Proposals for Reform which concluded that rates should remain the main source of revenue for local authorities. The storm aroused by the 1985 Scottish valuation list forced Ministers to reconsider their position.

CONCLUSIONS

Up to now the local rate has managed to survive in the face of great hostility. Two factors have aided the survival. One has been the problem of finding an acceptable alternative. The other has been the size of national grants which have substantially restricted rate demands. Further, it is widely accepted that the local rate does have great advantages as a method of taxation. It is firmly established and well understood; it is economical to administer; its visibility is high so it stimulates a high level of public attention. According to the Layfield Committee this visibility is a great merit, but it does expose local councillors to political pressure. Were all national taxes as visible as the local rate, Ministers would find that national expenditure decisions were more sensitive. In this context our framework of taxation has put local government at a great disadvantage compared with Whitehall and made it much easier for central government to intervene in local affairs.

The need to 'do something' about the rates is not a new issue. It has been pressed for decades by Ratepayers' Associations. The fresh prominence stems from the existence of a government deeply hostile to high public expenditure and to the personal intervention of the Prime

Minister. The lessons from the past in this sensitive area show that it is easier to tinker than to arrange fundamental reform; that tinkering has led to more central grants; that more central grants lead to greater government influence over local affairs. Any fresh assigned revenue, e.g. from non-domestic rates, will continue this trend. Local government must have a wider tax base if it is to keep its independence and the best way forward may be to provide a new form of local tax in addition to the property rate which still has great advantages. The latest suggestion for a new tax, the community charge or poll tax, has not featured in earlier discussions, no doubt because its inherently regressive nature was thought to make it even less acceptable than traditional property rates. Meanwhile the scale of local services and how they should be paid for will remain a fertile source for argument.

REFERENCES

Books and pamphlets

Conservative Party, 1974, 1979 and 1983, Election
    Manifesto
Crossman, R.H.S., 1975, The Diaries of a Cabinet Minister,
    Vol. 1, (Hamilton and Cape, London)
Foster, C.D., Jackman, R.A. and Perlman, M., 1980, Local
    Government Finance in a Unitary State, (Allen and
    Unwin, London)
Hepworth, N.P., 1984, The Finance of Local Government,
    7th ed. (Allen and Unwin, London)
Hicks, J.R., Hicks, U.K. and Leser, C.V., 1944, The Problem
    of Valuation for Rating, (Cambridge University Press,
    Cambridge)
Hildersley, S.H.H. and Nottage, R., 1967, Sources of Local
    Revenue, (Royal Institute of Public Administration,
    London)
Ilersic, A.R., 1965, Allen and After, (Rating and Valuation
    Association, London)
Institute of Municipal Treasurers and Accountants, 1968-9,
    papers on Sales Tax, Motor Tax, Local Charges, Local
    Income Tax, Rates, (IMTA)
Keith-Lucas, B. and Richards, P.G., 1978, A History of
    Local Government in the Twentieth Century, (Allen and
    Unwin, London)

Rhodes, R.A.W., 1986, The National World of Local
    Government, (Allen and Unwin, London)
Richards, P.G., 1975, The Local Government Act 1972:
    Problems of Implementation (Allen and Unwin, London)
Royal Institute of Public Administration, 1956, New Sources
    of Local Revenue, (R.I.P.A.)

Official publications

1901: Local taxation Report of the Royal Commission Cd
    638
1914: Local taxation Report of Departmental Committee Cd
    7315
1944: Valuation for rates Report of Departmental
    Committee Non-parl. Ministry of Health
1952: Rating of site values Report of Departmental
    Committee Non-parl. Ministry of Housing and Local
    Government
1956-57: Local government finance White Paper Cmnd 209
1964-65: Impact of rates on households Report of
    Committee Cmnd 2582
1965-66: Local government finance in England and Wales
    White Paper Cmnd 2923
1968-69: Local government in England Report of Royal
    Commission Cmnd 4040
1970-71: Future shape of local government finance Green
    Paper Cmnd 4741
1975-76: Local government finance Report of Committee
    Cmnd 6453
1976-77: Local government finance Green Paper Cmnd 6813
1981-82: Alternatives to domestic rates Green Paper Cmnd
    8449
1982-83: Valuation and rating in Scotland White Paper Cmnd
    9108

Chapter Three

THE POLITICISATION OF LOCAL GOVERNMENT

John Berridge

INTRODUCTION

'Politicisation', so far as local government is concerned, is usually interpreted to mean an increasing degree of activity in local government by political parties qua parties, in particular the two major national parties. This interpretation opens up an important line of enquiry, as the 1986 Widdicombe Report (Cmnd 9797) and the valuable research material produced for the Committee amply demonstrate (Young 1986a). However, a wide interpretation is both necessary and desirable to improve our understanding of the political climate of local government. The term 'politicisation' should be used more generally to indicate a considerably increased degree of political activity and a general rise in the political temperature on some issue, in which partisan or party politicisation is just one factor. We are so used to similar patterns of political party activity in democratic societies that we tend to equate party activity with political activity, and to measure politicisation by the degree of party activity involved. Yet surely if the term is to mean anything it must be applicable to the arrival on the political agenda of any issue, anywhere - including one-party or non-party systems.

'Politics' is of course present and active in all sorts of situations where party political activity is absent - in the election of a Pope, in the Senate of a University, in the decision by a previously all-male club to admit women members and, indeed, in the internal manoeuverings of political parties themselves - as well as in the inevitable emergence of party groupings at all levels of government as people of like mind group together to achieve their goals. But the intensification of political activity in small group politics is hardly sufficient by itself to justify the term 'politicisation'; something more is implied.

I suggest that the additional ingredients are (1) involvement in an area in which national or local government is also involved and (2) exposure to public debate, with the inevitable consequence that the political parties will take a position on the issue and that other participants will find themselves sucked into the minor whirlpools around the maelstrom of mainstream politics. The bishops found themselves in this situation recently when, because they felt the pastoral work of the Church gave them not just a legitimate interest but a duty to voice their concern, they spoke out on the issue of unemployment. They incurred the irritated disapproval of the Government backbenchers and of political activists who criticised their intervention on the grounds that 'the Church should keep out of politics'.

So the term 'politicisation' should be used to indicate the translation of a non-political institution or issue into the political arena as an active participant, or the evolution or transformation of what would normally have been an untroubled relationship in the political arena into an atmosphere of discord, and a struggle in which party politics may but need not be involved. For example, the relationship between the Universities and the Government, via the University Grants Committee, has become sharply politicised without partisan politics being involved at all. Indeed the educational trades union and professional asssociations, whilst becoming much more political in their approach to the central problem of funding for education, have been at pains to keep party politics at bay, recognising that they could not carry their multipartisan membership with them if they became identified with a particular political party.

POLITICISATION OF ISSUES, INSTITUTIONS AND PARTY GROUPS

What might be termed issue politicisation arises when concern is more widespread and not co-terminous with party loyalties, and political parties find that the matter is assuming increasing importance on the national political agenda whether they like it or not. In Scotland the raison d'etre of the Campaign for a Scottish Assembly is issue politicisation, and the organisation has so far been most anxious to remain non-partisan.

Institutional politicisation can be sporadic and issue-related - the bishops' foray on unemployment - or a longer-term change in the institution's perception of its role - for example the developments in the Royal Institute of British Architects following the election of a President, Rod Hackney, who is an exponent of 'community architecture'. Hackney's vision of community architecture (involving the architect in the design of a community, the provision of jobs, and the regeneration of the inner cities, not merely the design of buildings), makes him a non-partisan political activist, and to the extent that he succeeds in putting his theories into practice, architecture and the RIBA will have been politicised.

As for the politicisation of party groups, the Widdicombe Report detected a general growth in the geographical spread of politics, and itemised the different manifestations thereof (Cmnd 9797, Chapter 4). Significantly, all but one of these items were concerned with partisan politicisation and the increasing involvement of the national political parties. However, other influences have also increased politicisation in local government - influences in which party political activity is sometimes a cause and sometimes an effect. These are:

1. The entry of the Conservative Party, and subsequently the Scottish National Party (SNP), Plaid Cymru and others into local government;
2. The increasing attention paid by the national parties and the media to local election results as an indicator of central party popularity;
3. The internal politics of the Labour Party, which have given rise to manifestations at local level leading to friction or confrontation with the Government or the national Labour Party;
4. The actions of groups and individuals, who saw local government as a vehicle for the advancement of their cause or their self-interest, which increased tension in central-local relations, between parties and within party groups;
5. Attempts by the Government, for political reasons or for non-(party) political reasons which have political

consequences, to exert more control over local government. The vehicle is generally central government legislation, particularly (though not exclusively) the series of Acts relating to local government, but greater control has increasingly been exercised through 'guidelines' and other forms of quasi-legislation.

These five influences are not mutually exclusive. Rather, they may interact to intensify politicisation and be mutually self-reinforcing. They are now discussed in more detail.

(1) **Increased partisan politicisation**

Local government has certainly become more partisan. Gyford (1985) has shown how there were high and low points in this process as the Liberals declined and Labour came to be a major national party which was also involved as organised groups in local politics. The development of partisan politics in local government therefore centres on the growth of Conservative activity at local level. Conservative Central Office say they can trace no formal decision to get involved, simply a long-standing policy to increase participation which depended for its momentum on the energy and determination of successive Party Chairmen in urging local associations to put up candidates and organise party groups in local elections. They consider that the most significant surge came with the reorganisation of local government, but say that even now some branches refuse point-blank to field candidates against the Independents.

Conservative representation per se has a long history in England and Wales; it dates back to pre-war days, with a big increase in the 1945 elections - the first elections since 1938. Geographically it has been uneven, and until the reorganisation of local government there were still many councils where the opposition to Labour came from 'Ratepayers', 'Moderates' and other local groups. For a long time Central Office policy was to maintain the party's interest through liaison with such groups or through a co-ordinating 'front' organization such as the London Municipal Society, created for the sole purpose of maintaining close liaison with the right-wing group on the London County Council.

Partisan politics therefore predated widespread Conservative representation in local government in England and Wales. Ratepayers, Moderates and similar groups were organised local 'parties'; they had to be, if they were to have any chance of opposing the Labour groups on the councils. They operated as a group in the council chamber and in elections, and press reports commonly spoke of 'considerable gains by the anti-socialist groups', 'Right-Wing groups' and sometimes, to make sure their readers understood, 'Moderate (Con) gains in council elections'. Keesings' Contemporary Archives, reporting on the May 1969 elections in England, says 'Labour also lost South Shields to the Progressives, as the Conservatives are known locally' (Keesings 1969-70, p. 23364). But they were essentially <u>local</u> groups, with no wider organisational structure and nothing stronger than a liaisive link with the Conservative Party. Despite widespread personal political orientation towards the Conservatives - though there is evidence that this was less true in the South-West and in Wales (Grant, 1977, p. 3; Stanyer, 1976, p. 85) - these local right-wing groups could be robustly independent, and would not necessarily go along with Conservative government policies if they considered them to be detrimental to local interests. This was one factor in the Conservative Party's determination to increase its local representation.

In Scotland there <u>was</u> a definite decision that Conservatives should contest local elections, coupled with continuing pressure from Conservative Central Office in Edinburgh. But Conservative involvement in Scotland was much later than in England and Wales; the decision was not taken until 1967 or 1968, and even then progress was slow. The first official Conservatives in the four major cities emerged in Glasgow (1 seat) and Edinburgh (2 seats) in 1967, in Aberdeen in 1971 and in Dundee not until 1974. In Glasgow an alliance with the Progressives enabled a gradual and relatively smooth takeover by the Conservatives (25 Conservatives and 3 Progressives by 1973 compared with 1 Conservative and 52 Progressives in 1967) and in Edinburgh, despite some infighting between Conservatives and Progressives, there were 21 Conservative councillors by 1973. But in Aberdeen the Progressive/Conservative conflict was bitter, whilst in Dundee (in 1967) Conservative support for the Progressives was pledged in exchange for an agreement that they would all take a Progressive /Conservative label and finally stand as Conservatives in the

1974 elections for the new authorities. Scottish Conservative involvement therefore did not really take off until the reorganisation, since when candidate numbers have continued to increase - though seats won have declined since 1978 (see Table 3.1).

The Tory decision to get involved in local politics in Scotland was ostensibly taken because the Labour Party's annual participation in local elections provided valuable experience for the party activists whilst the Tory machine was only being exercised at bye-elections and General elections. Conservative failure to participate in local elections also meant that they were not able to assess the strength of their support as accurately as the Labour Party. Even at the General Elections in 1974, when the Conservative entry into local politics had theoretically been in force for some three years, many constituency associations were taken by surprise at the 'sudden' surge in SNP support and lost seats that had always been regarded as Tory strongholds. The reform of local government in Scotland had already provided a major stimulus to Conservative involvement in local politics; if anyone still needed convincing, the salutary shock of the lost strongholds provided the evidence.

It would be a mistake, however, to equate partisan politicisation in Scottish local politics solely with the entry of the Conservative Party. There are two reasons for this; as in England and Wales, there were already organized partisan groups in local politics anyway - most of Widdicombe's list of characteristics of local party politics were true of the Progressives in Scotland - and the entry of the SNP and later the Alliance led to a heightened degree of partisan politicisation and an effective four-party political system.

Progressives were almost all Tories as far as political ideology was concerned, and they were seen as such by the electors; a joint study of Scottish electoral behaviour by four Scottish Universities in the 1960s (Bochel et al., 1967) asked for the voters' perceptions of the Progressives, and subsequently asked the same question about the Tories. They invariably got the same answer - 'I've just told you my perception of the Tories'; clearly the elector did not appear to differentiate between the two. So the entry of the Tories under their own label into Scottish local politics did little to politicise local government in the towns and cities; to the average citizen it was very much 'business as usual',

Table 3.1: Conservative representation in Scotland since 1974

(254/112 = 254 candidates/112 seats won.)

| Year | Party | | | | | | |
---	Con	Lab	Lib	SNP	Comm	Ind	Others
1974 Regional	254/112	303/172	83/11	126/18	56/1	297/114	29/4
1978 Regional	292/136	284/176	37/6	225/18	38/1	151/89	20/5
1982 Regional	283/119	322/186	112/21	266/23	24/1	140/87	29/0
1986 Regional	259/65	317/223	245/40	330/36	13/1	141/79	85/1
1974 District	539/241	753/428	148/17	269/62	128/0	644/345	79/17
1977 District	543/277	719/299	136/31	465/170	90/2	521/318	97/20
1980 District	547/229	765/494	153/40	439/54	63/1	426/289	59/17
1984 District	571/189	830/545	417/78	493/59	-*	402/267	122/11

*The small Communist presence in 1984 is included in 'Others'

Source: Compiled from Bochel and Denver (1975 et seq.).

especially since the Conservative councillors were frequently the same people they had known as Progressives.

Contemporary with the creation of the Regional Councils, give or take a year or two, was the surge in national electoral support for the SNP, which entered the local political arena in Scotland in the heady atmosphere which followed Winifred Ewing's victory at the Hamilton bye-election. Inherent in the SNP's local representation there was always a national political dimension - of seeing that Scotland got a 'fair deal', even if this was by local increments, as well as the more practical purpose of providing candidates, councillors and party workers with experience. The Party leadership felt that if the SNP was to be taken seriously then they had to be active in all aspects of Scottish life and politics, and that certainly meant local government. The significant point for the purpose of this chapter is that the two major parties saw the SNP as an interloper in their private war, and the political temperature rose sharply as they lost no opportunity to attack the party and its councillors.

The SNP, and later the Alliance, have therefore played a direct part in the politicisation of Scottish local government. Both parties have recruited candidates and workers from people who had not previously been active in political life, and both have forced the two major parties to operate in what at the local level is a real four-party system - at the district level there are Alliance and SNP administrations, and at both levels there are places where they hold the balance of power.

(2) Increasing attention paid to local election results

Once the major political parties had become involved as organised groups in local politics, it was inevitable that more attention would be paid to local election results as an indicator of national party fortunes; Widdicombe's findings on electoral behaviour at local elections, in line with other research, suggest that electors tend to vote on national party lines (Miller 1986, p. 162) even though the majority disagree with politics at local government level (Young 1986b). Media coverage, which used to be quite limited, has grown to the point where TV programmes on local election night resemble the intensive live coverage which was reserved for General Elections.

Contemporaneously, party monitoring of public opinion for electoral purposes was becoming more sophisticated, and more attention was paid not only to local election results but to local election campaigning, in order to achieve a good result. It is now frequently suggested that the government of the day will refrain from or advance certain policies in the months preceding the local elections in the hope (or fear) that its party's showing might be affected; as a general election approaches, the local results may tip the balance in deciding whether to go for a General Election or not.

(3)   The internal politics of the Labour Party

There is a considerable element of politicisation not only between but also within the parties as factional disputes break out over the selection of candidates and the contents of the manifesto. Such disputes may involve friction between the party's Central Office and a local party or parties as well as internal battles at the local level, media reports of which will heighten public awareness of the significance attached to local politics. Most central-local intra-party disputes have centred on the Labour Party and alleged infiltration by the hard left, though there have also been minor flurries where Conservative candidates with alleged National Front connections have received publicity.

Internal party disputes can sometimes be intense and bitter, and may raise some fundamental questions about the nature of democratic politics. In recent years it has been the Labour Party which has suffered most from such internecine strife, and in the late 1970s the chief Labour agent Reginald Underhill (as he then was) was asked by the Labour Party to carry out an investigation into the infiltration of the Party by the extreme left.

In the event the party decided not to publish his report, and Underhill grew increasingly more concerned about what he felt was a grave danger to the party and indignant about the attacks that were made upon his evidence. As a Party official he was effectively gagged, but retiral and a life peerage gave him more independence and in 1980 he released some of his documentation on infiltration. Militant Tendency documents (disputed by the Tendency) were quoted which suggested infiltration was deliberately planned, and that it focused on the local level: 'We must consciously aim to penetrate every constituency party in the country, including even the rural ones ... A citadel in every constituency, a <u>base in every ward</u>'. Whether the allegations were true or false, dissension within the Party was bitter and local party groups were often the battleground, whilst the Conservatives saw it as evidence that the Labour Party had lost control and that extremists were taking over in local constituency organizations and council groups. Naturally the media followed the internal wranglings of the Party with great interest, and was an important factor in keeping the issue on the public agenda.

(4) The actions of groups or individuals

Reselection (or 'de-selection') of Labour MPs received more publicity, but the same process was also going on at local level as 'hard left' candidates replaced moderates, and the Conservative Government's concern in this respect focused particularly on the Greater London Council (GLC) and the Metropolitan Counties. The contemporaneous emergence of a number of individual local politicians who achieved a good deal of national publicity brought together two strands in the politicisation of local government - the prominent and often controversial individual and the intensification of inter and intra-party hostilities at both local and national level.

There have always been individuals who saw local government as an entry route to national politics, varying from those who saw it as a useful apprenticeship in politics to others who found it a way of providing themselves with a platform from which they attracted public notice. In the process, they can have a profound effect on the temperature of local politics and central-local relations; even the seemingly innocent pastime of town-twinning (Dundee with Nablus, in 1981, instigated by a Labour activist) can take on international political dimensions and cause bitter and prolonged debate in the council chamber. It is argued that this phenomenon has been more pronounced in recent years and has contributed to the politicisation of local government, sometimes in addition to and sometimes interacting with other factors.

Ken Livingstone's period of office as Leader in the GLC widened the debate about the proper boundaries of local government responsibility and exacerbated relationships inside and outside his own party. His election to the GLC in

1980, and the abrupt upheaval in the party group which made him its Leader illustrates the argument that actions by individuals may have a profound effect on the politicisation of local government.

After his election, and the capture of other Metropolitan Counties by the Labour Party, relationships between the Conservative Government and the authorities concerned deteriorated rapidly. Other councils, such as Liverpool, were not lacking in controversial figures and in any case some seemed hell-bent on a major confrontation with the Government. Their vociferous denunciation of Government policies, which they protested were destroying local government as such, was itself sufficient to politicise local government sharply and bring the issue on to the centre stage of politics. Furthermore, their varied attempts to defy the Government by finding ways around the expenditure ceilings (Parkinson, 1986) intensified the political battle both inside the councils and between central and local government. Both sides saw their actions as being forced on them by the other; the end result was the abolition of the GLC and the Metropolitan Counties (under the Local Government Act 1985) and the curtailment of local authorities' powers to contest their case through publicity (under the Local Government Act 1986).

One of the early disputes between the GLC and the Government centred on Ken Livingstone's introduction of cheap fares on London Transport. The motives behind this plan may possibly have been political, but it could validly be argued that such a move was a proper strategic decision by a large metropolitan authority; after all, low fares or even free public transport had been tried elsewhere in similar circumstances. Whatever the motives, the Government was irritated and the coefficient of friction increased.

Effectively, some fundamental questions about the proper remit of democratically elected local authorities were being posed that might in other circumstances have given rise to a fruitful debate. The next Livingstone initiative, however, choked off the debate before it began and made political confrontation with the Government inevitable. He invited representatives of Sinn Fein to visit the GLC for discussions, maintaining that terrorist bombing in London had given him, as Leader of the GLC, just cause to hold discussions with the political allies of the Provisionals in an attempt to stop the bombing campaign. But he must have been well aware that the Government would be outraged by the entry of a local authority into what it considered to be a priori central government business, and the wording of the invitation, which (as reported) included specific references to discussions of ways to bring about a British withdrawal from Ulster and the reunification of Ireland, was hardly calculated to temper their irritation. In the event the Government used its powers to ban three Provisional Sinn Fein members of the Northern Irish Assembly from entry into Britain. Livingstone retaliated by flying to Belfast in February 1983 at the invitation of the Provisional Sinn Fein leaders, though there were signs of backtracking by the GLC, whose officials stated that he was travelling in a personal capacity.

Through these and similar incidents Livingstone was able to maintain a high national profile from a local government base, and to represent Government moves to abolish the GLC and the Metropolitan Counties as a politically-motivated campaign against Labour councils and a personal attack on him. There are other examples, which also illustrate the interdependence of a number of the factors which helped towards politicisation, though space precludes a fuller exploration: Bernie Grant, as Labour leader in Haringay, particularly over his controversial attack on the police after the Broadwater Farm Estate riot, and Diane Abbott in Harrow, both of whom won seats in the 1987 election, had helped to politicise the issue of black people in politics and in the Labour Party. Derek Hatton and the Labour administration in Liverpool, in constant conflict with the government, and others such as 'Red Ted' Knight in Lambeth kept the issue of local government in the public eye.

(5) Increased central government control

The Government's attempts to reduce the powers of local authorities by statute took three forms - control of their spending powers, reduction of their functions and (in the case of the GLC and the Metropolitan Counties) simple abolition.

We have seen how central-local relations between the Government and metropolitan authorities were soured. By the Local Government Act 1985, the GLC and the Metropolitan County Councils were abolished and replaced by Joint Authorities, drawn from constituent borough councils but responsible to the Secretary of State, for police, fire and passenger transport. The creation of joint boards is an admission that in such a concentrated urban area some services need a wider administrative remit, and the fact that the Government did not conclusively demonstrate that local government was incapable of overseeing such services effectively must leave a question mark against its motive.

The tremendous battle which preceded the passage of the Act, in which the GLC in particular made extensive use of advertising, was undoubtedly the stimulus for the Local Government Act 1986, which prohibited Local Authorities from using publicity for such a purpose in the future. Publicity is defined in the Act as 'any communication of whatever form addressed to the public at large or a section of the public'. This might seem pretty draconian stuff, especially since central government does not suffer from any similar restraints; in fact it would have been even stronger, but the Government had already had to moderate the original wording in the face of backbench opposition and unhappiness.

Even before the Act, in R v ILEA ex parte Westminster City Council (1986 1 W.L.R. 28) it was held that retaining an advertising agency to conduct a campaign to inform the public of the effects of ratecapping 'and persuading them to the view held by the authority' was invalid on the grounds that the purpose of persuading was unauthorised - you could describe but not persuade, because persuasion materially affects the making of the decision. The Act further politicised central-local relations and left local authorities in a much weaker position to resist further encroachments on their area of responsibility.

There are however other ways in which the electoral support of the opposition may be put in hazard and the powers of local government reduced. The Housing Act 1980 established the right of 'secure' tenants (i.e. of three years standing or more, later reduced to two years) to buy their council houses at a substantial discount. Though this dealt a direct blow at the local Labour strongholds in the council estates, one cannot tell whether it was a deliberate Conservative attempt to begin the erosion of their main opponent's electoral power base or simply the natural extension of the concept of a property-owning democracy. But it was seen by Labour as a tactical attack on their support, and housing immediately became a politically super-charged issue - a classic example of issue politicisation in local politics. The Act very considerably increased the coefficient of party friction locally (local Conservatives were delighted and Labour furious, considering the Act a typical product of the Conservatives' 'dirty tricks department') and brought about strife and confrontation between Labour local authorities and central government, showing how issue politicisation can very quickly become partisan politicisation. The popularity of the Act, after a slow start to sales, has caused controversy inside the Labour Party ever since.

The most direct assault on local autonomy followed from the Government's belief that the whole of public expenditure must be reduced if inflation were to be kept under control, and that implied controls over local authority expenditure, an overtly valid argument given their economic philosophy. Whatever the reason, the effect of each successive Act was to heighten still further the confrontation between local authorities and the Government, particularly Labour authorities who saw in this yet another politically-motivated move. The method was brutally progressive; by the Local Government Planning and Land Act 1980 limits were placed on the expenditure of individual local authorities. In addition Government gradually but significantly reduced the annual grant, and those who exceeded the limits suffered a penalty cut.

Loopholes were closed one by one; local authorities which turned to the rates or the loans fund to restore their expenditure levels found the Government legislating to end supplementary rates (under the Local Government Finance Act 1982), control rate levels, and finally to impose penalties for expected as well as actual overspending (under the Rates Act 1984). Scottish Acts gave similar powers to the Secretary of State for Scotland. Unlike the Housing Act, these measures did not meet with an unqualified chorus of approval from Conservative authorities. In the main their comments were more restrained than Labour's, but most of them found the controls irksome, difficult to live with and sometimes downright unfair. There were complaints from some Conservative authorities that they had loyally cut back drastically on expenditure and tried to stick to the guidelines only to be penalised more heavily than others who had not made the effort and had sometimes been in open defiance of the Government. There was also genuine unease on the Tory benches in Parliament about the increase in central government powers, and an increasing trickle of Tory backbenchers abstained or voted against the Government during the passage of the Bills.

Other Acts had a different and more indirect effect. The Transport Act 1982 opened up passenger transport to competition, thus lessening rather than removing a function from local government. But the setting up of Urban Development Corporations (under the Local Government Planning and Land Act 1980), removes a responsibility which would normally be fulfilled by local government and transfers it to a central government 'creature'; the establishment of City Technology Colleges (already in train), allowing schools to 'opt out' of the State system, the creation of a national core curriculum for education and forcing local authorities to put more of their services out to tender (Queen's Speech, 1987) continue the theme. At one blow such policies increase not only central control but also central political influence, enabling the government of the day to shape to its own design large areas of policy over which it previously had little control. The argument that there should be local democratic control of local service provision can be rendered irrelevant if there are so few services provided locally that local government is no longer seen as an important influence in everyday life. In those circumstances the wheel would have come full circle, since such a system would hardly be highly politicised.

The attempts to control local authority expenditure could be classified as issue politicisation leading to greater partisan politicisation, though there is some doubt which is the chicken and which the egg. If the Conservative Government set out quite deliberately to attack Labour in its local power bases - the Prime Minister had spoken openly of her ambition to destroy socialism in Britain - thereby polarising opinion and maybe weakening the Alliance as a useful by-product, then the motivational force was partisan and issue politicisation the vehicle. On the other hand, if the Thatcherite obsession with the control of public expenditure was the motivational force and the other factors side-effects, albeit not unwelcome ones, then issue politicisation was the stimulus for greater partisanship and factionalism.

CONCLUSION

Local Government has always been Political (capital P) as

recognised by the Widdicombe Report (Chapter 4). As a specifically political institution established by law, and buttressed by the moral authority that comes from having its own electorate, it represents in Britain the closest thing we have to the Separation of Powers. Until recently the recognition by both central and local government of their different but intermeshing roles, and the environment of administrative politics in which they have operated, have enabled peaceful co-operation between two sets of elected authorities each incidentally acting, to some extent, as a balance to the other. In the main, then, neither local government and the services it provides nor central-local relations were highly politicised. What has changed?

The essence of the argument in this chapter has been that there are a number of different factors involved in the politicisation process, and that to limit the analysis to partisan or party politicisation is not necessarily the most important, nor indeed the most fruitful approach. An individual's action, or the emergence of a new issue, may immediately spark governmental opposition and pressure group reactions both at central and local level; positions will be taken, attitudes harden, parties align themselves with one side or another (or if they should happen to find themselves on the same side, quickly make clear that their juxtaposition is accidental and stems from entirely different causes) and other (non-partisan) political forces are drawn in.

An issue can thus easily become highly partisan-politicised very quickly, but the partisan politicisation followed the initial personal action, or developing issue-politicisation, and possibly the entry of other non-partisan bodies onto the battlefield. Presumably no one would deny that topics like abortion, divorce and child abuse can be highly susceptible to issue politicisation, but these are areas where political parties tread as if they were walking on eggs; the last thing they want is to make this a partisan political issue - until the issue politicisation debate has shown fairly clearly which way the majority opinion is moving.

The entry of the Conservative Party and others into the local political arena has not, in itself, been the major factor in politicisation. But once the parties were all involved locally, the increasing attention given by the party headquarters to the results of local elections as an indicator of the national parties' electoral popularity - an attention which creates its own dynamic - inevitably detracts from all facets of the 'local' dimension of local elections and turns them into a glorified public opinion poll. Once local parties believe that their chances of retaining or winning office depend not so much on their own record as on that of their national party, and once they accept that the party in office may manipulate policies to maximise its chances at the local polls, they are locked into a vicious circle which increases partisan politicisation and diminishes the role and status of local government. In the election year of 1987, it is arguable that the shadow of the general election date was at least as great a factor in the local elections as the records and perceived abilities of authorities at local level.

Add to that a spate of legislation which simultaneously increases the central government's area of discretion and limits that of local authorities (Loughlin, 1986, p. 192), and another vicious circle is created. Local authorities strive to find ingenious ways around the restrictions, as in Liverpool (Parkinson, 1986) and the Government responds with yet another Act to close the loophole which has been found. Increasingly, too, some Labour authorities and individual activists are behaving in such a way as to make national or international symbolic gestures (e.g. the declaration of nuclear-free areas, the invitation to Sinn Fein, and Liverpool's exercise in brinkmanship) which have infuriated a government prepared to exact retribution. There have been some past examples of this type of behaviour (e.g. Clay Cross: Ascher v. Lacey (1973) 1 W.L.R. 412) but the profile of local government opposition to central government has been much heightened of late. For all these reasons central-local relations are increasingly based on conflict rather than (as in the past) co-operation and no matter whether the initial culprit is central or local government it is the latter democratic institution that will be weakened in the short run. Ultimately the central government's will can be made to prevail.

It is difficult to see how all this can be to the benefit of the nation as a whole. A demoralised and severely restricted local government sector will hardly be attractive to officers as a career or to citizens as a form of public service, whilst the greatly increased range of powers available to the central government will be at the disposal of any party which manages, for whatever reason, to win a general election. At the end of the day, it seems that at both ends of the central-local spectrum democracy has been diminished.

REFERENCES

Bochel, J. et al., (1967) 'A survey of politics in Scottish cities'. The Universities of Aberdeen, Dundee, Edinburgh and Glasgow. (MIMEO)

Bochel, J. and Denver, D., (1975) The Scottish Local Government Elections 1974: Results and Statistics. Scottish Academic Press. (Annual)

Cmnd 9797 (1986) The Conduct of Local Authority Business: Report of the Committee of Inquiry into the Conduct of Local Authority Business (The Widdicombe Report) HMSO

Grant, W., (1977) Independent Local Politics in England and Wales. (Saxon House)

Gyford, J., (1985) 'The Politicisation of Local Government' in M. Loughlin, D. Gelfand and K. Young Half a Century of Municipal Decline 1985. (Allen and Unwin, London)

Keesings (1969-70) Keesings Contemporary Archives: A Record of World Events, (Longmans Group, London)

Loughlin, M., (1986) Local Government in the Modern State. (Sweet and Maxwell, London)

Miller, W., (1986) Local Electoral Behaviour. In Cmnd 9797 (1986)

Parkinson, M., (1986) 'Creative Accounting and Financial Ingenuity in Local Government: the case of Liverpool.' In Public Money, March Vol. 5 No. 4 pp. 27-32

Stanyer, J., (1976) Understanding Local Government. (Martin Robertson)

Young, K., (1986a) 'Widdicombe from the Researcher's Angle' In Local Government Studies November/December 1986

Young, K., (1986b) Elections and Party Politics. In Cmnd 9797 (1986)

Chapter Four

THE LEGAL LIMITS OF LOCAL AUTONOMY

Chris Himsworth

INTRODUCTION

The idea of autonomy has been of great importance in the
rhetoric of central-local relations in Great Britain and
within the general idea of autonomy, financial autonomy has
had pride of place - reflecting the key role of finance in the
determination of intergovernmental relationships in any
political system. The recurrent use of the term has not,
however, contributed to any great precision in its meaning.
Clearly it has something to do with the freedom of local
authorities, singly or collectively, to make financial
decisions in a way which is not wholly dictated to them by
central government. They are able, within limits, to
determine total levels of revenue raising and expenditure
and to allocate expenditure within those totals. But there is
no precise yardstick on which a scale of financial autonomy
can be measured. Such a yardstick tends to fade in the
shifting sands of the political and social condition of the
state and the pattern of intergovernmental relations within
it.

There is no wish here to adopt a naively instrumental
view of the law. Any implication that autonomy rests
merely on legal relations and is amenable to merely legal
change is not intended. It is, however, assumed that, in a
society in which law is accorded an autonomy of its own and
in which discussion of present structures and change is most
frequently directed towards existing law, a review of the
different legal bases for local authority financial autonomy
has its own value. Hence there follows a review of autonomy
guaranteed in international law, autonomy guaranteed under

a written constitution, autonomy implicitly guaranteed by constitutional convention and the autonomy which derives from the legal limitations which are imposed by Parliament upon central government for the time being. It will be found that, to an extent, discussion overlaps two or more of the four categories. There are not clear dividing lines between them.

Autonomy guaranteed by international law

There are at present no treaties or conventions and no international customary law which is both binding upon the UK and designed to guarantee local autonomy. Furthermore, international law has no immediately binding effect upon UK domestic law. In particular, it cannot bind Parliament in the exercise of its legislative power. It is also inherently unlikely that the content of any international rules in this sphere could ever have the precision to produce any noticeable impact upon the domestic scene. These objections amount to an argument that adherence by the UK to an international code would be a pointless irrelevance - a position firmly taken by some commentators (Grant, 1985, pp. 237-8).

However, there exists the European Charter of Local Self-Government, which is a Council of Europe treaty first opened for signature by member states on 15th October 1985. It is a younger cousin of the European Convention for the Protection of Human Rights and Fundamental Freedoms 1950 (also from the Council of Europe) (Jacobs, 1975) which is addressed to the rights of individuals and, born out of the fears of post-war Europe, seeks to protect the rights and freedoms it itemises from invasion by the law and practice of member states. To this extent it is intended to supplement the guarantees contained in the Universal Declaration of Human Rights 1948 (which has itself been followed by the International Covenant on Economic, Social and Cultural Rights 1966 and the International Covenant on Civil and Political Rights 1966).

The Convention contains in Section I a series of Articles spelling out the rights and freedoms to be protected but, just as significantly, establishes in Sections II and III the elaborate enforcement mechanisms - the Commission, Court and Committee of Ministers. The Convention provides that citizens of those states which admit this right may petition the Commission directly. The strength of the Convention's provisions should, however, not be exaggerated. They do not bite very deep and their sharpness is tempered by vagueness of definition. Enforcement, too, is hampered by Commission procedures and, in the UK, the Convention's provisions are not directly enforceable in the courts.

It is, in a sense, the function of the European Charter of Local Self-Government to provide for local authorities what the Convention provides for individuals in Europe. The preamble to the Charter recites inter alia the commitment of member states of the Council of Europe to greater unity for the purpose of safeguarding and realising the ideals and principles which are their common heritage; the belief in local authorities as one of the main foundations of any democratic regime; that the right of citizens to participate in the conduct of public affairs is most directly exercised at the local level; and that these ideals entail the existence of local authorities endowed with democratically constituted decision-making bodies and possessing a wide degree of autonomy with regard to their responsibilities, the ways and means by which those responsibilities are exercised and the resources required for their fulfilment.

These aims are spelled out a little more fully in the substantive Articles of Charter which follow. The principle of local self-government is to be recognised in domestic legislation, and where practicable in the constitution (Art. 2). Powers given to local authorities are normally to be full and exclusive. They may not be undermined or limited by another central or regional authority except as provided for by the law (Art. 4.4). Any administrative supervision of local authorities may be exercised only according to such procedures and in such cases as are provided for by the constitution or by statute (Art. 8.1).

The longest Article of all is Article 9 which relates to the 'Financial resources of local authorities'. It provides that local authorities are to be entitled (within national economic policy) to adequate financial resources of their own, commensurate with their responsibilities, of which they may dispose freely within the framework of their powers. Furthermore, the financial systems on which resources available to local authorities are based including local taxes and charges, are to be of a sufficiently diversified and buoyant nature to enable them to keep pace as far as practically possible with the real evolution of the cost of carrying out their tasks. Financial equalisation procedures designed to correct the effects of the unequal distribution of potential sources of finance and of the financial burden they must support are not to diminish the discretion local authorities may exercise within their own sphere of responsibility. The provision of grants shall not remove the basic freedom of local authorities to exercise policy discretion within their own jurisdiction. For the purpose of borrowing for capital investment, local authorities must have access to the national capital market within the limits of the law.

It is, however, permissible for a State to ratify the Charter and yet, if it wished, elect not to be bound by any of its financial provisions. Moreover, many of the Charter's provisions are very loosely drawn - in part, of course, because they have to be capable of application to a large number of diverse systems of local government without obvious absurdities. Then, in contrast with the Convention, the Charter contains no machinery at all for its own enforcement. Neither an individual nor a local authority from a participating state would have any direct way of ensuring investigation of nor remedy for an alleged breach of the Charter. These are serious criticisms of the Charter if it is to be viewed as a credible yardstick against which the behaviour of ratifying states may be measured and challenged. For the UK, these criticisms will, however, probably remain an irrelevance. Even if the Charter's terms are adopted by other states, it is clear that, under the present Government at least, this will not happen here. When the Charter was opened for signature the British government declared its opposition to it and its refusal to sign and ratify.

Constitutionally guaranteed autonomy

Here the objections are even more obvious. To talk of constitutional guarantees (actual rather than aspirational) is to assume a written constitution. The UK has no written constitution. Therefore, there can be no prospect of guarantees from this source. Even if there were, at some point in the future, a move towards the adoption of a written constitution - perhaps with the primary aim of protecting individual liberty in a Bill of Rights - it is far from clear that rules to establish and entrench financial security for local authorities or, indeed, a system of local government at all would be included. Whatever might be the other arguments for a written constitution, it could well be argued that the rules about local government should remain much more malleable, much more available for change within the political system than crystallisation in a written constitution would imply. The same sorts of considerations are as relevant here as they are to international protection - tension between the wish to entrench and the wish also to retain flexibility, the wish to avoid drawing courts into 'political questions'; and, above all, the suspicion that the reduction of principles to writing is, for all the more or less understood reasons why laws fail to achieve the efficacy to which they aspire on their face, no sure way to secure an impact on the ground.

Actual attempts in other countries to entrench systems of local government (as opposed to forms of federalism) do not appear to be common. The United States Constitution, for example, does not entrench forms of local government but it does entrench the federal system and is thereby instructive on two matters. The limits of the powers of federal and state governments respectively are prescribed and, in cases of doubt, the Supreme Court is available to resolve conflicts in the light of its interpretation of the provisions of the Constitution. No-one has ever pretended that this is a merely mechanical process but it is one which appears to have encountered increasing difficulties in recent years. The Supreme Court is skilled in the process of injecting meaning into the skeletal text of the Constitution but their efforts to develop, apply and defend tests for distinguishing those things rightly federal from those things rightly in the power of the states have broken down. The case of Garcia v San Antonio 469 US 528 is particularly instructive on this. If the US finds the federal-state divide increasingly difficult to police, how much greater would be the maintenance of a clear constitutional line in the UK between central and local powers?

Another development in the United States has been the emergence of a literature on the constitutional status of local government - and particularly the cities (e.g. Frug, 1980; Williams, 1986). This is something of simply United States domestic interest in so far as it represents moves towards the recognition of the institutions and values of decentralised government at the level of local authorities - even though this is not recognised at all in the text of the

Constitution. But, whatever the domestic significance of the debate, it produces arguments which, as they reach this side of the Atlantic, will fall on the sympathetic ears of those who have been attempting a similar exercise here. The comparison is not precise because of the very lack of written constitutional protections but, from that different starting point, there is the quest for local government values capable of being given real recognition not in a system with a written constitution which is silent on the matter but in a system with no written constitution at all and one in which the coherent recognition of fundamental constitutional principles is highly problematic.

Autonomy guaranteed by constitutional convention

The conventions here are those which, if not invented by him, were given such prominence by Dicey in his Law of the Constitution (Dicey, 1968) - first published in 1885 and used as a powerful analytical tool by British constitutional writers since. It is widely agreed that there is a need for a way of taking account of many of the practices within the political system which have acquired a normative character and giving them the status of rules, albeit non-legal rules, of the constitution. Conventions enable those areas of the political system for which very little provision is made by statute or common law but which are inhabited by the Prime Minister and Cabinet and their relationships with the Crown and with Parliament to be charted with rules. There are problems with these conventional rules. Since they do not owe their existence to any formal source there are uncertainties as to their content and there are questions about the consequences of breach of them. These problems lead many to be sceptical about the value of designating them as rules at all (Griffith, 1963, pp. 401-2).

Although most of the conventions of the text-books are concerned with central government, they can play a role too in local government. Just as in central government, there are recurring patterns of behaviour in local authorities which may be taken to be sustained by constitutional principles of great importance at that level. These give rise, for instance, to the conventional rules about the relationships between members and officers and between the different political groups in a council's membership. The statute book does not tell us much about these and conventional practices with some normative content fill in many of the gaps. Recently these conventions have come under stress. There is unhappiness in some quarters about how the rules are operating and the call has come from the Widdicombe Committee (Cmnd. 9797, Chapter 5) to have many of them reduced to statutory form. Statutory rules have the greater precision and inflexibility which, it is thought, are required.

That is one area in which conventional rules may be said to have a relevance for local government. The other is much closer to present purposes and is that of an asserted conventional autonomy for local government and especially for its financial position. Once again, we have the familiar position in British constitutional practice of a structural background contained in statute onto which, it is urged, should be grafted conventional understandings and rules designed to reflect constitutional values inadequately expressed in the statutory rules taken alone. They may be taken as moderating or qualifying the formal rules.

Thus Jones and Stewart described the claims of central government (which they opposed) to establish overall expenditure targets for local government without the statutory power to do so as an assertion of a constitutional covention enabling them to intervene (Jones and Stewart, 1983, p. 52). This would be a convention claiming to limit the local autonomy which might otherwise have existed under the merely statutory rules - in the interests of some presumed constitutional need for the general subordination of local authorities to be maintained and, in particular, the need for central financial and economic control over them.

Unsurprisingly, however, there has been greater interest, among writers on local government, in seeking to identify conventions supporting a stronger position for local authorities (Jones and Stewart, 1983, passim). Rather than conventions tending to the greater subordination of authorities, conventional rules have been asserted which would tend to moderate statutes in the direction of greater autonomy. This is what Elliott claims when he asserts the need for both sides in the central-local relationship to recognise each other as governments (Elliott, 1981, p. 96). Each should take account of the other's governmental status. Local government actions acquire thereby a legitimacy 'to such an extent that central government should restrict the width of local authority actions only after the most careful consideration'. Elsewhere he refers to the basis of local government in a 'commitment to a limited form of constrained local autonomy' (Elliott, 1983, p. 41). Meanwhile Loughlin, whilst acknowledging the formal constitutional subordination of local authorities, moves by way of the official language of 'partnership' to say that 'the conventional terms of that relationship (between central and local government) are so ambiguous as the network of linkages is complex' and that

> the constitutional status of local government is determined not only by formal structures but also by certain traditions, understandings and norms which have evolved through past practices ... it is not only the formal structures but also the <u>texture</u> of relationships which determines the status of local government (Loughlin, 1983, pp. 2-4)

This is not an uncontroversial position. From her own (Marxist) perspective it is denied in large measure by Cockburn for whom the very notion of a constitutional independence for local government is unacceptable (Cockburn, 1977, p. 46). It is also more widely challenged by sceptics reinforced in their views by both the formal rules which contradict the claimed conventional rules and recent experience which, they argue, completely denies the existence of traditions and understandings between centre and locality (e.g. Grant, 1985, p. 236).

In discussing the potential force of convention, we are dealing with ideas which are domestically familiar to British constitutional lawyers in which ways rules of international law and written constitutions are not. In that sense their claim to credibility and acceptance may be greater. They do not, however, escape the strong cutting edge of parliamentary omnicompetence.

Autonomy under the law?

No apology need be offered for what has been a deliberate attempt to explore hypothetical sources of a legal model of local financial autonomy but, in the real world, international conventions and the alleged conventions of central-local relations count for little. Governments have it within their legal power to give considerable spending freedom to local authorities but they also have the power, through their control of Parliament, to restrict that freedom. The concept of autonomy seems to be quickly emptied of meaning.

There are, however, a number of ways in which meaning may be given to financial autonomy. One lies in the freedom to spend which derives from powers and duties which are conferred in relatively broad statutory terms rather than in terms which specify minutely the objects of a spending power. Local authorities operate subject to the ultra vires doctrine and the illegal exercise of a statutory power will normally produce illegal expenditure. Thus a power which is broadly defined confers greater freedom to spend. Similarly, the effect of those sections of the Local Government Acts which permit authorities to do anything 'which is calculated to facilitate, or is conducive or incidental to, the discharge of any of their functions' confer the necessary spending freedom to achieve those ancillary purposes (Local Government Act 1972 s.111; Local Government (Scotland) Act 1973 s.69). The other important powers of this sort are those which permit authorities, subject to increasing numbers of qualifications incorporated by amendment, to 'incur expenditure which in their opinion is in the interests of their area or any part of it or all or some of its inhabitants' (Local Government Act 1972 s.137; Local Government (Scotland) Act 1973 s.83). There is clearly a sense in which these provisions confer a spending freedom which authorities would not otherwise enjoy. There is also a sense in which the freedom conferred is merely one to spend existing funds on a rather wider range of purposes - whilst spending less on others. These are, however, powers which have rightly been accorded some significance and have attracted a literature of their own (Crawford and Moore, 1983).

These provisions represent an important form of financial autonomy but are closely entwined with the related but wider ideas of a 'relaxation' of the ultra vires rule through the grant of a 'general competence' to local authorities. This connects also with proposals for the removal of the powers (particularly of surcharge) of one of its principal guardians - the external auditor. Because they necessarily invite much broader discussion of the general limits to local authority powers, they will not be further pursued here.

There are also other ways in which the ideas of freedom and autonomy are used in relation to local authority spending and which are concerned with the very sources of revenue themselves. Thus there is a strong sense in which a series of narrowly circumscribed specific grants from central government confer less freedom or autonomy upon the recipient authorities whereas a general grant which is not, at the point of receipt, explicitly allocated to particular purposes is said to allow greater freedom. Similarly, if we turn to the rating system, it may be the 'buoyancy' of the tax, to which a number of separate factors contribute, which provides a measure of the autonomy which it confers upon local authorities. Again, these are issues of the very highest importance in any debate about the financing of decentralised government. The autonomy (or lack of it) finally conferred is not, however, one owed primarily to the fact of that legal definition but to the characteristics of the tax or grant itself.

There is, however, a remaining distinguishable form of autonomy which has been of great importance in recent years. It is the residual freedom for manoeuvre which survives the concerted efforts of central government to restrain local government spending. This sounds like a very much more limited version of local financial autonomy but it has a foundation in reality so far denied to the rhetoric of the more ambitious models.

It is underpinned by two substantial principles. The first is that which was described by Chester nearly forty years ago as one of his 'clarifying assumptions' (Chester, 1951, Chapter 1). These were the propositions with which he opened his book on Central and Local Government to set the scene for his more detailed analysis. First among his 'assumptions' was that 'Government Departments and Local Authorities are Statutory Bodies' and from this he derived the fundamental proposition for central-local relations that, although there is a direct link between the power of ministers and the supreme law-making power of Parliament, they are not synonymous.

> So far as current action is concerned the Department is ruled by the actual law and not by the possibility that Parliament may be influenced to change it. And however much the senior civil servant may wish he had different statutory powers usually there are many obstacles between the wish and the fulfilment (Chester 1951, p. 3)

Parliament has never given Government Departments

unlimited discretionary powers to interfere in the affairs of Local Authorities. The right to approve borrowing, to audit local accounts, to hold local inquiries, to act in default, to demand statistical returns, to give and withhold grants and similar powers are all conferred by specific sections of Acts of Parliament. This being so, any action by a Department not supported by such powers is challengeable in the Courts in the usual way (Chester, 1951, p. 5)

Local government and the relations between local authorities and central departments may have changed since 1951, but these words continue to ring true today. It may be that Parliament will, in due course, be induced to change the law but, until the change is made, ministers are compelled to act under the law as it is - on pain of challenge in the courts. In theory, it may be supposed, ministers will be able, by as many legislative amendments as are necessary, to acquire for themselves the power totally to mould and to limit local expenditure to levels which they dictate but, in the meantime, they must obey the law. And it is in this obedience that there nestles a degree of local autonomy.

This may not sound much but we can expand it a little by invoking a second principle, familiar in the sociology of law, which reminds us that it is routinely the case that the law fails to operate as a simple machine (Miers and Page, 1982, Ch. 8). It is not an instrument whose handles may be pulled by government in the certain knowledge that what is aimed at will be achieved. The efficacy of law is not total and not only may intended effects be diluted but unintended side-effects may accompany legislative change. For this reason, the proposition made earlier that ministers could, in theory, take powers containing all the controls they might wish for has to be modified. Rather, the theory of the inefficacy of law tells us that they will always to an extent fail. The reasons for such slippage in the law are a matter of enquiry and will clearly vary from case to case but they may include not only imprecision or other ineptness at the point that a new law is devised and drafted but also, most importantly, the tightness and appropriateness of the processes of implementation and enforcement. The very openness to legal challenge of ministerial action taken in reliance upon existing powers conferred by Parliament may contribute substantially to the effective limits of those powers.

Thus, successive modifications of the grant legislation show that it may take ministers several years to acquire all the powers they need and, until then, authorities retain a degree of freedom, a degree of autonomy. Other traces of freedom may appear as, for example, when decisions by the Secretary of State to reduce the grant entitlements of Brent and five other London boroughs were temporarily struck down - even if the authorities' success was 'primarily symbolic' (Loughlin, 1983, p. 16). With more substantial challenge in prospect, the Local Government Finance Bill in the 1986-87 Parliamentary Session is designed to give the Secretary of State retrospective immunity as well as to ensure, once again, that for the future his own powers will be stronger.

That Bill also includes similar provisions relating to Scotland where, for some years, the Secretary of State has wanted to be able to penalise high spending authorities by reducing their grant. Section 5 of the Local Government (Scotland) Act 1966 contained useful powers to reduce by order the rate support grant of an authority whose expenditure had been 'excessive and unreasonable' but these powers had to be extended to cover proposed expenditure. This was done by means of the Local Government (Miscellaneous Provisions) (Scotland) Act 1981 and, under the 1966 Act as amended, the Secretary of State ordered the reduction of the grants of Stirling District Council and two other authorities but said, as he had also authorised himself to do under the Act, that the authorities could have some of the grant penalty returned if they reduced their rate. But the Secretary of State did not have the power to order reduction of the rate. The Controller of Audit, invoking the concept of the 'fiduciary duty' claimed that, even though the authorities were not under a statutory duty to accept the deal offered by the Secretary of State, the ratepayers were legally entitled to have their burden lifted (Himsworth, 1982). Long afterwards in the case of Commission for Local Authority Accounts v Stirling (1984 SLT 442) the Court of Session ducked the question of 'fiduciary duty' but, in the meantime, the Secretary of State had simply taken the powers he needed in the Local Government and Planning (Scotland) Act 1982. Then, wanting not only the power to penalise individual authorities but also to rate-cap generally, he took further powers in the Rating and Valuation (Amendment) (Scotland) Act 1984.

He also used the 1984 Act to cover up another chink in his armour of control. Some housing authorities had not, in the minister's view, been raising their rents sufficiently. They had instead been relying increasingly upon a contribution from their rate funds to finance expenditure from their housing revenue accounts. Initially, the Secretary of State did not have the power to limit directly the amounts of rate fund contribution so he leaned on authorities by relating their permitted levels of capital spending (which he could control) to their levels of rate fund contribution. Keep the rate fund contribution down (with the result that rents rise) and permitted capital spending would be increased. But, again, the Secretary of State did not have the power to <u>compel</u> a lower rate fund contribution. Thus, under the 1984 Act he took powers to prescribe levels of rate fund contribution. In the first year he did so, however, some authorities still tried to resist. The validity of his order was challenged in an action which was unsuccessful but must have made Scottish Office lawyers briefly nervous (Himsworth, 1985).

There has since followed a period of continuing 'creative accounting' whereby legal accounting devices are used to avoid control by reallocating expenditure between different accounts (Cmnd. 9714 para 1.30). A recent Scottish example of this came in September 1986 when the Government suddenly tired of the attempts of authorities to escape constraints on capital expenditure through the use of 'covenant schemes' and hastily brought forward (to September 1986) the date of a ban on such schemes which had been intended to operate from March 1987.

CONCLUSIONS: SOME OR NONE?

An important constitutional principle is acknowledged when the limits on the powers of ministers rather than authorities are asserted. There is an autonomy which exists just beyond the reach which is statutorily permitted to ministers for the time being. However, the power of ministers to extend their reach further by recourse to Parliament also reflects a working principle of the British constitution. The central question is whether there are or ought to be limits upon the operation of that principle. Of course, there are. There are the operational limits in drafting legislation (sometimes at speed) and beyond that, there are the limits which reflect wider bureaucratic constraints. These appear in Paying for Local Government (Cmnd. 9714 para 1.50) when ministers are seen to reject reforms which would not only increase central control over local spending but would also suck central government into a much more detailed, complex and expensive process of supervision than they would be prepared to permit. Even allowing for their role in an argument leading inexorably towards the community charge, these views have some separate validity of their own.

Central government will never exclude all local choice because it would be ultimately impracticable and counter productive. But this is indeed a low base-line. The extent to which that degree of autonomy, which initially lurks solely in the interstices of the ultra vires rule as it impinges on ministers and as moderated by the imperatives of bureacratic restraint, can be further expanded depends on the weight given to the 'conventional' arguments already discussed. Conventional constraints upon the invasion of local autonomy are not merely the product of wishful thinking by localists but may already be regarded as rules of constitutional morality which await greater definition and recognition.

REFERENCES

Chester, D.N. (1951) Central and Local Government (Macmillan, London)

Cmnd 9797 (1986) The Conduct of Local Authority Business (Chairman D. Widdicombe) HMSO London

Cmnd 9714 (1986) Paying for Local Government HMSO London

Cockburn, C. (1977) The Local State (Pluto, London)

Crawford and Moore, M. (1983) The Free Two Pence (Chartered Institute of Public Finance and Accountancy, London)

Dicey, A.V. (1968) Law of the Constitution (10th ed) (Macmillan, London)

Elliott, M.J. (1981) The Role of Law in Central-Local Relations (Social Science Research Council, London)

------ (1983) 'Constitutional Continuity and the Position of Local Government', in Young, K. (ed.) National Interests and Local Government (Heinemann, London)

Frug, G. (1980) 'The City as a Legal Concept' 93 Harvard Law Review 1057 (Cambridge, Massachusetts)

Legal Limits of Local Autonomy

Grant, M. (1985) 'Central-Local Relations: The Balance of
    Power', in Jowell, J. and Oliver, D. (eds) The Changing
    Constitution (Clarendon, Oxford) 229-49
Griffith, J.A.G. (1963) Editorial Public Law (Stevens,
    London) 401-2
Himsworth, C.M.G. (1982) 'Fiduciary Duties of Local
    Authorities' Scots Law Times (News) 241, 249. (Greens,
    Edinburgh)
------ (1985) 'Defining the Boundaries of Judicial Review',
    Scots Law Times (News) 369 (Greens, Edinburgh)
Jacobs, F.G. (1975) The European Convention on Human
    Rights (Clarendon, Oxford)
Jones, G. and Stewart, J. (1983) The Case for Local
    Government (Allen and Unwin, London)
Loughlin, M. (1983) Local Government, the Law and the
    Constitution (Local Government Legal Society Trust,
    London)
Miers, D.R. and Page, A.C. (1982) Legislation (Sweet and
    Maxwell, London)
Williams, J.C. (1986) 'The Constitutional Vulnerability of
    American Local Government: The Politics of City
    Status in American Law' Wisconsin Law Review 83
    (Madison, Wisconsin)

Chapter Five

A POLL TAX FOR BRITAIN?

Clive Martlew and Stephen J. Bailey

INTRODUCTION

In the latest of a series of consultative documents (Cmnd 8449 and Cmnd 9008) concerned with the financing of local government, the 1986 Green Paper 'Paying for Local Government' (Cmnd 9714) proposes the ultimate abolition of domestic rating, its replacement by a so-called 'Community Charge', and the standardisation under central government control of non-domestic rate poundages. The Community Charge would be payable by all adults aged 18 and over, and will be determined by individual authorities as a flat-rate payment. Central government would determine a national non-domestic rate poundage to be levied against non-domestic rateable values and the proceeds would be distributed to local authorities on a per adult basis. There would also be reforms made to the system of central government grants paid to local authorities.

The 1986 Green Paper gives the impression of having discovered a panacea to all the present maladies in the field of central-local relationships. The universal remedy is 'effective local accountability' which is seen as 'the cornerstone of successful local government' (p.vii). The present system is condemned as failing in this respect since business ratepayers have no local voting rights and too few domestic ratepayers actually pay rates in full or even in part. It is also stated that accountability is undermined because rates 'vary in a way that now has little or no regard to the use made of local authority services' (p.vii). All this is reinforced because the complexity of the system of central government grants obscures the true relationship between services and cost.

THE GREEN PAPER'S ANALYSIS

Before examining the Government's proposals in more depth it is perhaps worth highlighting a fundamental question, the answer to which will determine their success or failure. That question is: Does the proposed reform actually improve local accountability? If it does then there may be genuine grounds for believing reform will be both successful and long-lasting. If it does not, then at best the reform simply achieves a redistribution of the local tax burden and at worst it further exacerbates the current problems. It must be said that the signs are ominous as even at the most elementary level the precise purpose of the proposed reform is unclear. It has been argued elsewhere that the local accountability argument is merely a pretext for increased central control over local authorities and that 'Local accountability has become the official euphemism for attempted control by the centre of local spending' (Ward and Williams, 1986, p. 27). If this is the case then reform is predestined to fail and, indeed, is not intended to improve local accountability.

The impression that local accountability is indeed a euphemism for central control is not dispelled by the foreword to the Green Paper which states rather wistfully that if the costs of services are easier to perceive and 'fairly distributed' then electors will be able to make 'sensible choices' about the level and distribution of local spending. The Government's belief is that if the relationship between finance and services can be made 'clear' then electors will be 'sensible' - and they will vote against higher spending. This is amplified later in the Green Paper in the chapter on Scotland where it is stated that the failure of central government to achieve 'adequate control' over local authority spending is due to the 'mismatch between those who elect the local councillors taking spending decisions and the rate payers who have to bear the financial consequences' (p. 62). Thus the Government's attempt 'to maintain the pressure on authorities from their own electorates to spend responsibly' (p. 62), by progressively reducing grant, has been thwarted. The aim of the reform therefore appears to be to increase accountability in order to reduce spending - objectives which cannot necessarily be achieved simultaneously. This leads one to suspect that if spending falls then this will be a triumph for 'local accountability' while if it rises then local accountability will be said by the Government to have failed.

(a) Non-domestic rates

Over half the total rate income in Great Britain comes from the non-domestic sector (54% in England, 56% in Wales and 62% in Scotland). However, in certain areas this is much higher (up to 75%) and it is said in the Green Paper that this provides a substantial cushion against the effects of higher spending on domestic ratepayers. 'Authorities therefore find themselves in a position to increase spending on services for the voting domestic ratepayer largely at the expense of the non-voting, non-domestic ratepayer. This provided little incentive to economy' (p. 6).

The Government's preferred option on the non-domestic rate is that the power to set the poundage should be transferred to central government. There would then be a common national poundage to produce a yield equivalent to the present one which would then be index-linked to the rate of inflation. The product would be pooled and distributed on the basis of the number of adults in each authority. However, a national system will not be possible until a revaluation of all non-domestic property has taken place in England, Scotland and Wales in 1990 and in the meantime the poundages in force in Scotland will be nationalised and index-linked to the rate of inflation.

(b) Grants

The diagnosis of the 1986 Green Paper is that the present grant arrangements do not contribute to accountability. The aim of reform is to create a grant system which allows changes in local expenditure levels to be reflected in changes in tax bills, and to operate it in a way that enables local residents 'to see the extent of the support that is being provided' (p. 28). This requires stability. However, the present grant system is not stable because of for example changes in the distribution methodology and data. Grant entitlement can also vary within a year as the calculations are based on actual expenditure. An authority's grant can change because of its expenditure varying from estimates and through combined effects of the decisions of other authorities.

The Green Paper sets up a number of objectives for a new grant system: simplicity, stability, accountability (to enable taxpayers to see a link between changes in their tax bills and their local authority's expenditure) and equalisation for needs (because 'it would be unreasonable to leave people in high-need areas to bear a heavier burden than people in low-need areas in order to provide the same standard of service') (p. 33). Resources equalisation and relief for domestic ratepayers would no longer need to be objectives of the grant regime when rates are replaced by the Community Charge.

The Government's proposal is to create a grant system with 2 elements: a needs grant to compensate authorities for differences in the cost of providing a standard level of service to meet local needs, and a standard grant to provide an additional contribution from national taxation towards the cost of local services. The Government would fix the total grant available. Specific grants would be deducted and needs grants would be distributed on the basis of a local authority's expenditure need per adult. Standard grant would be distributed as a per adult amount. The total grant for each authority would be fixed at the beginning of the financial year and would not be affected by what the authority actually spent. Higher than planned actual spending will then have to be borne entirely by the poll tax whilst lower than budgeted spending will provide surplus funds to the authority.

(c) **Local domestic taxes**

The Green Paper asserts that there are three main criteria a local tax should be evaluated against: technical adequacy, fairness and accountability. Technical adequacy includes things like cost effective administration and the need for the local taxation system to fit with the national tax system. It also includes the need to promote 'proper financial control' in the sense of the yield being predictable and not 'lumpy'. It should also be suitable for all tiers of local government. Fairness must take account of both the 'beneficial' and 'redistributive' principles. The Green Paper states that domestic rates are 'accused of inadequacy in

Table 5.1: Households paying full, partial and no rates

Householders paying:

	Full rates	Partial rates	No rates
England	66%	18%	16%
Wales	67%	15%	18%
Scotland	62%	21%	17%

Source: Cmnd 9714.

both respects' (p. 20), in that they do not reflect the use made of services nor the ability to pay. Local accountability, says the Green Paper, is 'now of crucial importance' and 'is the key to an approach to local government finance that rests on responsible local spending decisions and a reduction in central government intervention' (p. 21).

In order to secure accountability the Green Paper states that the tax base should be wide to ensure that 'a substantial proportion of electors have a direct financial interest in the decisions of their authority' and that 'there should be a clear link between changes in expenditure and changes in the local tax bill' (p. 21). It goes on to argue, as did its predecessor in 1981, that only four categories of taxation could independently raise enough finance - property taxes (i.e. domestic rates), local sales taxes, local income taxes and residence taxes.

(i) Domestic Rates - The Green Paper accepts that domestic rates score well on the technical criteria and they retain a 'much attenuated' link with the original 'beneficial' and 'redistributive' principles (p. 21). However, it argues that while rates are perceptible to ratepayers they do not promote accountability because of the low proportion of the electorate who pay. This appears to be the main criticism levelled at the rates: the mismatch between voters and those who pay domestic rates. This link it is argued is further weakened by rebates which damp the effects of higher spending and so 'under the present arrangements those who receive full relief can vote for higher services without having to pay anything towards them' (p. 6).

In all three countries of Great Britain householders comprise roughly 50% of the electorate. In Scotland, for example, there are 3.9 million electors and 1.9 million householders. Using Table 5.1, it can be seen that only 30% of electors therefore pay rates in full in Scotland. 'So domestic rates fail the first test of a suitable local tax. They fall on too few shoulders' (p. 22).

The 1986 Green Paper also argues that domestic rates 'fail the test of giving clear signals to those who pay' (p. 22) as revaluations lead to shifts unrelated to expenditure decisions and even very regular revaluation would remove this link. Of course this last point ignores the fact that there have been no revaluations in England and Wales since 1973! Revaluations in Scotland have been seen as exacerbating the problems of rates (Bailey, 1986).

(ii) A Local Sales Tax (LST) of 6.5% could replace the yield of domestic rates. It would have wide coverage. However the 1986 verdict is the same as that in 1981, that because it is not perceptible it would not promote accountability. It would be administratively complex, the yield would be lumpy and badly distributed, and major economic side-effects and distortions could result because, for example, regional shopping centres would benefit at the expense of their neighbours.

(iii) A Local Income Tax (LIT) would have to be levied at 4.5p to replace domestic rates. The Green Paper states that its introduction would mark the abandonment of the 'beneficial' principle in favour of the 'redistributive' principle. That is, local taxation would be related to ability to pay and not at all to the use made of services. The Green Paper rejects LIT on four grounds. First, an extension of taxation on incomes would run counter to the Government's commitment to reducing the burden of tax on incomes. Second, a local income tax would not underpin local accountability. Third, 'it would not be appropriate to rely too heavily on a redistributive tax to fund local authority services.' Fourth, it would make management of the economy more difficult (p. 23).

First, converting rate bills to an LIT would produce a range in England from 2.5p to 11p meaning that in some areas there could be substantial increases in income tax. Second, the assertion that LIT would not promote accountability was directly contradicted by Layfield (Cmnd 6453, pp. 298 and 189). It argued that 'LIT is a necessary condition of greater local responsibility' and that 'a local income tax, with locally variable rates of tax and levied on the basis of the taxpayer's place of residence meets the test of accountability'. The degree of 'coverage' of the electorate which a tax provides is obviously the key so far as the Government is concerned but in ruling out LIT on the grounds that 'only' 57% of voters will pay it seems to be setting the criteria unreasonably high. It also assumes LIT is the only local tax but the degree of coverage would rise substantially if LIT was combined with domestic rates. An LIT would be cheaper to administer than the Community Charge since it would be easier to allocate national taxpayers to local authority areas than to identify residents from scratch. Kay and Smith (1987) argue that end-year assessments could be easily incorporated into the PAYE system at little additional cost.

Third, it has not been established why 'it would not be appropriate to rely too heavily on a redistributive tax' (p. 23). It appears that a value judgement has been made that a local tax should be as much like a charge as possible. LIT of course is redistributive and in no sense could be construed as a charge. On the other hand relating local tax bills to ability to pay would be seen as one of the great strengths of LIT by its supporters.

Fourth, the argument that LIT poses problems for the management of the national economy has been criticised as 'bad economics' (Crawford and Dawson, 1982) on the grounds that an increase in local current expenditure financed entirely from local taxation (including a Community Charge) has no impact on macroeconomic objectives, except for balanced-budget multiplier effects which are negligible. This is especially the case where 'crowding out' is significant and so it has been argued that 'there is a strong case for removing the rate-financed component of local government spending from the ambit of demand management policy' (Jackman, 1982).

(iv) A Residence Tax. The Green Paper proposes a residence tax called the Community Charge. The search for a local tax is seen as being an attempt to reconcile the 'beneficial' and 'redistributive' principles. The Green Paper states that 'no tax could satisfy both aims simultaneously' and only rates and a tax on residence are 'technically capable of being applied at the local level in a way that has regard to local accountability' (p. 24). Of the two the Green Paper finds the tax on residence to be more acceptable for four reasons. First, it argues that rates 'are no better related to the ability to pay than a flat rate charge would be'. Second, rates are less well related to the use of local authority services 'which now more closely reflects the number of people in a household than the value of the property occupied'. Third, rates fall on a narrow section of the local electorate while the coverage of the Community Charge would be much wider. Fourth, a Community Charge would be more perceptible than rates (p. 24).

The Community Charge would be determined by each authority and payable at the same rate by all adult residents of a local authority. The Green Paper states that there would be 'some assistance' for those households on low incomes. It goes on to say that 'moving from rates to a flat-rate Community Charge would mark a major change in the direction of local government finance back to the notion of charging for local authority services', and asserts that a Community Charge 'would provide a closer reflection of the benefit from modern people-based services than a property tax' (p. 25).

A Critique

The derivation of accurate figures to illustrate the levels of Community Charge likely to be levied is subject to many methodological problems and any published figures must necessarily make a number of assumptions which, if not valid, can give a very distorted picture. For example, in order to model the outcome of the reform one needs to know whether local authorities will continue to receive as grant those funds presently disbursed under domestic rate relief. If not then local tax bills will be higher since relief is presently 18.5p in the pound in England and Wales and 7p in the pound in Scotland (the poundage reduction applied to rateable value). Furthermore, centralisation of the non-domestic rate can be done on an all-Britain basis or separately for England, Wales and Scotland. Such assumptions will have dramatic effects on the levels of Community Charge raised by local authorities. Attempts to calculate figures are available in Hale (1986), Martlew and Bailey (1986) and Smith and Squires (1986). Hence the following analysis concentrates upon the validity of the Green Paper's analysis rather than the tax outcomes.

(a) **Non-domestic rates**

In its discussion of non-domestic rates and in arriving at the conclusion they should be 'nationalised' the Green Paper blatantly ignores research results. For example, it notes that 'hard evidence of the effect of rates on business is scarce' (p. 13) without acknowledging that what there is does <u>not</u> show any significant impact of rates on manufacturing employment. There has been a substantial amount of research on the factors influencing industrial location but as Crawford <u>et al.</u> (1985) have stated, 'None of these studies highlights the level of rates as an important factor - or even a lesser contributory factor - in driving firms out of some areas and into others' and 'that with the exception of office employment in and around London, it is not possible to detect an influence of rates on the location of employment'. The statistical methodology of Crawford's research has been criticised (Bennett, 1986) but there is certainly no evidence (other than at a purely anecdotal level) to suggest that serious economic distortions arise from geographical variations in non-domestic rate bills.

Another example of the Green Paper's ignorance of research results is in its claim that 'most costs that businesses face are fairly uniform across the country. But the rate burden can vary considerably even between neighbouring authorities' (p. 13). This is not supported by recent research (Tyler <u>et al.</u>, 1984) which found significant geographical differences in the costs of labour, transport, insurance, industrial services and rents as well as in rates. Hence the Green Paper is again at fault for adopting a blinkered outlook, only taking a very partial view of the factors influencing industrial location. Furthermore, if grant is cut most heavily for urban authorities with above average levels of unemployment and if these authorities increase their rate income to compensate for loss of grant, then high rates will become associated with high unemployment. There is however no direct causation. Rather the cause is the Government's failure to accurately assess their need to spend by failing to take proper account of the extra costs imposed on such urban authorities suffering from economic and demographic decline. These extra costs may be considerable and yet are not fully reflected in Central Government's assessments of their need to spend (Jackson, 1982; Bailey, 1982). Hence the Government is confusing changes in grants with changes in rate-financed expenditure.

A further problem with the Green Paper analysis is that while it is true that local authorities are not directly accountable to non-domestic ratepayers in the sense of there being no 'electoral' link, nevertheless only in 1984 did the present government introduce 'consultation' procedures which were explicitly intended to reduce this so-called problem. Although early experience with consultations has not produced dramatic effects (Martlew, 1986), it is certainly far too early to make a proper judgement on their success or failure.

The Green Paper states that: 'Businesses will be concerned to ensure that the new arrangements do not lead to an increase in the proportion of local government spending financed by their rates' (p. 16). For this reason the national average poundage will simply raise the same total amount as at present. However, while it may be true that representative business organisations are concerned primarily with the overall balance between non-domestic rates and other local taxes it can in no sense be presented as the view from an individual business. Each business will be interested primarily in what it, and it alone, pays in non-domestic rates. Setting a national average poundage obviously implies that businesses currently in high poundage areas will in future have lower rate bills while those in low poundage areas will have to face higher bills. The precise effects of centralising non-domestic rates once again depend on the assumptions one makes. One approach is worked through in Martlew and Bailey (1986).

There must also be some concern in local government about what index the Government will use to calculate the annual increases in poundages. The Green Paper advances two possibilities - the 'actual' figure of inflation as represented by the Retail Price Index (RPI), which is the method proposed in the Bill to implement the changes, or a Government forecast of inflation. In the former case there would be a question mark about the relevance of RPI as a measure of local authority costs which are, of course, heavily influenced by labour costs. In the latter case Government forecasts may be more a statement of a policy goal than a realistic estimate of what will actually happen. In either case if the annual increase did not reflect actual cost increases in local government (which in any case will vary from area to area) the difference would have to be made up from the Community Charge.

Finally, in terms of local accountability, the effect of the national non-domestic rate is, of course, to make local government reliant on central government for its income from non-domestic rates (i.e. it becomes in effect an assigned revenue, distributed on a per adult basis). For example at present domestic ratepayers meet only 13% of net rate fund expenditure in Scotland so that in future 87% of local authority funding will be controlled by central government. This would appear to directly contradict the Government's stated aim of enhancing local accountability in that local government will be even more answerable to and dependent upon the centre. Non-domestic rates will simply be an 'assigned revenue' - a form of funding for local government that has consistently been rejected in Britain. There would no longer be any rationale for non-domestic rates as a local tax and to refer to them as such would be misleading. In effect local government is losing a local tax.

(b) **The community charge**

So far as the new Community Charge itself is concerned the 1986 Green Paper makes a number of invalid or inconsistent statements. First, a major flaw in the Green Paper is that it considers that the proposed Community Charge 'would mark a major change in the direction of local government finance back to the notion of charging for local authority services' and 'a Community Charge would provide a closer reflection of the benefit from modern people-based services than a property tax' (p. 25). On closer reflection, however, this assertion is untenable. It is precisely those people who will have to pay the Community Charge and who are not presently paying rates as householders, who make least use of local government services (i.e. mainly young adults aged 18 to 24.) The major categories of expenditure are directed towards young children and the elderly.

A second and related problem, which receives little attention in relation to a Community Charge, arises from the fact that the gains from local expenditure of the more affluent will be likely to be disproportionately high relative to their payments. The idea that families of the same size should pay the same charge because they use the same amount of services flies in the face of the great amount of evidence which shows that middle class residents receive much higher benefits than others from local authority (Le Grand, 1982). To the extent that rateable values reflect site values, they will reflect part of the benefit of providing services such as parks, schools etc., in each area. Higher rateable values reflect these higher costs of service provision as well as the scarcity of the site area.

Thirdly, another invalid proposition is that the Community Charge will automatically increase accountability. This is simply an assertion. There is no supporting evidence or theory presented in the Green Paper about the effect of local taxes on voter behaviour, nor is any data presented about who actually votes or abstains from voting. Although the turnout in local elections among the young is very low in other respects 'local government voters are almost perfectly representative of the full electorate' (Miller, 1986, p. 143). The Green Paper makes the implicit assumption that those people not paying local taxes (in full or in part) vote for ever-increasing expenditures. Most damning of all to the Government's case on this issue are the comments of the Widdicombe Report on the Conduct of Local Authority Business.

> Our own survey of public attitudes suggests that the linkage between voting and paying rates might not be quite as poor as the figures quoted (in the Green Paper) would suggest. When asked whether or not their household pays rates 94% of electors said 'yes' and only 4% 'no'. This indicates two things. First, most electors who do not themselves pay rates are members of a household that does. Second, many electors perceive of themselves (or their households) as 'ratepayers' even where their rates are partially or wholly rebated. It was only through a subsequent more detailed question that our survey was able to discover that many of the 94% receive rebates, and even then this was probably under-stated by respondents (Cmnd 9797 p. 40)

As Miller states in his analysis of the same figures: 'Psychologically local electorates are ratepayers, whether or not they actually pay them.' Hence a Community Charge (for which both spouses are to be made jointly liable) will make no practical difference and therefore have no effect on accountability in this respect.

Fourth, a major contradictory argument is the claim that changing from rates to a Community Charge will have negligible impact on the distribution of local tax burdens but that, nonetheless, there will be a radical improvement in accountability. The Green Paper states that the combined effect of changes to local taxation and grant would mean that 'over 70 per cent of gains and losses would be less than

£2 a week' and that 'the main gainers would be single adult households, primarily one-parent families and pensioners, while the main losers would again be young single adults because they would become liable to pay local tax for the first time' (p. 41). In fact the Green Paper claims that the Community Charge is less regressive than domestic rates. However, that assertion assumes that the minimum payment of 20 per cent, as proposed in the White Paper 'Reform of Social Security' (Cmnd 9691), is already introduced. This latter change will particularly disadvantage those pensioners who presently receive full rate rebates and young non-householder unemployed adults. Taking both the proposed reforms together (i.e. in the 1986 Green Paper and the White Paper 'Reform of Social Security') the conclusion that rates are more regressive that the Community Charge is quite easily reversed. The new system will be much more regressive than the present system. Whilst it is difficult to quote precise figures, given the almost deliberate attempt of the 1986 Green Paper to mislead the reader, it is clear from Figure F7 (p. 107) that the totality of reform makes households with net actual incomes below £200 per week considerably worse off whilst those over £200 per week are made considerably better off. The totality of reform is undoubtedly regressive. The Green Paper is therefore at fault in making misleading and poor use of data.

More generally, a fifth point is that the Community Charge will be difficult to enforce. In the 1981 Green Paper (Cmnd 8449) a Community Charge was said to meet all the technical criteria of yield, suitability for all tiers, and financial control, but it was perceived as being difficult to enforce. A register of residence would have to be created and maintained. This will be very costly and in any case unreliable and hence the Community Charge was rejected as a viable option. Other problems relate to the proliferation of small financial transactions and debt recovery procedures. Clearly the political will has now been found to overcome the practical problems associated with identifying the tax base. 'These problems are not insuperable. In view of the overriding importance of increasing local accountability through the introduction of a Community Charge they must now be tackled' (p. 26). However, it has been argued elsewhere 'that the problems associated with implementation are insuperable' and so the Community Charge 'falls at the very first hurdle of technical adequacy' (Scottish Consumer Council, 1986, pp. iv and v).

The Audit Commission for England and Wales has stated that limits should be placed on the value of debts referred for legal action and that limits should be placed on the uneconomic pursuit of small or uncollectable debts - a category which is likely to cover most non-payers of the 20% minimum (Audit Commission, 1986). The same point will apply to the Community Charge and non-householder taxpayers will have little in the way of seizable assets. Hence accountability is hardly promoted.

(c) **Other deficiencies**

First, the Green Paper is solely concerned with the distribution of the local tax burden and its effect on accountability. However, local service users are not just concerned with accountability at the input or financing stage. They are also concerned with the accountability of local government for service provision at the output stage. For example, they are concerned with the maintenance of council houses and schools, with the adequacy of teaching materials, of social services for the elderly and so on. The Green Paper completely ignores the distribution of local service outputs, despite its constant reference to narrowing the gap between those who vote for, those who pay for and those who receive local outputs.

Second, the Green Paper assumes that abolition of domestic rates will leave housing as an untaxed area of consumption. This is surely naive. Rates are equivalent to about 15 per cent of total housing costs, taking account of mortgage payments after tax relief, repairs, maintenance, insurance, etc. It would be a very attractive source of expenditure against which to apply Value Added Tax, Capital Gains Tax or some other variant of housing tax in the future. In the meantime removing housing from all taxation is likely to lead to effects on house prices and hence affect other areas of social policy. Annex E to the Green Paper estimates the effect on prices to be 5% at least and possibly as high as 15% if supply does not respond to increased demand. These effects are discussed further in Chapter 7.

Third, central government leaves unresolved how it will maintain consistency between local expenditures and macroeconomic policy, if authorities once again have complete freedom to set the level of local taxation. What the government appears to be hoping is that this regressive poll tax will provide a stranglehold on local government spending and that capping of local taxes and grant regimes that penalise overspending will therefore not be required. There is of course no guarantee that 'greater accountability will lead to more 'sensible' expenditure decisions. 'Community charge capping' represents yet another attempt at a 'middle way' which Layfield (1976) denounced as unlikely to lead to a long-lasting solution.

CONCLUSIONS

The reforms proposed by the 1986 Green Paper are not the panacea they are heralded to be. Indeed every claim in the foreword to the Green Paper is open to dispute. The 'searching examination of the way we pay for local government' is not very searching. It is narrow and partial in focus. Nor does it answer the opening question 'What is the role of local government in this country'? The proposed reforms do not leave an independent viable structure. Capping of local taxes will still be used. Whilst agreeing with the foreword that 'local electors (should) know what the costs of their services are' and that 'effective local accountability must be the cornerstone of successful local government', the proposed reforms achieve neither precondition. Central government sees the main problems at present as being that non-domestic ratepayers have no vote, domestic rates are paid by a minority of local electors and complicated central government grants conceal the real cost of local services from the electorate.

On the other hand the rating system has many strengths as a local tax which have tended to be forgotten in the rush to replace them. They are practical, suitable for all tiers of local government, difficult to evade, perceptible (and, in the past, have therefore been seen as good at promoting local accountability), administration costs are low and their yield is predictable. Most of the faults of rates are not inherent in the tax but rather the product of the failure to modernise the system as local government and society has changed.

The burden of local taxation could be spread more widely by introducing a Local Income Tax (LIT) in either full or partial replacement of rates. If it was thought that LIT was inappropriate for the lower tier authorities the retention of rates could be an option. This would make rough

89

sense in that personal services (largely provided by the upper tier) would then be funded by LIT while property and environmental services (largely provided by the lower tier) would be funded by a property tax. Abolition of the Metropolitan Counties and GLC (and proposals to do likewise to the Scottish Regional Councils) undermines this proposal.

Such reforms would have the prospect of being long-lived, practical, equitable and consistent with subsequent reforms of functions and structure and even devolution. They are not a panacea, but they are a better solution than the muddled reform proposed in the 1986 Green Paper.

REFERENCES

Audit Commission for England and Wales (1986) Improving Cash Flow Management in Local Government HMSO

Bailey, S.J. (1982) 'Do Fewer Pupils Mean Falling Expenditure?' in Rose, R. and Page, E. (eds) Fiscal Stress in Cities (Cambridge University Press, Cambridge)

------ (1986) 'Rates Reform - Lessons from the Scottish Experience' Local Government Studies May/June Vol. 12, No. 3, pp. 21-36

Bennett, R.J. (1986) 'The Impact of Non-Domestic Rates on Profitability and Investment' Fiscal Studies Vol. 7, No. 1, pp. 37-8

Cmnd 6453 (1976) Local Government Finance: Report of the Committee of Enquiry (Chairman Frank Layfield), HMSO

Cmnd 8449 (1981) Alternatives to Domestic Rates, HMSO

Cmnd 9008 (1983) Rates: Proposals for Rate Limitation and Reform of the Rating System, HMSO

Cmnd 9691 (1985) Reform of Social Security: Programme for Action, HMSO

Cmnd 9714 (1986) Paying for Local Government, HMSO

Cmnd 9797 (1986) The Conduct of Local Authority Business: Report of the Committee of Inquiry (Chairman David Widdicombe Q.C.), HMSO

Crawford, M. and Dawson, D. (1982) 'Are Rates the Right Tax for Local Government?' Lloyds Bank Review No. 145 July pp. 15-35

Crawford, P. et al. (1985) 'The Effect of Business Rates on the Location of Employment' University of Cambridge,

Department of Land Economy

Hale, R. (1986) 'Who Will Pay for Local Government' <u>Public Finance and Accountancy</u> 16 May pp. 6-10

Jackman, R. (1982) 'Does Central Government Need to Control the Total of Local Government Spending?' <u>Local Government Studies</u> Vol. 8, No. 3, May/June

Jackson, P.M. et al. (1982) 'Urban Fiscal Decay in UK Cities' <u>Local Government Studies</u> Sept/Oct pp. 23-43

Kay, J. and Smith, S. (1987) <u>Administration Options for a Local Income Tax</u> (Institute of Fiscal Studies, London)

Le Grand, J. (1982) <u>The Strategy of Equality: Redistribution and the Social Services</u> (Allen and Unwin, London), p. 128

Martlew, C. (1986) 'Consulting Non-Domestic Ratepayers in Scotland: The First Year' <u>Local Government Studies</u> Vol. 12, No. 1, Jan/Feb, pp. 57-66

Martlew, C. and Bailey, S.J. (1986) 'Local Taxation and Accountability: An Assessment of the 1986 Green Paper 'Paying for Local Government and its Effects in Scotland', <u>Public Finance Foundation</u> Discussion Paper No. 10, London

Miller, W. (1986) Local Electoral Behaviour (in Cmnd 9800 <u>The Conduct of Local Authority Business Research</u> Vol. 3 of The Committee of Inquiry, pp. 105-72) HMSO

Scottish Consumer Council (1986) <u>The Community Charge: SCC's Submission on the Government's Proposals</u> Glasgow

Smith, S.R. and Squires, D. (1986) 'Who Will be Paying for Local Government?' IFS Commentary, <u>Institute of Fiscal Studies</u>, Chapter 2, London

Tyler, P. et al. (1984) 'Geographical Variations in Industrial Costs' <u>University of Cambridge</u>, Department of Land Economy, Discussion Paper 12

Ward, I. and Williams, P. (1986) 'The Government and Accountability Since Layfield' <u>Local Government Studies</u> Vol. 12, No. 1, Jan/Feb, pp. 21-32

Chapter Six

LOCAL FREEDOM AND CENTRAL CONTROL - A QUESTION OF BALANCE

Tom Wilson

1. OBJECTIVES AND POLICIES

The Government's objectives in shaping its policies on local government finance since 1979, as set out in its 1986 Green Paper (Cmnd 9714 para 1.19), may be summarised as follows:

(1) To contain local government expenditure at what are described as 'affordable' levels.
(2) To encourage the local authorities to carry out services more efficiently and to introduce private competition where possible.
(3) To reduce detailed controls over local government.

Experience has shown, however, that it may not be possible to pursue all three objectives simultaneously. There has been some conflict between (2) and (3) and particularly sharp conflicts between (1) and (3). The Government's determination to check the growth of total public

---

Footnote: When the Department of the Environment embarked upon a new examination of the finance of local government in the autumn of 1984, four assessors were appointed: Lord Rothschild, Professor (now Sir) Christopher Foster, Mr. Leonard Hoffman Q.C. and Professor Thomas Wilson. This chapter is a revised version of a paper by Professor Wilson published in the Journal of Policy Studies, October 1986.

expenditure and, if possible, reduce it, has led to a tightening of the restrictions on local spending by means of targets and rate-capping, and this has been in conflict with objective (3). As well as the natural resentment of the local authorities directly affected, there has been more general concern about this strengthening of the power of Whitehall.

If one of the purposes to be served is the expression of local diversity of choice about local expenditure and local taxation, can it really be proper for the central authorities to try to hold down such expenditure and taxation below the levels that these authorities, for their part, regard as 'affordable'? If a local electorate would prefer more public services and would be prepared to pay for them, why should their preferences be overruled?

In reply, it can be said that these pleas on behalf of local democracy would be more convincing if democracy at the local level worked more effectively. With only a small fraction of the electorate voting at elections fought largely on national issues, the link between electoral preferences and local government spending policies is somewhat tenuous. The situation is further complicated by the fact that only about half the local electorate is liable to pay local taxes - a point that is given central emphasis in the Green Paper. Moreover to a degree, and sometimes to a considerable degree, the higher local taxation of individuals is shifted back to central government through the social security system. The arrangements for the provision of grants have also encouraged higher local spending in the past and the subsequent reform of these arrangements may not therefore be as genuine a grievance as is often implied. Proper allowance must also be made for inconsistency in personal behaviour. Thus the pressure for higher public expenditure may not be accompanied in practice by a genuine readiness to accept lower real disposable income, and attempts may be made to obtain offsetting increases in gross income. The demand for more central government expenditure may, of course, be distorted at least as much in this way as the demand for local government expenditure, but the local authorities are not responsible for macro-economic policy and can therefore ignore the consequences to an extent that central government cannot.

The most effective method of fostering consistent behaviour is to finance the supply of services by charging directly for them when they are supplied. Views differ as to the extent to which it would really be feasible to extend charging in this sense, and some may feel that the Green Paper underestimates the scope for using the market. The fact remains that a substantial part of the supply of local services will not be financed in this way. The aim must then be to reform the fiscal system in order to strengthen local accountability.

2. GRANTS, LOCAL TAXES AND ACCOUNTABILITY

It has often been maintained that local accountability is weak because the local authorities derive too large a proportion of their current revenue from central government grants. The position in England and Wales in 1984-5 - the reference year in the Green Paper - may be summarised as follows:

domestic rates	13.2%
non-domestic rates	20.5%
fees, charges, rents and sales	15.7%
central government grants	50.6%

If local revenue-raising powers could be so increased as to permit the elimination of grants from central government, all local spending would have to be locally explained and locally defended. A powerful constraint might thus be imposed on extravagant policies and there might also, at the opposite extreme, be less danger of restrictions on expenditure more severe than local people would prefer. For they should then have a better chance of getting what they wanted - wanted to the extent of being themselves prepared to pay for it through local taxation. This, in simple terms, is the case for financial self-sufficiency. If that self-sufficiency cannot be made complete, should it not, at least, be increased?

Self-sufficiency, however, is no clear guide to accountability. Attention must also be paid to the characteristics of the taxes employed, and non-domestic rates have serious defects as a local tax. For this is a case of taxation without representation. The local authorities are not accountable to the firms and other organisations that pay these rates and their vulnerability has undoubtedly been exploited by some Labour councils. It is true that business rates over the country as a whole may be passed on to purchasers, like any other indirect tax, although the scope for doing so without some loss of markets will naturally depend upon the macro-economic situation. But firms in areas where taxation is particularly heavy may not be able to pass on the local excess without a loss of trade, and such areas will become relatively depressed. This might not deter the irresponsible minority of local authorities, especially when any consequential decline in the tax base would be offset under a grant system that included a resources element.

The complete abandonment of grants, in favour of complete fiscal self-sufficiency at the local level, would imply a drastic change in social policy, even if it could somehow be achieved. For this would mean the abandonment of equalisation payments by which the poorer areas benefit at the expense of those better off. It is true that such transfers could be organised without the central government acting as intermediary. This is what happens in West Germany. The fact remains that, however organised, transfers are required, given the framework of social policy (Grewal et al. 1980, Musgrave 1961, Oates 1972, Wilson 1984).

The Green Paper proposes that there should be changes in these transfers, partly as a consequence of the proposed changes in the rating system. With non-domestic rates collected at a uniform poundage and distributed between localities on a per capita basis, a measure of equalisation would be implicitly achieved. Secondly, with domestic rates ultimately replaced by a poll tax that is quite unrelated to ability to pay, a taxable capacity base for the transfers ceases to be relevant. For both these reasons, there will no longer be any case for a resources grant designed to equalise the tax base. Grants will be provided, however, to cope with special needs such as a relatively large number of children or of old people. But this is not all. For there is also to be a standard grant and it is necessary to ask how this can be explained or rationalised. As we shall now see, the attempt to do so raises a basic question about the purpose of devolving authority to local government.

3. LOCAL FISCAL AUTONOMY – REAL OR APPARENT?

It is a fact of critical importance that a substantial part of local government expenditure is carried out in order to meet the statutory obligations placed upon the local authorities by the central government departments. These obligations may be partly justified by the presence of what is described in economic jargon as 'externalities' - that is to say, because the effects of many local measures extend beyond a particular locality. Education is the obvious example. Or there may be a paternalistic concern lest some local authorities should not do the 'right thing' by local inhabitants. An example is the obligation to provide accommodation for old people. In the case of specific grants for specific purposes this is made clear, and it might be inferred that all grants, apart from what is needed for equalisation, should be specific. In fact, the role of specific grants has been played down in recent years not only in Britain but in some of the federal states as well. But the block grant in Britain, notwithstanding its name, is by no means available for free disposal by the local authorities.

In a minority reservation to the report of the Layfield Committee (1976), Professor Alan Day, with the support of Professor Gordon Cameron, proposed that the central government should pay in full for all it required to be done and should leave the local authorities free to meet their locally chosen expenditure from their own local resources. The adoption of this proposal would have a dramatic effect on local authority finance. Even if the change were to be confined to education, the consequences would be very large. But the proposal encounters the obstacle that the centrally imposed obligations are not usually presented in hard quantitative terms that could then be turned into clear financial obligations. Furthermore the role of local government would be changed in a rather important respect if they were to be so presented. For it is held that one of the functions of local government in Britain is to give a local interpretation to these centrally determined objectives and obligations and to the ways in which they can best be met. This is what administrative devolution is said to be about. This need not, of course, be the end of the matter, for this interpretation of the role of local government could, after all, be changed.

A case for change could be made on the ground that responsibility is fudged under the present arrangements with local authorities accountable to both their local taxpayers and to Whitehall. Indeed their obligations to the latter could cut across what they might deem in some areas to be their obligations to local taxpayers. Suppose, for example, that there was a preference in a local government area for abandoning the provision of personal social services with a corresponding cut in local taxation. This change would not be permitted. Public expenditure, whether financed from grants or local taxation, cannot be freely determined at local level. This leads, of course, to situations in which local authorities can complain, in response to Treasury criticism of high levels of expenditure, that they are only doing what other Whitehall departments require them to do. Although no attempt will be made in the present context to assess the conflicting considerations for and against current practice, it is right to point out that we have here an important instance of the need to avoid confining the debate to narrowly defined financial provisions to the neglect of wider objectives that the devolution of authority is designed to achieve.

The Green Paper does not go into these matters and its explanation of the case for a standard per capita grant is somewhat vague. It will be appreciated, however, that if the role of the local authorities is not to be fundamentally changed, a case can be made for such grants. For, if Whitehall requires that certain services should be provided, Whitehall can be reasonably expected to contribute to their cost. This is so in general terms although the obligations so imposed on the local authorities are not presented - deliberately not presented - in a form that can be unambiguously translated into financial terms.

Given this framework of policy, it would seem that too much attention has sometimes been directed to the proportion of local expenditure that is locally financed. A more important question may be the extent to which the local authorities can vary their expenditure at the margin, if they so desire. In Britain, as in a number of federations, grants have been designed in order to reward 'tax effort' at the sub-central level. That is to say, the grant made to an authority would be increased if it raised both local expenditure and local taxation and decreased if it did the reverse. In the USA, in particular, the case for rewarding tax effort and the appropriate means of doing so have received much attention. In Britain, however, the need in recent times - as envisaged by Labour Governments as well as by Conservative ones - has been to restrain local expenditure, and this has entailed penalties for the heavy spenders.

It may be objected, however, that the central government should not use the grant system either to encourage or to penalise increases in local outlays, and this view is now in effect endorsed in the Green Paper. For what is proposed is a neutral grant system. If a local authority spends more than its centrally assessed norm - its Grant Related Expenditure, or GRE - it will receive no extra grant and will have to obtain the additional revenue from its own taxpayers. If it spends less, it will not have its grants cut and will therefore be able to reduce local taxation by the full amount of the saving. In my view, a grant system that is neutral in this sense has been the right one to advocate and its adoption in the Green Paper is to be applauded. (In effect, we should be following the Australian pattern in this respect.)

Under the grant system, each local authority would be free to raise or lower its expenditure relatively to its GRE as it saw fit, subject to the condition that the implications for local taxation must be accepted. So far, so good. Local accountability should be strengthened and local autonomy respected. But there remains the other familiar question: what taxing power will be available to the local authorities and what will be its characteristics? What the Green Paper proposes is a Community Charge or poll tax as the sole source of revenue <u>at the margin</u>. Could this really be satisfactory?

4. THE CASE AGAINST A POLL TAX

A flat-rate tax per head of the adult population has long been regarded as a text-book curiosity of no relevance to a modern developed society. We must, however, be fair to antiquity. There were a number of poll taxes in England in the past, not only in the middle ages but even as late as the seventeenth century. These were poll taxes in the sense that a payment had to be made by all adults, apart from the very poor. But some of the more important ones were graduated. Thus the tax introduced by Henry II was quite steeply graduated with regard to rank and status, as rough proxies for ability to pay. Dukes had to pay 10 marks, earls 6, barons and knights 3, esquires 1/2, attorneys 1/2, farmers 1/4 to 1/2, other people one groat, with the exception of those who were real beggars (Dowell 1884).

We must also be fair to the Government. The objection to a flat-rate poll tax is its regressivity. But it is obviously necessary to compare such a tax with the rating system it would replace in order to ascertain whether regressivity would in fact be substantially increased. The domestic rate has been regarded traditionally as a regressive tax and this verdict was substantiated by the Allen Report (Cmnd 2582, 1965). Subsequently the position has been modified at the lower end of the scale by the introduction of rebates and allowances for those on social benefits. A similar procedure would be followed with the poll tax. Both would be affected, however, by the proposal that even those on benefit should pay 20% of the local tax. If this measure, rejected by the Lords, is nevertheless preserved, it could be modified by raising benefits sufficiently to offset the charge and thus prevent people from being forced below the Government's own social security minima - 'churning'. This would not be a case of putting money pointlessly into one pocket in order to take it out of another. For the compensation would be calculated at 20 per cent of the taxation required to meet average expenditure at GRE (Grant Related Expenditure) levels. Those who lived in high spending areas would get no extra help; those in low spending areas would be able to keep any surplus. There has, however, been no clear indication so far that the Government is committed to 'churning'.

It is obvious that, as compared with rates, a poll tax would benefit households with few members and add to the burden of large households. As it happens, a substantial proportion of persons with very low incomes live alone and they would benefit. The Green Paper contains the estimate that in total about 10 million households would gain and about 10 million would lose. An attempt is made to emphasise that the effect would be small. Only 15 per cent would lose £2 or more a week; only 3 per cent £5 or more. These figures look less reassuring when it is recalled that the average bill for rates is barely £5 per week.

As one would expect, there are some statistical complications in comparing rates with the proposed community charge. Thus it is necessary to direct attention to the net demands after remissions have been taken into account. It is also desirable to pay attention to household composition as well as to size of income group. It is therefore more informative to look at the appendices to the Green Paper, in particular appendix F, rather than the main text. Table 6.1, based on F5, shows clearly that the higher income groups would benefit from the proposed change. Nor is this all. For the effect of the change would be to raise the

Table 6.1: Ranges of equivalent net income in pounds per week: GB, 1984-5 prices

	Under 50	50-75	75-100	100-150	150-200	200-250
Gain (+) or loss (-) from substitution of net community charge for net rates in £ per week	+0.10	-0.03	-0.29	-0.26	+0.04	+0.58
Gain (+) or loss (-) in £ per annum	+5.20	-1.56	-15.08	-13.52	+2.08	+30.16
Gain (+) or loss (-) as % of net equivalent income	+0.2	-	-0.2	-0.1	-	+0.2

	250-300	300-350	350-400	400-500	500+*	All households
Gain (+) or loss (-) from substitution of net community charge for net rates in £ per week	+1.53	+2.20	+3.42	+4.16	+5.84	+0.04
Gain (+) or loss (-) in £ per annum	+79.56	+114.40	+177.84	+216.32	+303.68	+2.08
Gain (+) or loss (-) as % of net equivalent income	+0.5	+0.6	+0.9	+0.9	+0.8	-

* In the income group £500+ the figures for the gains are minima which would be much exceeded at higher levels of income.

value of house property and from this the better-off would gain substantially more.

In the Green Paper it is held that when there are certain public services that cannot conveniently be sold on the market, a compulsory uniform community charge is appropriate. But according to welfare theory, such a method of charging would not be at all appropriate for public goods - goods (such as defence) which confer a general benefit rather than one that could be confined to identifiable individuals with others excluded. For, if the charge takes no account of ability to pay, expenditure will have to be held down to what can reasonably be extracted from those with very low incomes. Expenditure will be then less than the better-off would prefer. Indeed, in a rather special way, this would be an <u>anti-libertarian</u> policy, with everyone held down to expenditure on a scale that could be financed from the poll tax. There would therefore be frustration and a denial of preferences. There is no way of determining what the 'right' scale of charges should be in this case but it is generally assumed that a levy roughly proportional to income would at least be much preferable to poll tax.

The same reasoning applies to local public goods. It is true that a substantial part of expenditure at both the national and the local level is not on goods of this kind. Moreover, there may be services for which the income elasticity of demand is negative. The personal social services are a possible example. Even so, it is hard to believe that a tax low enough to be paid by the poorest residents would finance expenditure on a scale that the bulk of the other residents would prefer. (This is, of course, apart altogether from any desire to shift the distribution of income deliberately in favour of those less well-off.) Even in the Green Paper it is conceded that a flat-rate tax would impose too severe a constraint on expenditure. This concession is made implicitly by embodying the DHSS proposal that persons on social security should have eighty per cent of the community charge remitted. There is a much larger implicit concession in the fact that the community charge is expected ultimately to finance only about an eighth of total current expenditure which means, of course, that the package as a whole is very much less harsh than some of its political critics have implied. But the poll tax would ultimately become the only means of financing <u>marginal</u> expenditure above GRE - financing, that is to say, those departures from an average pattern that are supposed to be one of the main reasons for having local government.

5. THE DOMESTIC RATE AND THE COMMUNITY CHARGE - THEIR DISTRIBUTIONAL EFFECTS

In the Green Paper, the Government is addressing itself to the problem of preventing fiscal extravagance without the use of detailed controls over the behaviour of the local authorities. This is an important issue for any central government and a difficult one and its solution requires a delicate balancing of conflicting considerations.

It is stated quite clearly that: '... the community charge would bear the full weight of any variations in an authority's expenditure from its assessed needs'. If the contribution of domestic rates in 1984-5 is a guide this would mean that the poll tax would finance, on average, just over 13 per cent of expenditure. Suppose, then, that a local authority were to raise its expenditure by, say, 10 per cent above GRE - scarcely an extravagant margin. The poll tax would have to go up by about three-quarters. If £190 can be taken as a reasonable estimate of the poll tax at GRE level of expenditure, it would now rise to about £330. For a low income household of two adults this would be a substantial amount. Even a couple on social security would then pay about £130 a year if the 20 per cent rule had come into force.

One does not need to be indifferent to the case for fiscal restraint in order to feel that the barrier thus erected against marginal increases in expenditure would be too forbidding. There are two grounds for saying so. The first is the familiar case, stressed above, for some measure of autonomy for local government - real autonomy, not just a formal freedom that could be exercised only at unacceptable cost. The second is that in putting forward these proposals, the Government is implicitly expressing vast confidence in its ability to assess local 'needs'. Of course appeals could be made and adjustments negotiated, but this means time and effort. If a local authority were finally left with a GRE that it believed, perhaps on quite good grounds, to be unduly tight, it would have to put up with it or itself finance some excess expenditure - which would mean, under the new regime, a rise in the poll tax.

It is true that each and every constituent of the fiscal system need not be progressive. On the assumption that progressivity is the aim, this surely applies to the fiscal package as a whole. The central government could - if it chose to do so - offset the regressivity of the community charge but, in the nature of the case, it could do so only on an <u>average</u> basis. If the local authorities are to exercise a reasonable degree of autonomy, they should have at their disposal a source of <u>marginal revenue</u> less regressive than a poll tax. We have referred so far only to <u>hypothetical</u> departures from GRE, but many authorities are, <u>as a matter of fact</u>, spending well above their respective norms. It is part of the Green Paper strategy to impose pressures that will reduce these 'excesses' and up to a point this seems right. But how fast? And how severely?

It is scarcely surprising that a gradual adjustment was proposed with ten years initially suggested for the period over which domestic rates would be eliminated in England. A lengthy transition period seemed all the more necessary because differences in poundages mean that there are substantial differences in the revenue from non-domestic rates, and these are to be removed. A safety net is also to be introduced, which will mean that no local authority will suffer as a consequence of the proposed changes in the first year. The details of safety nets for local authorities and businesses are still uncertain but those for individuals have been abandoned. In view of these complications, it is hard to estimate the final pattern of dispersion for the community charge that would emerge if, on the expenditure side, the pattern remained unchanged. An illuminating attempt to do so has, however, been made by Smith and Squire (1986) who find a very wide range between £129 and £560 with an average of £189.

There can be little doubt that the uniform <u>per capita</u> charge proposed in the Green Paper would cause intense resentment. It would not only be a question of rich and poor. There would be a sense of unfairness right up the income range. A family of, say, two adults living in a small tenement in a poor location would come to realise that they were paying as much as another couple in a much better place. The skilled worker in a small modern bungalow would observe that the bank manager in a larger villa was paying just the same. The bank manager might look with resentment at the large house of the company chairman or at the country house of the local squire and begin to growl because they were all making the same contribution, given family size, to the cost of local government. The size and location of a house may be an inadequate indicator of ability to pay but it is surely better than none at all. Moreover, although the total fiscal package is what should matter, local eyes would still turn with concern to the fairness or unfairness of local taxation, viewed in isolation.

The Government is opposed to a local income tax, as the Green Paper makes clear. What has not been recognised is that if rates are abolished and a poll tax substituted, this is most unlikely to be a permanent solution. The proposed community charge would be only a stepping stone to a local income tax.

Would a local income tax be feasible and also desirable? Is the Government wrong on this score? Even after computerisation had been completed, the Inland Revenue would still be faced with the problem of keeping records by place of residence. There could be troublesome complications, especially if some 500 local authorities were in a position to ask for income tax to be levied at varying rates and perhaps with varying provisions for allowances. Two points must, however, be made.

First, any administrative difficulties of this kind would be less serious than those presented by the levying and collection of the proposed poll tax. Special registers would have to be compiled and constantly revised as people changed residence, a collection system would have to be established and some form of effective penalties devised for offenders. It would present the most serious administrative difficulties, which receive too little recognition in the Green Paper. Moreover the problem of running a local income tax would be easier if it were confined to the higher level of local government with domestic rates still preserved on a reduced scale at the lower level. In order to assess the case for such a combination, it would be necessary to consider the structure of local government and the services assigned to the different tiers, both under the present arrangements and under any new arrangements that might be thought appropriate. Once again we are drawn beyond the financial issues towards a wider context.

Secondly, it may be objected that with basic direct taxation, including national insurance, then running at close to 40 per cent of income, any further increase would be most undesirable. A rise to about 45 per cent would in fact be needed to replace rates. Offsetting action could, however, be taken. For the national income tax could be reduced correspondingly and the loss of revenue made good by higher rates of VAT. Thus a rise in indirect taxation would be indirectly substituted for domestic rates, with income tax on average unchanged. (The direct substitution of VAT at the local level would not be appropriate for, like other taxes of this kind, it could be evaded by trading across local authority boundaries, unless the differences in local VAT rates were quite small.) This would imply exceedingly favourable treatment of expenditure on housing unless VAT were extended to new houses. But the purchasers of new houses, together with the building industry, would be penalised while the owners of existing houses went unscathed. It might then seem right to recommend that a national schedule A be restored with income tax levied on the imputed rents of houses - for which, of course, a case can be made that is unrelated to the problems of local government finance. There is another interesting variant that has not, I think, been much discussed: that a local income tax should take the form of a new schedule A and should be confined to this schedule. But a schedule A, whether local or central, would require imputed annual values, and it is the difficulty of assessing annual values that is one of the weaknesses of the rating system in its present form. If, however, a tolerable solution could be found in the case of schedule A, this could also be applied in order to remove the same defect from the rating system.

Clearly a local income tax offers much greater scope for local fiscal autonomy than a poll tax could provide, but this, if satisfactory from one point of view, is ominous from another. If the local authorities had uncontrolled access to this vast tax base, the less responsible minority could be expected to push rates of tax up to damagingly high levels. In raising the burden of income tax in this way, the local authorities responsible might stimulate migration and might also raise unemployment, but these considerations could well fail to deter. Naturally the weight attached to this consideration will depend upon one's faith in the effectiveness of local democracy. May I express the view that if there were to be a local income tax, it would be essential to have it 'capped' - and this would in itself become a fresh grievance?

My own initial inclination was to favour a capped local income tax, and I should still regard this as vastly preferable to the proposed community charge. I have, however, begun to doubt whether a local income tax would really be so much preferable to domestic rates as appears so often to be assumed. First of all, as explained above, a local income tax suffers from its own defects. Secondly, the case against rates in their present form is by no means conclusive and is greatly weakened when the scope for making improvements in the procedure for assessing rateable values is taken into account. To quote from the 1983 White Paper (Cmnd 9008), rates '... are highly perceptible to ratepayers and they promote accountability. They are well understood, cheap to collect and very difficult to evade. They act as an incentive to the most efficient use of property'. Moreover less harm is done to work incentives than would be done by a local income tax. These are surely important advantages not be lightly pushed aside - as the Republic of Ireland discovered after its abolition of rates (NESC 1985).

The existing rating system could be reformed. Capital values would not only simplify the exercise of valuation but should reduce the danger of those apparently inexplicable variations between similar properties which give rise to a sense of unfairness. The capital values of properties, including the sites they occupy, would be reasonably intelligible to most people who will have at least some notion of what houses are fetching, whereas the estimates of annual rental value are often unintelligible and, partly for these reasons, viewed with suspicion.

The retention of rates would encounter the objection that many local voters do not pay rates, but too much can be made of this point. Of the 17-18 million who do not pay, about 11 million are spouses who are certainly not indifferent to rates, and many of the remainder will also be concerned. Admittedly the burden is less for larger households, but they are making less claim on housing space and less also on scarce site space - a consideration strangely neglected in the Green Paper.

Some combinations of local taxes would be possible. A local income tax together with rates would increase the number who paid, although a local income tax in isolation would be only slightly better in this respect. Or the combination of a community charge with rates, proposed in the Green Paper as an interim measure, might be made permanent. It could be so devised as to reduce the regressivity of the former. If CC is the community charge, V_i the capital valuation of a particular property and $\bar{V}$ the national average valuation, then the total tax bill for a householder would be:

$$CC \left(1 + \frac{V}{\overline{V}} \cdot b\right)$$

A high value for b would obviously make the scheme less regressive. A formula of this kind would at least be preferable to an unadulterated community charge but it does not follow that it would be worthwhile to attempt, even in this way, to introduce such a charge. For the appalling problems of administering the charge would still remain and would probably outweigh any benefit it was likely to confer. If the rating system is to be combined with some other, it would be more sensible to combine it with a capped local income tax, with one tax allocated to one tier of government and the other tax to another tier. Whether any such combination of local taxes would warrant the administrative cost is, of course, another matter.

6. CONCLUDING REFLECTIONS

The need to reform local government finance has long been recognised but action has been long postponed. If the recommendations of the Green Paper are adopted, an important step forward will have been taken in a number of respects; but these proposals viewed as a whole, do not form the basis for a generally acceptable and therefore durable system. A long transition period with its complicated provisions would scarcely help to commend the scheme, and the final arrangements to which they are intended to lead would be marred by the abandonment of domestic rates in favour of a still more regressive community charge, or poll tax. It is hard to believe that this tax would survive. There is no basis here for the broad consensus required for a reform of this kind but every reason to suppose that it would become intensely unpopular with the electorate when people realised more fully than they do at present what a poll tax really implied.

There seems no escape from the conclusions that another attempt will have to be made to review these issues and to make fresh recommendations. When this is done local government - or rather sub-central government, local and regional - should be viewed in all its inter-related aspects. The importance of these interrelations has, indeed, become apparent time and again even in the present paper on finance. As we have seen, the financial provisions cannot be adequately assessed without regard to the objectives to be achieved by devolving responsibility and to the particular functions thought to be appropriate for sub-central government. The structure of government and the assignment of responsibility between the different tiers must be taken into account. The basic question is the extent to which local government in modern Britain can be regarded as genuinely representative of local opinion or can be made more so. For the answer to these questions must largely determine the extent to which financial autonomy at the local government level can be defended as socially desirable.

REFERENCES

Cmnd 2582 'Report of the Allen Committee of Inquiry into the Impact of Rates on Households' HMSO, 1965

Cmnd 9008 'Rates: Proposals for Rate Limitation and Reform of the Rating System' HMSO August, 1983

Cmnd 9714 'Paying for Local Government' HMSO January, 1986

Dowell, S. (1884) A History of Taxation and Taxes in England from the Earliest Times to the Present Day (Longmans and Co., London)

Grewal, B.G., Brennan, G. and Mathews, R.L. (1980) The Economics of Federalism (ANU Press, Canberra)

Layfield, F. (1976) 'Local Government Finance: Report of the Committee of Enquiry' Cmnd 6453, HMSO May, 1976

Musgrave, R.A. (1961) 'Approaches to the Fiscal Theory of Political Federalism' in Public Finances, Needs, Sources and Utilization (National Bureau of Economic Research, Princeton N.J.)

NESC (1985) 'The Financing of Local Authorities' National Economic and Social Council, Dublin

Oates, W.E. (1972) Fiscal Federalism (Harcourt Brace Jovanovich, New York)

Smith, S. and Squire, D. (1986) 'Who Will be Paying for Local Government?' Institute of Fiscal Studies, March, 1986

Wilson, T. (1984) 'Fiscal Decentralisation' Anglo German Foundation

Chapter Seven

RATES REFORM AND THE HOUSING MARKET

Gordon A. Hughes

INTRODUCTION

After many hesitations the government has now brought forward legislative proposals to abolish domestic rates in Scotland and to institute a modified poll tax - the community charge - in its place with effect from 1989. It had been expected that a similar reform of the rating system in England and Wales would follow some years after the Scottish reform had been completed but the government now intends to speed up this process.

For obvious political and social reasons most of the discussion of the consequences of the proposed reform have concentrated either on its short term distributional consequences or on its effects on the financial and administrative problems facing local authorities. The latter issue is discussed in other chapters in this volume and, in addition, firm conclusions on both issues cannot be drawn until more information is available on various crucial details

Footnote: I am grateful to Andrew Dilnot, the Institute for Fiscal Studies and the Department of Employment for providing the data from the Family Expenditure Survey on which this paper is based. I am also grateful to Steve Bailey, John Muellbauer, and other participants at seminars at the CEPR and the Centre for Housing Research, Glasgow for comments on the earlier versions of this paper. I am, of course, entirely responsible for the analysis and views expressed in this paper.

concerning the implementation of the community charge. The final distributional effects of the change will, for example, depend upon any associated adjustments in social security benefits and on the nature of the rebate scheme designed to mitigate the burden of the community charge on low income and elderly households. This illustrates the point that it is often quite misleading to examine the distributional impact of a particular tax proposal in isolation. What matters is the overall distributional impact of the tax and benefit system as a whole and whether this is significantly altered by the reform. This depends not only on changes in the specific tax payments made by households but also on adjustments in patterns of consumption and household welfare in response to changes in the relative prices of goods and services.

In the case of the reform of local taxation it is likely that these price effects will be substantially more important in the longer term than the income effects associated with changes in the direct burden of taxation. This is because domestic rates may best be regarded as an indirect tax on housing services, similar to VAT but with lower tax rates applicable to low income households. From this perspective the crucial feature of local tax reform is the replacement of a large specific commodity tax on housing consumption by taxes whose primary impact is on household income - this includes a general local sales tax as well as a local income tax or a local poll tax. The presumption established by the theory of optimal taxation is that specific commodity taxes tend to be inefficient relative to income or broad-based sales taxes in the sense that they involve a large sacrifice of social welfare per pound of net revenue collected. This social loss - the 'deadweight loss' of the tax - is roughly proportional to the product of the relevant tax rate and of the change in the demand for the item due to the imposition/removal of the tax. Since the supply of housing is relatively inelastic, at least in the short run, any change in the demand for housing resulting from the abolition of domestic rates is likely to be reflected in a rise in house and land prices, so that the reform may be expected to have a major impact on the housing market as well as exacerbating existing planning conflicts over housing development on the outskirts of major cities.

In this chapter I will summarise the main results of a study of the impact of the abolition of domestic rates on the housing market. The technical details of the underlying model are presented in other papers - see Hughes (1987) - so that I will concentrate here on the possible magnitude of the changes in housing demand following the abolition of domestic rates and on the implications of shifts in the composition of housing demand for the planning system and related aspects of the housing market. The next section examines the importance of domestic rates as a tax on housing services, which provides the basis for the estimates in the remainder of the chapter. In section 3 I will discuss the results of using a (relatively) simple demand and supply model to analyse the impact of various local tax reforms on the demand for and price of housing. For obvious reasons of data, etc. this model is based on aggregate demand and supply at a regional level which may mask important changes in the composition of housing demand. These are discussed in later sections along with the broader implications of the estimated changes for the housing market and housing policy.

DOMESTIC RATES AS A TAX ON HOUSING SERVICES

Analyses of the incidence of domestic and business rates have tended to treat them as being similar to the American property tax, which is a major source of revenue for local and state governments. The general conclusion of the recent US literature on the property tax is that the burden of the average tax rate on property falls on the factor incomes accruing to the owners of capital while local differences in tax rates will be borne by local consumers of property services, so that the only local differences in tax rates will be capitalised in property values - see Topham (1983). However, there is a critical difference between the US property tax and British rates: the former is, in principle, applicable to all capital assets - including movable assets such as machinery - whereas the latter is strictly a tax on real estate, i.e. land and buildings. Further, agricultural real estate is exempt from rates while differential rating provisions have applied to industry in England and Wales in the past and still apply in Scotland. It follows that rates should not be treated as a general tax on capital which is the basis of the American conclusions. Instead, British rates are a tax on real estate services applied to certain sectors of the economy. To the extent that these services absorb a significant proportion of the nation's capital stock it is possible that rates may reduce the post-tax return on capital received by owners of capital but otherwise they result in an increase in the cost of real estate services to industry, the service sector and households. Differences between the rates burden across localities may be capitalised in property or land prices, but the extent of this depends upon the operation of the planning system which controls the nature and volume of land development.

It is not possible to estimate the effect of the reform of local taxation on the return to capital, especially as some crucial details concerning the implementation of the proposed uniform business rate remain obscure. In this paper I will assume that the abolition of domestic rates will lead to an equivalent fall in the price of housing services if house prices do not change. To estimate the importance of domestic rates as a tax on housing consumption it is necessary to calculate the value of housing services generated by the houses occupied by different households. Ideally this calculation would be based upon market rent data, but rent controls and the scale of the public rented sector mean that such an approach would be inappropriate in Britain. In the absence of market prices it is possible to estimate the long run supply price of housing services and to use this as the basis for valuation. This calculation is based on the requirement that the owners of houses will expect to make a 'normal' real return on their investment after covering costs of maintenance and depreciation. Since there is no evidence for any significant depreciation of the British housing stock, provided that it is adequately maintained, we may value housing services as the sum of a standard rate of return on capital valuation plus estimated maintenance costs. The 'normal' real rate of return is taken as 3% p.a., which is typical of the long term return on indexed gilts since housing has been a very secure investment throughout the last 40 years, while estimates of capital values are based on cross-section data taken from surveys of building society mortgages. Maintenance costs are estimated from information on local authority maintenance expenditures and amount on average to about 1% of the capital value per year.

With the aid of household data from the Family Expenditure Survey (FES) for 1980 on payments of domestic rates, other expenditures and housing characteristics, I have calculated regional averages for domestic rates as a percentage of household consumption of housing services in

Table 7.1: Domestic rates as a tax on gross housing services

(% Tax rate by region, 1974-85)

Region	1974	1980	1985
North	22.7	23.6	30.9
Yorks-Humber	20.7	23.6	31.0
East Midlands	20.1	20.2	26.7
East Anglia	23.8	23.5	26.2
GLC	23.0	27.4	35.8
South East (excl. GLC)	26.2	28.6	30.4
South West	25.8	26.1	30.5
Wales	18.1	21.9	25.9
West Midlands	25.1	27.7	35.7
North West	26.3	27.6	38.9
Scotland	25.0	34.4	47.7

Source: Author's calculations based on the General Household Survey 1974, Family Expenditure Survey 1980, and CIFPA Finance and General Statistics 1980-81 - 1985-86.

1980. These are presented in Table 7.1 together with similar figures for 1974 which were estimated in a similar manner from data taken from the General Household Survey (GHS) and for 1985 which were obtained by adjusting the 1980 figures to allow for changes in house values and rate poundages after 1980. The estimates show that domestic rates constitute a much heavier indirect tax on housing services than is imposed on any other items of consumption except for alcohol, tobacco and petrol. By 1985 the average tax rate on housing services was over double the general rate of VAT. Between 1985-86 and 1987-88 rises in rate poundages in Scotland substantially outstripped the rise in house prices so that by 1987 domestic rates represent a tax of over 50% on Scottish housing. One reason for the relative rise in the implicit tax rates for Scotland is that successive revaluations have shifted a significant proportion of the overall rating burden away from industrial property onto residential and commercial (retail and office) property. On top of this the larger Scottish local authorities have tended to increase their rate-financed expenditures rather faster than the average for Britain as a whole. It is thus hardly surprising that domestic rates are particularly unpopular in

Scotland.

As my previous work on the incidence of domestic rates - Hughes (1982) - has shown, the overall burden of this tax is distributed in a mildly progressive manner, largely as a result of the effects of rate rebates (housing benefit) in reducing the rate payments made by low income and elderly households. The correlation between payments of domestic rates and household income is low, so that the generally progressive character of domestic rates as a tax in distributional terms is undermined by its erratic nature. As one would expect, the correlation between payments of domestic rates and consumption of housing services was quite high in 1974 - immediately after the last rating revaluation in England and Wales - but this has probably declined substantially as a result of successive postponements of rating revaluation. After allowing for systematic differences associated with region and tenure it turns out that domestic rates as a proportion of housing services tends to increase very slightly with income. This progressivity, is, however, swamped by biases in rating assessments which will be discussed later. These could easily be corrected in the course of a general rating revaluation, especially if the basis for assessment was shifted to capital values rather than imputed rental values. Thus, the principal economic objection to reliance upon domestic rates as a tax base for local government arises from the high implicit tax rates on housing consumption and the consequential welfare losses.

HOUSING DEMAND AND SUPPLY

The elimination of a substantial tax on any important item of consumption may be expected to generate large price and income effects on the demand for the item. Since the supply of housing is quite inelastic in the short run, the impact of any change in the demand for housing as a consequence of the abolition of domestic rates will initially be experienced as changes in the prices of existing houses and of land zoned for residential development. The longer run impact of the reform will depend upon the response of housing supply to changes in demand, which will involve either new building or conversion of existing buildings. Evidence for the UK suggests that even in the long run the supply of housing is not especially elastic. As we have seen during the mid-

1980s, there is great resistance to any expansion in housing supply which involves encroachment on Green Belt areas in the South-East, so that the adjustment of housing supply to changes in demand patterns will be neither rapid nor easy in parts of the country. Further, the composition and location of the extra demand for housing will not be equivalent to a uniform increase in the existing housing stock because there seem to be systematic variations between types of housing and between different locations relative to city centres in the implicit tax rates on housing services associated with domestic rates.

In order to assess the potential impact of the abolition of domestic rates I have constructed a simple supply and demand model of the housing market in each region using the household data taken from the 1980 FES to predict changes in housing demand resulting from the replacement of domestic rates by a community charge (CC) or, as an alternative, by a local income tax (LIT). The details of the community charge differ slightly from that proposed in the Scottish Act because, at the time the work was carried out, there was no information on the way in which the rebate system might operate. Thus, the levels of the community charge are calculated on the assumption that all adults pay the full charge. It turns out that the differences between the alternative tax bases as replacements for domestic rates are quite small in terms of their impact on the housing market, so that my work provides a satisfactory basis for assessing the consequences of the proposed reform. The reason for the similarities between the alternative reforms is that the most important aspect of all the reforms is the replacement of a specific commodity tax, whose impact is equivalent to a large price change for an important item of consumption, by a broad-based tax whose impact is equivalent to a reduction in household income.

A key parameter in modelling the impact of the reform is the price elasticity of the demand for housing - or, more generally, the nature of the equation determining household demand for housing services. In order to indicate the sensitivity of my conclusions to alternative assumptions about this equation I will report two sets of estimates:

(A) The first set are based on an equation which implies a typical price elasticity of housing demand of about -0.75. I regard this as the best estimate of this elasticity, especially in the longer term, so these results are reported as the 'main estimates' in the tables.

(B) Some studies have suggested that a much lower (absolute) price elasticity would be appropriate. I believe that these estimates are based upon mis-specified models, but to take account of them the calculations have been performed for a demand equation with a typical price elasticity of -0.25. These results are reported as the 'low estimates' in the tables.

The two sets of estimates are based on econometric work reported in King (1983) which was based on FES data similar to that used in my model. In each case demand for housing services is obtained from an estimated expenditure equation based on the Almost Ideal Demand System - Deaton and Muellbauer (1980) - which splits household expenditure between expenditure on housing and on other consumption. For the purpose of investigating other local tax bases such as a local sales tax, expenditure on other consumption can be subdivided between expenditure on food and other expenditure categories using demand equations which I have estimated using pooled FES data for a number of years. The crucial difference between the two housing demand equations is that the principal equation is derived from a model which allows for the effect of short run rationing in the housing market, i.e. households cannot easily adjust the quantity of housing that they consume or gain entry to their preferred tenure, whereas the low elasticity is derived from a model which ignores such constraints. The rationing model seems to capture important features which one would expect to influence housing behaviour in Britain and its price elasticity of demand is similar to long run elasticities which have been obtained from the time series studies.

The effects of replacing domestic rates by alternative local taxes are calculated for each region by an iterative procedure involving two steps at each iteration:

(i) Using the values of prices and other variables from the previous iteration, the magnitude of the tax base for the new tax is calculated by summation over all the sample households in the region, taking account of any induced changes in expenditures. This means that the tax rates required to raise the same revenue as domestic rates can be directly calculated, from which changes in post-tax incomes and the price index for non-housing consumption may be computed.

(ii)   This income and price information combined with the previous iteration's estimate of the change in the price of housing services is then used to estimate the change in the aggregate demand for housing in the region, again by summing over all sample households. It is assumed that housing supply responds to changes in house prices according to a simple constant elasticity supply function so that a revised estimate of the change in housing prices needed to equalise supply and demand can be calculated. This iterative procedure is continued until estimates of the new tax rate and of the change in housing prices are obtained for each region.

In the very short run it is reasonable to assume that the elasticity of housing supply is close to zero. This means that house prices must rise to choke off any short term increase in demand for housing as a result of the abolition of domestic rates. However, the assumptions underpinning the estimation of the main demand elasticity imply that this reflects the medium or long term response of demand to price changes whereas the lower demand elasticity might be more relevant to the analysis of the short term effects of the reform. The uncertainties surrounding the immediate impact of any major tax change are such that it is not worth attempting to produce estimates of short term price changes, so I will concentrate on the medium and long term effects where these are distinguished by the elasticity of housing supply assumed in each case.

The tax rates for three alternative local taxes required to generate the same revenue in 1985 as domestic rates are shown in Table 7.2. Tax rates for a local sales tax are included in order to illustrate the consequences of broadening the base of local commodity taxation. The median local sales tax rate by region is 6.9% which is very similar to the sales taxes imposed by many US state governments while the differences in tax rates between neighbouring regions are quite small - except perhaps for that between the GLC and the rest of the South East - so some of the standard objections to a local sales tax do not appear to be valid. The median local income tax rate is 7.6% and again it seems unlikely that regional differences in tax rates would result in significant fiscal mobility. It should be noted that, in computing the revenue for a local income tax, it has been assumed that the tax is levied on taxable income as assessed for the national income tax. The community

117

Table 7.2: Tax rates for alternative local taxes to replace domestic rates, 1985

Region	Community charge £ per adult	Local income tax, %	% Sales tax excl. food
North	146	8.0	6.5
Yorks-Humber	124	7.9	5.8
East Midlands	144	6.4	6.0
East Anglia	129	6.0	7.0
GLC	231	7.7	8.7
South East excl. GLC	176	6.7	6.9
South West	144	7.6	7.3
Wales	104	5.6	5.8
West Midlands	179	8.4	7.6
North West	165	7.7	6.9
Scotland	161	7.1	7.6

Note: The community charge does not allow for the rebates of up to 80% of the charge for low income and elderly households.

Source: Author's calculations.

charge per adult varies substantially more across regions than do the other tax rates because of higher levels of household income and expenditure in London and the South East. As explained above, the average community charge for Scotland in 1985 is rather lower than the equivalent figure derived from the government's estimate of £221 for 1986-87 because of the different treatment of rebate arrangements but this has a trivial effect on the remainder of the analysis. Note that the high implicit tax on housing services in Scotland resulting from domestic rates is not matched by high tax rates for the alternative local taxes. This reflects the heavily skewed distribution of rateable values and relatively low average consumption of housing services per person in Scotland, which are associated with the high proportion of council housing in the total housing stock.

For a medium term analysis of the impact of the reform on house prices I have assumed an elasticity of housing supply of 1.0. This is almost certainly rather higher than the probable supply elasticity over a period of about 5 years, so that my estimates of the consequential increase in housing prices should be understated. Nonetheless, the

Table 7.3: Rise in house prices due to the abolition of domestic rates

(% increase over medium term)

Region	Main estimates		Low estimates	
	CC	LIT	CC	LIT
North	17.5	18.2	10.0	10.3
Yorks-Humber	12.9	13.3	7.5	7.9
East Midlands	13.6	13.7	4.6	4.8
East Anglia	12.5	13.0	7.0	7.4
GLC	13.1	13.7	4.6	5.1
South East excl. GLC	11.6	11.9	3.5	4.1
South West	11.9	12.4	6.2	6.7
Wales	11.5	12.1	6.8	7.4
West Midlands	14.5	14.9	5.0	5.6
North West	16.4	16.7	7.7	8.0
Scotland	23.1	23.8	14.2	14.9

Notes: CC = Community Charge; LIT = Local Income Tax.

Source: Author's calculations.

model suggests that house prices will increase by 12% in the South East and 23% in Scotland using the demand parameters in A above - see Table 7.3. The low elasticity set of demand parameters in B above imply price increases of between 4% for the South East and 14% for Scotland. The Green Paper on rates reform - Department of the Environment (1986) - briefly discusses the possible magnitude of the impact of the abolition of domestic rates on house prices (Appendix E, paras E10-E12) but it does no more than present illustrative calculations and suggest that the likely average price rise for England as a whole would be no more than 5%. The authors suggest that the price elasticity of housing demand lies between -0.5 and -0.8, so that the first of my sets of estimates is directly comparable. My calculations imply an overall price increase for England of three times that quoted in the Green Paper. In addition, it is now envisaged that the switch to a community charge in place of domestic rates would take place with little or no transitional period rather than over 10 years, so that the impact of the change will be much more substantial relative to the other factors influencing

Table 7.4: Aggregate increase in housing demand due to the abolition of domestic rates

(% increase by region, main estimates)

Region	Medium term supply elasticity = 1.0		Long term infinite supply elasticity	
	CC	LIT	CC	LIT
North	17.8	18.5	32.1	33.4
Yorks-Humber	13.0	13.4	23.9	24.7
East Midlands	13.6	13.7	24.6	24.9
East Anglia	12.7	13.1	23.1	24.0
GLC	13.5	14.1	24.1	25.2
South East excl. GLC	11.9	12.2	21.3	21.9
South West	12.3	12.8	22.1	23.1
Wales	11.8	12.4	21.4	22.5
West Midlands	14.7	15.0	26.7	27.4
North West	16.4	16.7	30.5	31.2
Scotland	23.1	23.8	44.2	45.7

Notes: CC = Community Charge; LIT = Local Income Tax.

Source: Author's calculations.

movements in house prices.

Since the elasticity of housing supply has not been assumed to be zero, the price changes will be accompanied by substantial changes in the size of the housing stock. The main estimates imply an increase in regional housing demand of 12% in the South-East and 23% in Scotland - see Table 7.4. These quantity changes imply a large increase in the level of housing construction, since in recent years the net annual addition to the housing stock has been less than 1% a year. In particular, it seems rather implausible to assume that the housing supply elasticity could be as high as 1.0 for London and South East in view of the severity of the constraints on large scale housing construction imposed by present planning policies, especially with respect to the avoidance of any encroachment on the Green Belt. I have therefore examined the implications of a supply elasticity of only 0.5 rather than 1.0 for these two regions. Using the main demand estimates this leads to a rise in house prices of approximately 17% in the South East and 19% for the GLC as compared with figures of 12% and 14% respectively for the supply elasticity of 1.0. The aggregate increases in housing demand are only slightly reduced by the higher price increases to approximately 8% in the South East and 10% in the GLC, which still imply that the rate of increase of the housing stock would need to exceed 1.5% p.a., much higher than in the recent past.

For the longer term I have used a perfectly elastic supply of housing in order to illustrate the consequences of the reform on the assumption that its impact will be solely on the size of the housing stock while house prices are unaltered. Again, this assumption is exaggerated, but it provides a basis for calculating the maximum possible impact of the reform on the demand for housing. Using demand parameters A (the main estimates) the increase in housing demand by region varies from 21% in the South-East to 44% in Scotland. The alternative set of demand parameters imply increases in the range 5% to 20%. It is, I think, inconceivable that the stock of housing in Scotland could be increased by over 40% without any rise in both land and housing prices, so that the long run impact of the reform might in practice fall somewhere between the sets of estimates obtained by using supply elasticities of 1.0 and infinity. It should be remembered that this long term increase in housing demand due to the abolition of domestic rates would be in addition to increases associated with rising living standards and demographic factors - such as new household formation and the effects of a high level of marital breakdown.

Domestic rates are a very erratic tax on the value of housing services, partly because of the vagaries of an out-of-date valuation system and partly because of rates rebates and housing benefit. As a result the dispersion of the changes in the price of housing services relative to other consumption experienced by different households is very large. This is illustrated by the figure in Table 7.5 which details some of the characteristics of the distribution of medium and long run price changes for households in Scotland. This example is particularly interesting because rating revaluations have not been postponed in Scotland, so that the wide dispersion of price changes undermines the argument that domestic rates would be a satisfactory tax if only politicians were prepared to keep valuations up-to-date. It is difficult to justify on any grounds a commodity

Table 7.5: Distribution of changes in housing demand and the price of housing services for Scottish households (as % of original values)

	10th percentile	Median	90th percentile	Average
A. Price of housing services relative to other consumption				
1. Medium Term (supply elasticity = 1.0) Community Charge or Local Income Tax	-39.5	-26.8	-3.3	-24.1
2. Long Term (infinite supply elasticity) Community Charge or Local Income Tax	-51.1	-40.9	-23.8	-38.5
B. Housing demand by household				
1. Medium Term (supply elasticity = 1.0) Community Charge	-2.3	23.1	43.2	21.6
Local Income Tax	0.9	23.1	43.0	22.7
2. Long Term (infinite supply elasticity) Community Charge	14.8	44.9	66.6	42.6
Local Income Tax	19.7	45.8	68.2	44.5

Source: Author's calculations.

tax whose effective tax rates vary between households to the extent shown in the table.

The median and average price changes are quite close, though the upper tails - i.e. smaller than average price falls - are longer than the lower tails. The range between the 10th and 90th percentiles is longer for the medium term than for the long term price changes. Both ranges are so large that it is clear that the reform will affect otherwise similar households in widely divergent ways, so that the reform may be perceived as leading to a significant degree of horizontal inequity. This is an excellent example of the difficulties inherent in attempting to reform erratic but well-established taxes. The new tax arrangements may be 'better' according to standard criteria for judging the distribution of the total tax burden, but this certainly need not apply to the distribution of the changes in tax payments which is what most people concentrate on in judging proposals for tax reforms. Unfortunately, it is the erratic nature of domestic rates which makes the process of reform so painful since its replacement by any alternative local tax must lead to a substantial degree of reshuffling of the tax burden between similar households.

The large dispersion of changes in the cost of housing services inevitably means that there will be a similarly large dispersion in the changes in housing demand across households, as Table 7.5 shows. This explains the necessity of analysing the impact of local tax reform using a model which is based on calculations concerning the behaviour of individual households rather than some kind of aggregate demand function. Note also that the differences between the dispersions of the changes in housing demand for the community charge and the local income tax are quite small, which reinforces the point that it is the abolition of domestic rates that is the crucial aspect of local tax reform with respect to its effects on the housing market.

EFFECTS ON THE STRUCTURE OF HOUSING DEMAND

In addition to the aggregate impact of the abolition of domestic rates on house prices and the demand for new housing construction, the reform is likely to lead to significant shifts in the composition and location of the housing demand. These effects are associated with systematic biases in the ratios of rateable values to capital values, and thus to the values of housing services, for different kinds of housing, biases which have been exacerbated in England and Wales by relative movements in house prices since the last rating revaluation in 1973.

(A) Council housing vs owner-occupation

In my previous work I showed that domestic rates represent a higher implicit tax on council housing than on owner-occupied housing, which suggests that the demand for housing by council tenants will increase by more than the

123

average for all households. On the other hand, households may find it difficult to satisfy their increased demand for housing within the public sector. There is considerable housing mobility among council tenants as they are able to organise moves or swaps within the housing stock owned by their local authority, but this mechanism could not cope with a general upward shift in the demand for better or bigger housing by council tenants. The shift in the overall cost of housing relative to other consumption may persuade some households to switch from council tenancy to owner-occupation but this would only relieve the pressure on public housing to the extent that those on council waiting lists or existing tenants choose to buy in the private sector rather than buying or planning to buy their council accommodation. The extent of the shift from council tenancy to owner-occupation cannot easily be estimated because the short term capital gains accruing to owner-occupiers as a result of the abolition of domestic rates could provide the basis for a classic speculative bubble in house prices - of the kind that took place in 1972-73 and in 1985-86 in London and the South East - which might encourage a larger switch from council tenancy to owner-occupation than would result from a steadier increase in house prices over a longer period of time.

A general increase in the demand for housing by council tenants may be manifested in a desire for better quality rather than bigger accommodation. This would exacerbate the problems that housing authorities already experience in letting small, poor quality flats in unpopular estates, so the benefits of good management and maintenance of council housing are likely to become even larger than at present. One obvious response would be to follow a much more market-oriented policy in setting local authority rents - a trend which is already apparent in some local authorities - and in determining the resources devoted to renovation or maintenance.

(B) **Household formation**

Ignoring the influence of other social and economic trends one would expect a fall in the price of housing relative to other consumption to increase the (potential) rate of new household formation, since it will become both more attractive and more feasible for young people to leave home in order to occupy their own accommodation. Similarly, at the margin the social factors which influence new household formation - marital breakdowns, the desire of the elderly to remain independent, etc. - will be shifted in the direction of less sharing of accommodation and a greater number of separate households. Much of this demand will be for rented rather than owner-occupied accommodation, so that the present situation of excess demand for privately rented housing will be exacerbated. An appropriate combination of renovation and more flexible letting and pricing policies by local authorities might ensure that currently unpopular blocks of flats could meet some of this excess demand, though recent experience suggests that housing associations may be more innovative and competent than local authorities in this sphere.

(C) **The distribution of central government grants to local authorities**

The criteria for the allocation of grants from central to local government will shift from an emphasis on the equalisation of rate poundages to the equalisation of community charge levels for a uniform service level, so that areas with a low rateable value per head will tend to lose relatively. This shift will tend to favour higher-rated urban areas at the expense of lower-rated rural areas, subject to the caveat that some central city authorities may lose quite heavily as a result of the move to a uniform business rate. At the margin this change will raise the proportion of the total cost of local public services borne by local taxpayers in rural areas which, combined with the higher average cost of providing such services, is likely to decrease the attractiveness of housing in rural areas. The major beneficiaries from the redistribution of central government grants seem likely to be the suburban and small town local authorities in southern England, which will reinforce the already strong pressures for further housing development in such localities.

(D) **Urban vs rural housing**

There are indications that rateable values as a fraction of capital values are higher in urban than in rural areas. The abolition of rates will thus reduce the cost of urban housing services by more than that of rural housing services. Further, the reform implies a reduction in the cost of housing services relative to the cost of transport services for commuting, so that the locational choices of households will shift in favour of higher quality or bigger houses with relatively short travel to work times. These relative price changes, as well as the effects of grant redistribution discussed in (C) above, will mean that the increase in the demand for urban housing, especially in central city or inner suburban locations, will be significantly larger than that for rural housing. Since the supply of housing is particularly inelastic in such locations, the increased demand may be expected to lead to a rise in the average price of inner urban housing relative to the average price of rural housing. On the supply side the change should greatly strengthen incentives to renovate or redevelop older housing in inner city areas. As usual such improvements would tend to shift housing up-market and out of the rented sector so that the availability of low cost rented accommodation in cities would be reduced.

All of these changes, including the general increase in the demand for housing, imply that the planning system is likely to be subject to unprecedented stresses. Some of the effects will reinforce present trends and policies - e.g. the rehabilitation of good quality housing in inner urban areas will be encouraged. On the other hand, any shift of housing demand from rural to urban or suburban areas will increase conflict over the granting of planning permission for residential development, particularly for green-field sites on the edges of towns and cities. The increased demand for housing will also tend to push industrial and commercial development yet further out from the centre of towns and cities by bidding up the value of land zoned for residential development, which will reinforce existing disputes over the merits of out-of-town shopping and industrial developments.

CONCLUSION

The analysis outlined in this paper suggests that the abolition of domestic rates will have a major impact on the housing market. By removing a substantial tax on the consumption of housing it should lead to a large increase in the potential demand for housing. At an aggregate level the response of housing supply to the additional demand will determine how far the change will lead to increased actual consumption of housing or to higher capital values for land and houses. In addition to the changes in aggregate supply and demand for housing there will also be important changes in the composition of housing demand which will present local authorities with major problems to resolve as managers of public housing and as planners responsible for making decisions about the zoning of land for development. The elasticity of housing supply will be determined in large part by the manner in which the planning conflicts between those who wish to convert the existing housing stock or to develop new housing on the edges of towns and cities and those who wish to retain the present restrictive policies on land development for environmental reasons are resolved. Thus, the division of the overall impact of the reform between price and quantity effects will ultimately depend upon political decisions about planning and land use.

While the abolition of domestic rates may lead to substantial income changes for many households and other transitional difficulties, it should not be assumed that its long run effect on economic welfare will be detrimental. This is a classic case of removing a specific commodity tax which generates a large deadweight loss, so that it is possible that the reform may be Pareto-improving in the sense that everyone could be made better off. The distributional effect of the reform will depend critically upon the nature of the tax which is substituted for domestic rates. Reliance upon the community charge will slightly reduce the progressivity of the tax system as a whole, whereas a local income tax would slightly increase its progressivity. However, even using a social welfare function incorporating a large degree of inequality aversion any adverse distributional effects are swamped by the welfare gains accruing to households as they adjust their housing consumption in response to the relative price changes.

Ignoring the beneficiaries of any capitalisation of the effects of the reform, it turns out that the elasticity of housing supply is the critical variable in determining the overall welfare gains and losses. In the very short run - i.e. with a zero supply elasticity - the reform simply amounts to a redistribution of the tax burden, so that the overall effect is almost invariably detrimental once allowance is made for the implications of the reform for horizontal equity as well as vertical inequality. Over longer time periods the median value of the real income gains accruing to households increases along with the elasticity of housing supply. For an infinite supply elasticity the median gain is of the order of 10% of original income for a community charge or a local income tax and all but a very few households are better off, whereas for a supply elasticity of 1.0 the median gain is approximately 5% for the same two alternative local taxes and about 12% of households are worse off.

These results show why the planning issues raised by the abolition of domestic rates are so important. Their outcome will determine the extent to which the potential social gains from the elimination of a (relatively) inefficient specific commodity tax are actually realised in the form of real income gains for a majority of households. Of course, the planning system exists in order to ensure that proper account is taken of the environmental costs of land development, but it is difficult to believe that an increase in aggregate housing supply would cause environmental diseconomies amounting to more than 5% of total household income. This is, however, a classic 'insider-outsider' problem. The beneficiaries of new housing development will be households who do not currently own houses in the areas where there would be most pressure for additional development. Those who do own such houses have more to gain by restricting new building, which would increase the capital gains accruing to existing owners as a result of the reform. Since development may be possible in other locations, the incentives to resist additional development are more complex than this simple model suggests, but nonetheless a planning system which allows 'insiders' - i.e. existing owners - an important influence on whether new developments should proceed will tend to transfer much of the economic gains generated by the reform from 'outsiders' to these 'insiders'.

These and related consequences of the abolition of domestic rates on the housing market have received little attention by the government or by others concerned with the reform of local taxation. It is important to remember that the impact of this reform is primarily due to the elimination of a specific tax on housing, so that my conclusions would not be substantially altered if another government were to replace the proposals for a community charge by a local income tax. Thus, once the arguments over the short term distributional effects of the reform have subsided, I hope that it may be possible for the Department of the Environment and local authorities to turn their attention to the way in which they should respond to the changes in housing demand identified in this paper. Without such forethought they will find themselves being obliged to take important decisions which will influence the evolution of the housing market over many years without any coherent view of how to mediate between the conflicting interests which will inevitably put the planning system under great stress.

REFERENCES

Deaton, A.S. and J. Muellbauer (1980) 'An almost ideal demand system', American Economic Review, vol. 70, pp. 312-26

Department of the Environment (1986) Paying for Local Government, HMSO, Cmnd 9714, London

Hughes, G.A. (1982) 'The incidence of domestic rates and alternative local taxes', Fiscal Studies, vol. 3, March, pp. 23-38

------ (1987) 'Housing demand and the impact of local tax reform' (University of Edinburgh: mimeo)

King, M.A. (1983) 'Rationing and the UK housing market: estimation and welfare analysis' (University of Birmingham: mimeo)

Topham, N. (1983) 'Local government economics' in R. Millward et al. Public Sector Economics (Longman, London), pp. 129-98

Chapter Eight

THE FUTURE ROLE OF GRANTS IN LOCAL GOVERNMENT FINANCE

David King

INTRODUCTION

The 1986 Green Paper Paying for Local Government ended
(Cmnd 9714 p. 76) with three main conclusions, namely that
domestic rates should be replaced by a poll tax called the
'community charge', that non-domestic rates should be
levied at a uniform poundage with the proceeds distributed
to local authorities as a common amount per adult, and that
the grant system should be radically simplified. This chapter
has two main purposes. First, it investigates the proposed
simplified system of grants and suggests that - in some
respects at least - this system is not as satisfactory as the
one it will replace. Secondly, it argues that from a local
authority point of view, the proposed changes in the
arrangements for non-domestic rates would effectively
mean that the revenue from this source would be equivalent
to grant receipts rather than tax receipts. This has
important implications for local autonomy. However, before
examining these two major themes, it is necessary to look
briefly at both the present structure of grants to local
authorities and the proposed new structure. Discussion is
largely confined to England. The main conclusions can be
applied to both Scotland and Wales and so only notable
differences are highlighted.

THE PRESENT GRANT SYSTEM

(a) **Specific grants**

Local authorities receive a wide variety of grants at present, but it is convenient to divide these into two groups, namely specific grants and general grants. It should be stressed at the outset that these groups between them account for a very large proportion of local authorities' current income. This point is illustrated by the figures in Table 8.1, which shows the components of current income for English local authorities in 1984-85 and for Scottish authorities in 1985-86. It can be seen from columns (2) and (4) that grants accounted for 44.5 per cent of current income in England and 54.1 per cent in Scotland.

Specific grants are grants whose receipts must be spent on services specified when the grants are paid. The Green Paper (pp. 36-7) indicates that the government is undertaking a review of specific grants. However, no proposed changes have been announced, and so it will be assumed in this paper that no changes are made. Table 8.1 shows that specific grants in England account for less than a quarter of total grant income while in Scotland they account for little more than a tenth.

(b) **Rate rebate grants**

The revenue from general grants is not tied to particular services. General grants are effectively paid under three separate headings. Grants paid under the first heading are termed rate rebates. The objective of rate rebates is to reduce the burden of domestic rates on people with low incomes. In effect, but with considerable oversimplification, central government allows local authorities to set their rate poundages and it then assesses the impact of these poundages on poor people. Where the impact is felt to be excessive, central government requires local authorities to ease the burden on the people concerned while it makes up the lost local tax revenue by means of these tax rebate grants. Table 8.1 shows that rate rebates account for a little over 4 per cent of local authorities' current income.

Table 8.1: Sources of current income for local authorities in England (1984-85) and Scotland (1985-86)

Source	England (1984-85) £bn (1)	% (2)	Scotland (1985-86) £m (3)	% (4)
Domestic taxes*	4.4	14.9	470	11.9
Non-domestic taxes	6.8	23.0	1,012	25.7
Specific grants	2.8	9.5	236	6.0
General grants	10.3	35.0	1,896	48.1
rate rebates	1.2	4.1	166	4.2
domestic element	0.7	2.4	102	2.6
other	8.4	28.5	1,628	41.3
Miscellaneous	5.2	17.6	326	8.3
Total	29.5	100.0	3,940	100.0

* Net of rate rebates

Source: Derived from Paying for Local Government, pp. 28, 59-60 and 78.

(c) **Domestic relief grants**

The second general grant shown in Table 8.1 is termed the domestic element. Actually this is its title in Scotland; in England it has the more cumbersome title 'the domestic rate relief grant'. The objective of this grant is to ease the burden of rates on all domestic ratepayers. In effect, the government allows English domestic ratepayers off the first 18.5 pence of the poundages imposed by their local authorities and gives the authorities a grant to compensate for the lost revenue. In Scotland the figure is 8p. This is lower than the English figure since poundages in Scotland are lower than in England; this is because rateable values are higher in Scotland on account of the more recent (1985) Scottish revaluation of rateable values compared with England (1973). Domestic relief grants account for around 2.5 per cent of local authority income.

(d) **Block grant**

The third general grant is by far the most important. It is termed 'other' in Table 8.1, but in England and Wales it is known as the Block Grant and hence the use of capitals hereafter. In England, it accounts for 28.5 per cent of current income; in Scotland its equivalent is split into two elements known as the resources and needs elements which between them account for 41.3 per cent of current income. The description given here relates to the Block Grant system in England, similar to that in Wales and the combined effect of the Scottish elements is very similar. To understand the operation of the Block Grant it is useful to take two hypothetical authorities A and B which are referred to in Figures 8.1 and 8.2 respectively. For the purposes of this explanation, it will be assumed that the sole sources of revenue available to A and B are rates (both domestic and non-domestic) along with the Block Grant, and it will be assumed that A and B are comparable areas in that they are responsible for similar bundles of services.

The horizontal axes in these figures show the poundages which A and B could set. The vertical axes seek to measure the service levels which they could attain. An area's service levels will be held to depend on two factors, namely its total tax and grant income and its level of needs. A 'high needs' local authority is one with, for example, a relatively large

Figure 8.1

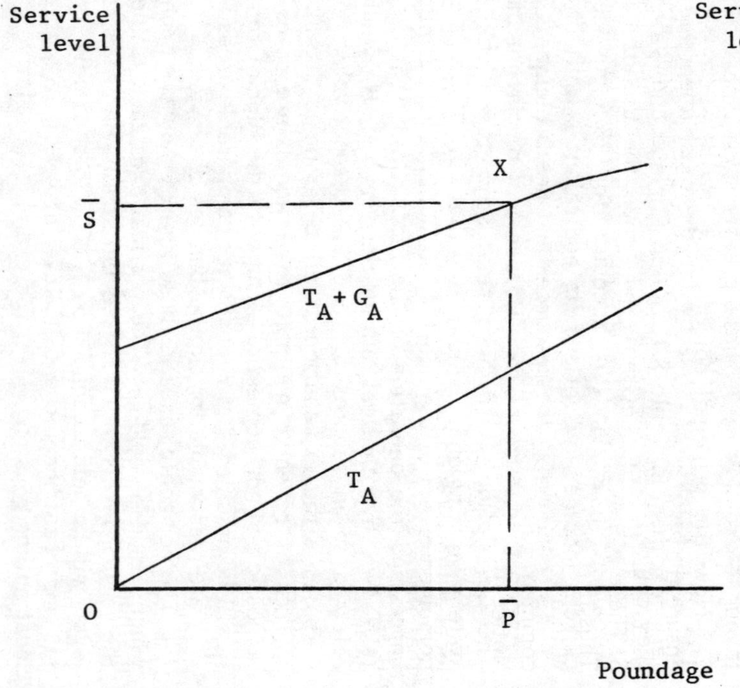

Figure 8.2

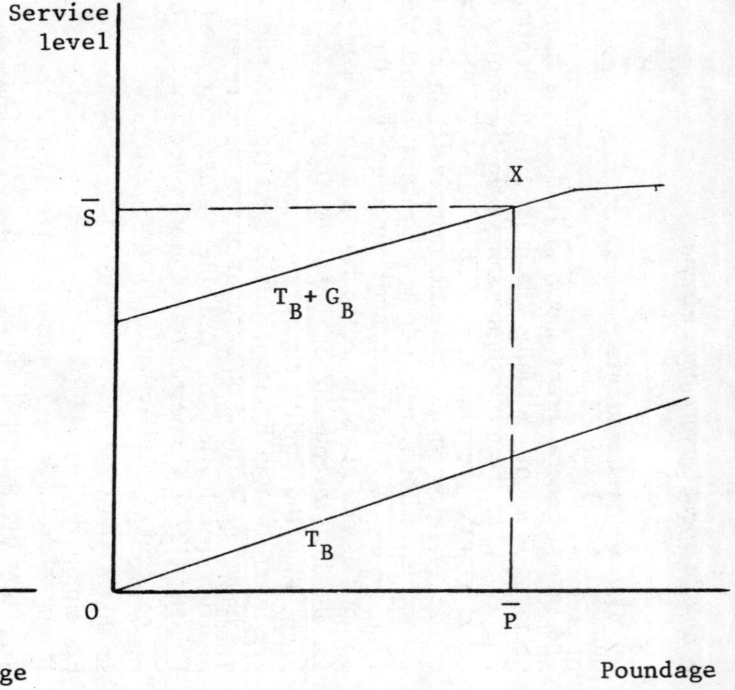

number of school age children or a relatively large number of premises from which refuse has to be emptied. It will be appreciated that if a high needs area and a low needs area each spent identical per capita sums, then services would typically be at a higher level in the low needs area, for such an area could afford a higher staff-pupil ratio in its schools and it could afford more frequent emptying of dustbins.

The lines T_A and T_B in Figures 8.1 and 8.2 show the service levels that A and B could afford if they had to rely on their local taxes (rates) alone. It will be seen that if they set the same poundage - say $\bar{P}$ - then A could have higher service levels than B. A similar result would arise if each area set any other common poundage, such as $0.8\bar{P}$ or $1.2\bar{P}$. There are two possible explanations for this. First, A could have a higher rateable value per head, so that a given common poundage produces more tax revenue per head there than applies to B. Secondly, A might have lower needs, so that a given revenue per head produces higher services. For simplicity, assume that both factors are at work in A's favour to explain why T_A has a greater slope than T_B.

Now the principal objective of the Block Grant is to ensure that if the areas set some standard poundage, $\bar{P}$, then they could afford to provide some standard level of service, $\bar{S}$. These standards are laid down by the central government. Thus if A and B each chose to set $\bar{P}$, then they would end up with a tax plus grant income which would take them to the common point X, enabling them to have services at $\bar{S}$. Notice that the point X is well above the tax lines T_A and T_B. This reflects the fact that, in practice, virtually all local authorities do rely heavily on Block Grant. Notice, too, that in assessing the grant which each area would be paid if it set the poundage $\bar{P}$, the authorities must take account of both its rateable value per head and its needs.

The most interesting aspect of the Block Grant scheme concerns its treatment of those local authorities which choose not to set the standard poundage $\bar{P}$. Since local authorities are free to set their own poundages, most - if not all - will in fact set one either below $\bar{P}$ or above. The simplest approach the government could use would be to work out what each area would get if it set $\bar{P}$, using the method just outlined, and then give it that amount irrespective of the poundage it actually sets. However, the government has always operated a scheme in which an area's grant receipt does depend on the poundage it sets.

Until recently, the approach adopted was one which

meant that most areas found that increases in poundages led to increased grants. The philosophy behind this was, broadly speaking, a view that those areas making the most effort to help themselves with high taxes deserved the highest grants. Recently, however, the Block Grant scheme has been modified in a way which means that virtually all areas find that increases in poundages lead to lower grants. This arrangement is embodied in Figures 8.1 and 8.2 where grants are paid in such a way that the areas end up with the relationship between poundages and service levels shown by the kinked lines $(T_A + G_A)$ and $(T_B + G_B)$. It will be seen that the gaps between these lines and the respective lines T_A and T_B diminish as poundages rise, showing that grants have less impact on the service levels attainable - that is to say grants become smaller - as poundages rise.

It must be stressed that although $(T_A + G_A)$ and $(T_B + G_B)$ pass through the common point X, the two lines are differently sloped to the left of the kinks - and indeed they also have different slopes to the right of the kinks. The different slopes are a result of the formula used for determining the effect of poundage changes on grant receipts. The rule for 1986-87 is that to the left of the kink, each area's poundage has to rise by 1.1p to secure a rise in tax plus grant revenue of £1 per head. Now areas with high rateable values per head will find that a 1.1p rise in poundages brings in far more than an extra £1 per head in rate income, so they would lose a lot of grant. A few areas will find that the rise in 1.1p brings in less than £1 per head so they would get rather more grant. The vast majority of areas find they would lose some grant, though some lose more than others. A and B represent this majority though A loses more than B; thus the gap between $(T_A + G_A)$ and T_A diminishes more rapidly than the gap between $(T_B + G_B)$ and T_B.

Now the fact that the scheme causes each 1.1p rise in the poundage set to lead to a £1 per head rise in income means that rises in poundages cause service levels to rise. Hence $(T_A + G_A)$ and $(T_B + G_B)$ have positive slopes. However, the fact that common rises in poundages for A and B lead to similar rises in the per capita income does <u>not</u> mean they lead to similar rises in service levels. It will be recalled that B has higher needs than A. If, for example, B has twice the needs of A, then it would take £2 per head in B to have the same impact on service levels that £1 per head would have in A. Put another way, each 1.1p rise in poundage will have the same impact on expenditure in A and B but more impact on service levels in A than B. Hence $(T_A + G_A)$ is steeper than $(T_B + G_B)$.

It remains to discuss the situation to the right of the kinks. The effect of the kinks is to put each area on to a flatter schedule at high poundages. This makes poundage increases very unrewarding once the kink is reached and the objective of the kinks is to deter areas from setting high poundages. Once an area reaches its kink, then it finds the grant formula changed in a way which means that an extra 1.5p poundage is needed to secure a £1 rise in tax plus grant revenue - in other words poundage rises lead to much greater losses in grant receipts. An area hits the kink if its expenditure exceeds the sum needed in its area to finance the standard service level $\bar{S}$ by an amount equal to 10 per cent of the sum needed to finance that level in an area with average needs. Thus area B, with its high needs, will hit the kink at a slightly lower service level than A, though this cannot be clearly brought out on small scale figures.

PROPOSED CHANGES IN GRANTS

(a) Needs and standard grants

The most important change in grants proposed by the Green Paper concerns the new needs and standard grants. The needs grant would compensate authorities for differences in the cost of providing a standard level of service to meet local needs whilst the standard grant would provide an additional contribution from central government taxes towards the cost of local services. They would both be distributed on a per adult basis. They are hereafter referred to as block grants.

The effects on areas A and B of the new arrangements are shown in Figures 8.3 and 8.4. For simplicity, it will be assumed again that the only current income available to A and B comes from local authority taxes and the block grants. Of course, the only tax whose rate can be determined by A and B will be the community charge on adults, so the horizontal axes in Figures 8.3 and 8.4 refer to the level of the community charge. The vertical axes refer to service levels as before.

The lines C_A and C_B show the service levels which A and B could achieve if they had to rely on the community

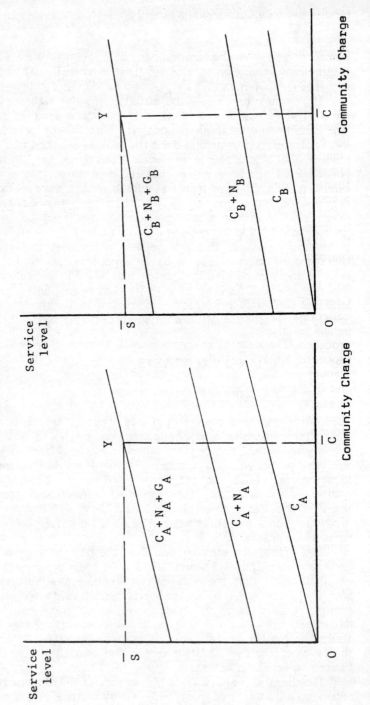

Figure 8.3

Figure 8.4

charge alone. Two points should be made about these lines. First, they are lower than the corresponding lines T_A and T_B in Figures 8.1 and 8.2. This reflects the fact that the yield of the community charge is meant to be comparable only to the yield of domestic rates, not to the yield of rates as a whole. Thus a standard community charge, say $\bar{C}$, would on its own produce a much lower level of services than a standard rate poundage. Secondly, the slopes of C_A and C_B are different. Indeed, the fact that C_A has a greater slope than C_B implies that a given charge is held capable of producing higher services in A than B. This could come about if there are proportionately more adults in A than in B. It could also come about if needs were lower in A than B. It will be supposed that, in practice, it comes about for both reasons.

As it happens, the community charge will not be the only tax raised for the benefit of local authorities under the Green Paper proposals. Non-domestic rates will still be collected. They will be collected by local authorities on behalf of the central government which will be given the proceeds. The central government will then distribute these proceeds to local authorities, giving each area the same amount per adult. The effect of this distribution on areas A and B is shown by the lines $(C_A + N_A)$ and $(C_B + N_B)$. These lines show that the proceeds raise the level of services each area could provide above the level the community charge alone would secure, and they are respectively parallel to C_A and C_B to show that the impact is the same at each possible community charge level since A and B will find their receipts from this source independent of their community charge levels. Notice that the gap between $(C_A + N_A)$ and C_A is larger than the gap between $(C_B + N_B)$ and C_B. This is because A and B will receive equal amounts per adult. This has more impact on services in A where a greater proportion of the population is adult - so that A receives more per head of population - and where, too, needs are lower.

On top of these non-domestic rate financed transfers, A and B will receive new block grants. As at present, the principal objective of these grants will be to ensure that A and B can finance a standard level of services, $\bar{S}$, if they set a standard level of community charge, say $\bar{C}$. Thus each area would be at point Y if it set the charge $\bar{C}$. What will happen to their block grant receipts if they set different community charge levels? The proposal is that these receipts would be unaffected. Thus the final lines for each area, $(C_A + N_A + G_A)$ and $(C_B + N_B + G_B)$ are parallel to the lines $(C_A + N_A)$ and $(C_B + N_B)$ showing that in each case the block grants should have the same impact on services irrespective of the level of poundage the area sets. Notice that these final lines are also parallel to C_A and C_B respectively.

(b) Other grants

The implications of the slopes of the final lines in Figures 8.1 to 8.4 will be considered in the next section. Before looking at these implications, it is useful to note briefly the Green Paper proposals for changes in non-block grants.

As far as specific grants are concerned, the Green Paper mentions (pp. 36-7) that a separate review will be undertaken. It seems this will consider ending some present specific grants and, presumably, raising block grants in compensation; and it will also consider creating some new specific grants and, presumably, cutting block grants in compensation.

Rate rebate grants and domestic rate relief grants will both disappear. This is because there will be no more domestic rates to impinge on people with low incomes in particular or on domestic ratepayers in general. However, there will be new community charge rebate grants to soften the impact of the community charge on people with low incomes in much the same way that rate rebate grants now soften the blow of domestic rates on such people.

THE OLD AND NEW BLOCK GRANTS COMPARED

(a) The key difference

In order to compare the present Block Grant and proposed block grants, it will be supposed for simplicity that the only sources of current income available to local authorities are those shown in Figures 8.1 to 8.4. Thus it will be assumed that at present they rely on rates (both domestic and non-domestic) plus Block Grant; and it will be supposed that in future they will rely on the community charge, the redistributed yield of non-domestic rates, and the new block grants.

The discussion so far makes clear that the key

difference between the present and proposed arrangements is that at present the Block Grant paid to each local authority is 'effort-related', so that a change in an area's poundage will affect its grant receipts, while under the proposed arrangements the block grants will be 'lump-sum' grants, so that a change in an area's charge will not affect its grant receipts. Now at present an area's grant will usually fall if it raises its tax rate, so it might be thought that the effects of tax rate increase on services will become more marked in future when grant payments will stay the same. However, this is not so.

That it is not so can be seen from the figures by considering what would happen if the areas raised their tax rates from $0.5\bar{P}$ (or $0.5\bar{C}$) to $\bar{P}$ (or $\bar{C}$). There will in fact be more effect on service levels at present than in future for $(T_A + G_A)$ in Figure 8.1 is steeper than $(C_A + N_A + G_A)$ in Figure 8.3 while $T_B + G_B$ in Figure 8.2 is steeper than $(C_B + N_B + G_B)$ in Figure 8.4. This result may seem paradoxical but the reason is straightforward. At present, if an area doubles its tax rate then it will receive twice as much income from domestic rates plus twice as much income from non-domestic rates; against this there will be a usually modest loss of grant. In future, an area which doubles its tax rate will get double the amount from the community charge, which can be seen as equivalent to a doubling of its income from domestic rates. True, it will not lose any grant, but equally it will receive no extra income from non-domestic taxpayers, and the absence of this gain will far outweigh the beneficial effect of a lump-sum grant.

The upshot is that local tax rate increases will in future be less rewarding in terms of their effects on service levels. Accordingly, it will be more difficult - that is to say more costly in terms of domestic taxes - to raise service levels. Thus areas may be less likely to seek high service levels. Indeed, the government no doubt hopes that the new regime will actively encourage areas to consider setting low taxes.

(b) **A closer look at the change**

It is possible to use an example to give some idea of just how much more difficult it will be for areas to raise their expenditure levels and hence their service levels. Tax rebates will be ignored in this example. In the new scheme, an area wanting to spend £1 per head more must raise £1 per head more in domestic taxes. This can be compared with the present situation for an English authority (outside London) where the average rateable value is around £130 per head. To finance an extra £1 per head expenditure under 1986-87 rules, such an authority would be required to raise its poundage by 1.1p provided it is to the left of the kink in the grant schedule. An extra 1.1p on a rateable value per head of £130 is £1.43, but since more than half rateable values are accounted for by non-domestic properties, only around 69p will fall on domestic taxpayers.

It can be seen that, at present, domestic taxpayers in (non-London) English authorities need, on average, to raise only 69p extra taxes to finance an extra £1 in expenditure. In future, these taxpayers will have to raise a full extra £1 in taxes. On efficiency grounds, there is much to be said for the proposed new arrangements provided, of course, it is assumed that the citizens concerned get the full benefit of the extra services, for at present increased service levels are 'subsidized' by increased non-domestic taxes (though part of the subsidy is offset by lower grant). However, it is worth making two observations about the new arrangements.

First, simply as a statement of fact, it will become much harder for citizens to raise local expenditure levels. It is interesting to recall that in 1981-82 they would have been able to raise expenditure by £1 merely by increasing domestic taxes by 35p! For in those days there would have been not only a rise in non-domestic rate receipts of 38p but also a <u>rise</u> in grants of 27p!

Secondly, the efficiency argument applies only if it is assumed that the full benefit of increased local service benefits domestic taxpayers alone. If some benefit accrues to businesses in their areas, then the new arrangements will not promote efficiency, for citizens will refuse to pay an extra £1 in taxes for an increase in services which yields, say, only 95p benefit to them, even though it might yield extra benefits worth 10p more to businesses in their areas and so produce total benefits worth more than £1 overall.

(c) **The varying impact of the changes in the grant system**

The discussion of Figures 8.1 and 8.2 explained how it is now harder for high need/low resource areas like B to raise their service levels than it is for low need/high resource areas like A, a point reflected by the fact that $(T_A + G_A)$ is steeper than $(T_B + G_B)$. Likewise, the discussion of Figures 8.3 and 8.4 showed that the same situation would apply under the proposed new grants, a point reflected by the fact that $(C_A + N_A + G_A)$ is steeper than $(C_B + N_B + G_B)$. It has also been explained that individual areas will find it harder in future than it is at present. However, it is necessary to point out that the situation is going to deteriorate more for areas like B than it is for areas like A.

To see the reasons for this, it is useful to compare a low resource/high need area such as Cleveland with a high resource/low need area such as Surrey. Consider, first, the present arrangements. Suppose Surrey wants an increase in service levels costing £10 per head. Then it must raise its poundage by 10 x 1.1p, that is 11p. Suppose Cleveland wants the same rise in service levels. It will actually cost some £13.50 per head there as needs are about 35 per cent higher than they are in Surrey (DOE 1985 Table D.3.1). Thus Cleveland must raise its poundage by 13.5 x 1.1p, that is 14.85p. In short, a given rise in service levels means raising taxes 35 per cent more in Cleveland than in Surrey.

Next consider the proposed arrangements. Suppose once more that Surrey wants an increase in service levels costing £10 per head. It will have to raise the community charge sufficiently to cover this rise. Now the community charge will fall only on adults - and adults comprise about 76 per cent of Surrey's population - so each of them will have to pay £13.16 to raise £10 per head of the population as a whole. Suppose Cleveland wants the same rise in its service level. This will cost £13.50 per head, as explained in the last paragraph. It will have to raise the community charge sufficiently to cover this. The community charge will fall only on adults - and adults comprise about 72 per cent of Cleveland's population - so each of them will have to pay £18.75 to raise £13.50 per head of the population as a whole. So a given rise in service levels which adds £13.16 to the community charge in Surrey will add £18.75 - that is 42 per cent more - in Cleveland. Admittedly this example selects the most extreme shire counties in England, but the inequality will actually be far greater between districts than between counties, so the example should not be seen as a freak result.

It is not easy to defend this result. It is true that both Cleveland and Surrey are able to provide the standard level $\bar{S}$ at the standard community charge $\bar{C}$ and that if both want a higher level then it's up to them alone. But these facts do not seem to offer a very satisfactory defence of a situation where, if both did initially set $\bar{C}$, then the citizens of Cleveland would find it much harder than Surrey to finance a common level in excess of $\bar{S}$; nor, to look at it in another way, do these facts seem to defend a situation where taxes will fall far more in Cleveland than in Surrey if both areas decided to set a common level below $\bar{S}$!

There is an interesting corollary to the point made here. Cleveland's problems arise because it has high needs and low resources per capita, a situation which will be common to all areas with proportionately large numbers of school children for they raise education needs and also mean that tax resources - adults - are proportionately low. Suppose an area wants high service levels above $\bar{S}$, and so has a community charge level above $\bar{C}$. What would happen if it permitted a housing development with residences suitable for families? Its needs would rise and its per capita resources would fall. Accordingly, its $\bar{C}$ schedule would get flatter, pivoting about O. In turn its $(C + N + G)$ schedule would get flatter as this must be parallel to the C schedule. In fact its $(C + N + G)$ schedule would pivot about Y as it must pass that point. Thus the new $(C + N + G)$ schedule will be higher than the old one to the left of Y - or $\bar{C}$ - and below it to the right. Given that the authority's charge exceeds $\bar{C}$ its present community charge level would in future provide poorer services. It follows that it will be tempted to oppose such a development. On the other hand, if the area had service levels below $\bar{S}$ with a charge level below $\bar{C}$, then it would be tempted to support such a development, for this time the flatter $(C + N + G)$ schedule would mean that its present charge level would provide better services. It seems a little odd to design a scheme where it is areas with the poorest services, and so perhaps the poorest schools, which will be the ones most eager to encourage children to become residents!

It must be stressed that the Green Paper proposals are not actually creating a new problem. Instead, they are just making an existing problem worse. However, the existing problem may not be as serious as the Cleveland-Surrey example suggested. Unfortunately, this means, in turn, that the worsening of the problems is actually more serious than it looks. The problem today is that poundages must rise 50 per cent more in Cleveland than in Surrey. This may not be as bad as it looks because rateable values are higher in Surrey than Cleveland. So the higher rise in Cleveland's poundages may not mean that Cleveland's domestic taxpayers actually have to pay more money for a given rise in services. Indeed, the reverse is likely!

How can the Green Paper proposals be modified to remove the problem? Removing it completely requires the community charge to be accompanied by a block grant which creates identical $(C + N + G)$ schedules for each area. These could have any slope desired. It must be noted, though, that only by chance would a given area find the common slope of the $(C + N + G)$ schedule equal to the slope of its individual C schedule. In other words, grants would ordinarily have to be effort-related grants, not lump-sum ones.

It is sometimes implied that it does not matter if one area, say Cleveland, needs a higher tax rate than another, say Surrey, to finance a given service level, say $1.2\overline{S}$. For it is suggested that house prices will fall in Cleveland relative to those in Surrey in such a way that the differential compensates prospective immigrants to Cleveland for their higher taxes by offering them cheaper housing. Hence it is claimed that tax capitalisation dispels equity problems (Topham 1985, p. 9). However, existing Cleveland owner-occupiers would suffer a capital loss. This point should be sufficient to show that relying on capitalisation effects does not eliminate any problems of inequity. A further discussion is provided by King (1984, pp. 146-7).

THE INCREASED ROLE OF CENTRAL GOVERNMENT GRANTS

Previous sections have focused on changes in the grant system. It is now necessary to take a broader look at the changing pattern of the current income accruing to local authorities. The present composition is shown in columns (1) and (2) of Table 8.2 for England (in 1984-85) and in columns (1) and (2) of Table 8.3 for Scotland (in 1985-86). These figures merely reproduce those given in Tables 8.1 and 8.2. It will be recalled that the figures for domestic taxes in these tables show payments of domestic rates after deducting the contribution made by the central government in the form of tax rebates, that is to say rate rebates. It will be seen that domestic taxes account for under 15 per cent of total income in England and for under 12 per cent in Scotland. Against these figures, non-domestic taxes - that is

Table 8.2: Sources of current income for local authorities in England (1984-85)

Source	Arrangements in force		Green Paper proposals	
	£bn (1)	% (2)	£bn (3)	% (4)
Domestic taxes*	4.4	14.9	4.4	14.9
Non-domestic taxes	6.8	23.0	-	-
General grants				
tax rebates	1.2	4.1	1.2	4.1
domestic element	0.7	2.4	-	-
block grant	8.4	28.5	15.9	53.9
Specific grants	2.8	9.5	2.8	9.5
Miscellaneous	5.2	17.6	5.2	17.6
Total	29.5	100.0	29.5	100.0

*   Net of tax rebates

Source: Derived from <u>Paying for Local Government</u>, pp. 28 and 78.

rates paid on non-domestic property - account for some 23 per cent and 26 per cent respectively.

However, the largest contribution comes from the central government in the form of grants which account for a total of 44.5 per cent of current income in England and 54.1 per cent in Scotland.

Columns (3) and (4) of the tables show what might have happened in the years covered by the tables if the proposed new system of finance had been in operation.

The tables imply that under the new system local authorities would cease to get any income from either non-domestic taxes or the domestic element, and that the revenue losses resulting would be precisely offset by increases in 'other' general grants. Before commenting on the implications of this change, it is helpful to explain one assumption which lies behind it.

It is assumed that local authorities cease to levy a non-domestic tax and have the revenue made good by a further increase in 'other' grants. The mechanics are clear cut in that the government propose to determine a uniform poundage at which non-domestic rates must be levied in all

Table 8.3: Sources of current income for local authorities in Scotland (1985-86)

Source	Arrangements in force		Green Paper proposals	
	£bn (1)	% (2)	£bn (3)	% (4)
Domestic taxes*	470	11.9	470	11.9
Non-domestic taxes	1,012	25.7	-	-
General grants				
tax rebates	166	4.2	166	4.2
domestic element	102	2.6	-	-
resources and				
needs elements	1,628	41.3	2,742	69.6
Specific grants	236	6.0	236	6.0
Miscellaneous	326	8.3	326	8.3
Total	3,940	100.0	3,940	100.0

*   Net of tax rebates

Source: Derived from Paying for Local Government, pp. 59-60. (The figure for miscellaneous income assumes this item accounted for the same proportion of income in 1985-86 that applied in 1984-85.)

areas. The proceeds will then be pooled and redistributed to local authorities at an equal amount per adult. The only question which arises is whether these new procedures mean that non-domestic rates should continue to be seen as a local tax, as implied in the Green Paper, or as a new grant, as implied in Tables 8.2 and 8.3. The case for regarding the revenue as extra grant revenue seems overwhelming. There would be no room for argument on this point if the central government actually collected the tax itself, for in that case it would clearly be a central tax and the distributed proceeds would clearly be grants. However, the fact that local authorities will initially collect the tax on, in effect, an agency basis and then hand its proceeds over to the central government for redistribution, is of no real significance at all.

The figures in Tables 8.2 and 8.3 suppose that nothing would change under the new system except the items just considered. This reflects the broad theme of the Green

147

Paper which proposes no changes in specific grants or in the use of fees, charges and rents which make up the bulk of 'miscellaneous' income. Likewise the paper suggests that local authorities would raise the same revenue from domestic taxes that they raise now, though of course it will be from a community charge instead of domestic rates. This, in turn, implies that there could be the same need for tax rebates to help poor people as there is now. However, the greater impact on the poor would probably mean that more tax rebates were now needed. In turn, the tax yield net of rebates would fall. Furthermore, the new system will tempt some areas to cut their service levels and others to raise theirs, and the resultant effects on total local authority expenditure may not cancel out. For example, if area E has a low rateable value per head and area F a high one, then E's citizens will at present be paying less than F's for a given standard of service; in future E's would have to pay more and F's less. E's citizens may vote for lower budgets and F's for higher ones but symmetrical responses cannot be guaranteed given the likely differing slopes of their (C + N + G) schedules.

IMPLICATIONS AND CONCLUSIONS

The main effect of the change in the system of finance is that the proportion of income accruing from grants - or, to put it another way, the proportion financed ultimately from taxes whose bases and rates are entirely at the central government's discretion - will rise greatly. It would rise from 44.5 per cent to 67.5 per cent in England and from 54.1 per cent to 79.8 per cent in Scotland. So the central government will be providing the great bulk of the revenue that local authorities spend. Now the central government is responsible to the people from whom it collects its taxes for the way in which the revenue from these taxes is spent. It is thus likely to want to exert even more control than it does now over what local authorities do with their income. This seems a pity because a major objective of a system of democratically elected local authorities is surely to allow individual areas to spend money in varying ways in accordance with the diverse wishes of different local electorates.

Local taxes will amount to just under 15 per cent of total income in England and under 12 per cent in Scotland.

An implication of these figures is that even if English authorities trebled their initial community charges then their total income would rise by under 30 per cent; if Scottish ones trebled theirs, then their income would rise by under 24 per cent. This suggests that raising expenditures will be very hard.

The upshot of the line of argument in the last section is that the Green Paper proposals are likely to lead to more central control of local authorities. In turn, it is likely that local spending patterns will converge more. Also, it has been argued that the proposals will deter high spending. Given that existing minimum standard regulations deter low spending, it seems clear that spending levels are likely to converge more. It seems, then, that local authorities are likely to be much less responsive to disparate local wishes. These conclusions raise the question of whether there will be any point in continuing to have a system of local government at all.

REFERENCES

Cmnd 9714 (1986) Paying for Local Goverment, HMSO, London

Department of the Environment (1985) The Technical Handbook of Grant-Related Expenditures 1985-86 (London)

King, D.N. (1984) Fiscal Tiers (Allen and Unwin, London)

Topham, N. (1985) 'A new framework for local government finance', Public Finance and Accountancy, 13 December, pp. 7-9

Chapter Nine

NON-DOMESTIC RATES AND LOCAL TAXATION OF BUSINESS

Robert J. Bennett

INTRODUCTION

The present system of local business taxation of Britain is a non-domestic property tax on the net annual value (NAV) of business property to which is applied a locally variable tax rate (rate poundage). The 1986 Green Paper (G.B. Government, 1986) proposes to replace the local discretion over tax rates by imposing a nationally uniform rate poundage: this gives a so-called unitary business tax - UBT. It is proposed that the proceeds of the non-domestic rates will then be redistributed between local authorities according to their adult residents' population. In addition local authorities may be left the discretion to levy an additional local tax rate at 5% of the national UBT tax rate. The proposals are being implemented in Scotland to come into effect in 1989.

The UBT proposal is one part of the Government's complex package of reforms for local government finance, and consideration of it cannot be divorced from the rest of the package. However, the issue of local business taxation gives rise to a number of specific questions separate from the main thrust of the Green Paper which emphasises the residential tax base reforms. Hence the discussion which follows below gives chief consideration to the local taxation of business although this is set in the context of the total pattern of relations between central and local governments.

THE GREEN PAPER: THEORY AND COUNTER-THEORY

In suggesting a UBT the Government has been responding to concern by industry and other commentators on the supposed deleterious effects of business rates. Such major concern is a fairly recent phenomenon, although there have been other periods in which non-domestic rates have attained a similar prominence, e.g., in the 1920s (see Mair, 1986).

In the recent past business rates have been looked upon as largely 'free income' by local authorities, and central government and industry have been relatively happy to accept this. Since the late 1970s, however, there have been increases in both the level and range of burdens. The increase in aggregate burden has become the more onerous since it coincided with recession, when profits were low, and since 1982 with cuts in central corporation tax rates which has decreased the benefit to be derived from deductibility of rates from corporation tax. The range of burdens between localities has increased in part because of central government actions to reduce local authority expenditure by selective reductions in Rate Support Grant, and in part by the actions of local authorities which have sought to expand expenditure. These local actions are particularly evident in local authorities with self-acknowledged 'new left' councils (Boddy and Fudge, 1983) where it has been sought to develop a contrary economic policy to that of central government. The range of burdens of rates in England and Wales has also increased between economic sectors. As a result of not keeping valuations up to date actual net annual values have progressively deviated from assessed NAV. This has increased the relative burden on manufacturing compared to commerce, with shops particularly lightly burdened (see Hedley, 1985; Bennett and Krebs, 1987).

There are a number of obvious criticisms of the UBT proposal. At a minor level there are difficulties in the valuation of mixed properties in a system of non-domestic rates which is combined with poll tax. At a more substantive level various analyses have confirmed that there are likely to be substantial shifts of rate burden under UBT, with increases for southern, suburban and rural areas, and decreases for many central city and older industrial areas (see, e.g., Hedley, 1985; CIPFA, 1986; Hale et al., 1985; Smith and Squire, 1986; Westminster City Council, 1986). The changes will be quite dramatic and hence it is accepted

151

in the Green Paper that substantial safety nets will be required. This considerably delays the effective implementation of UBT.

Redistribution of the UBT proceeds through a population grant, as well as the national setting of UBT rates, places very considerable additional powers in the hands of central government. This has been attacked by many commentators. It is feared that these powers might be manipulated in the future to disproportionately burden business (see, e.g., Hepworth, 1986; IOD, 1986; Webb, 1986; Zimmermann, 1986, 1987). For example, the IOD (1986, p. 23) see the severing of the link between domestic and non-domestic rates removing any brake on increases of the latter. It thus reduces protection for 'business ratepayers under a Government out of sympathy with the wealth-creating sector of the economy'. UBT is also unsatisfactory to all those interests concerned to preserve the autonomy of local government (see, e.g., Jones et al. 1986; Quirk, 1986). The Rating and Valuation Association (Hill, 1986, p. 36), for example, note that 'From the constitutional point of view, it is undesirable for one tier of government to determine a large element of the tax rate of another, albeit inferior, tier'. Others attack UBT on the grounds that its main desired outcomes can be achieved by other, simpler, means - by rate capping (CIPFA, 1986; CBI, 1986; Westminster City Council, 1986; IOD, 1986), by reduction of domestic rate relief grant, or by derating of industry as in Scotland (Mair, 1986; Webster, 1982).

The most significant criticism of the UBT, however, is that it totally undermines any link of local authority and local business. It is a major contradiction of the Green Paper proposals that, on the one hand, the domestic tax reforms certainly increase the number of tax payers and hence perhaps improve accountability, whilst the proposed non-domestic reform completely disconnects business from the locality in which it is situated, except for the minor effects of the proposed discretionary 5% non-domestic rate levy. Hence Westminster City Council (1986, p. 25) concludes that 'the proposals represent a sea-change in local authority finance in terms of much-reduced local autonomy: we do not accept that, over time, the uniform business rate would be seen as anything other than part of the national tax framework. Local government would be largely paid for by central government; the link between local business and local government would be effectively broken'. Again the

IOD (1986, p. 24) see UBT as 'a policy of despair - despair at ever achieving a proper system of responsible and accountable local government and despair at the possibility of achieving any effective relationship between the local business community and local government'. That the same views are echoed by AMA (1986, pp. 18-19) demonstrates that the same criticisms come from all parts of the political spectrum.

Two forces seem to have been at work promoting a UBT. A first argument for UBT is to be found in the increasingly dominant view of the theory of tax policy. The general theoretical discussion of business tax reforms in Britain and the USA has concentrated on the need to streamline national tax systems in order to free resources for greater investments in economic growth. Two major aspects of the resultant reform proposals are, first, to reduce the total level of tax on business, and secondly to remove distortions induced by taxation on different sectors, assets, sources of finance, or owners. The theoretical discussion is exemplified by, e.g. Feldstein (1978), Auerbach (1983), King (1977), and King and Fullerton (1984). The use of these arguments for the case of the UK corporation tax system is evident in the Meade Committee (1978) and particularly in G.B. Government (1982) and H.M. Treasury (1984). The outcome has been progressive reduction of corporation tax rates from 52% up to 1981, to 32% in 1986 as well as important reforms of specific capital allowances. These changes have been a major influence on increasing the burden of local business rates (since reduced central corporation tax rates also reduce the benefit of deductibility of rates to those firms having assessed taxable profit).

As a result the rates have come increasingly to be seen as the major remaining distortion which requires removal. This is essentially the case advocated by Lloyds Bank (1982) and Crawford and Dawson (1982). Bailey (1986, pp. 26-7) has interpreted this argument as central government's 'fiduciary duty' to protect ratepayers from local authority abuse of its discretionary powers. That rates are indeed distortionary is evidenced by Bennett (1986). However, the policy conclusion to be drawn is not necessarily the need for a uniform tax rate, as argued later below.

A second argument for UBT is to be found at central government level. Central government, it can be argued in the context of the present discussion, has three major

153

responsibilities with respect to local government activity. First, it must ensure that the economy contains as few impediments to the competitiveness of business as possible. This leads to the development of a policy of 'fiduciary duty' along the lines of tax reform noted above. Second, central government has seen itself as the agent of control of the level of total taxation and public expenditure in the economy as a whole. This leads naturally to the case to restrict local government financial freedom. Third, central government has a responsibility to seek equalisation between the resource bases and needs of local authorities in order to eliminate inequities and distortions. The non-domestic rates are the major source of inequality in local tax bases in Britain. (The range of rateable values per capita is 1:3.7 for domestic, 1:12.7 for non-domestic, and 1:12.6 for total rateable value in 1982.) Hence, elimination of the major part of these differences by UBT would greatly simplify central government's responsibilities through grants. However, UBT is not the only possible means of achieving this goal.

There are two alternative counter-theories to the UBT option. These will be referred to below as the 'benefit principle' and 'partnership principle'. The benefit principle is essentially an extension to local government of the macroeconomic theories regarding elimination of tax distortion. The benefit principle is that enshrined in the poll tax proposal (although in fact the community charge does not in any way approximate to a benefit tax). The benefit principle seeks to find a tax or charging scheme in which the impact of local government taxes or charges exactly equals the cost of provision of marginal service benefits. In this case the business tax system has zero impact: local government behaves like a market actor in which goods are delivered and charged on a cost-plus basis.

This principle is assumed by many public finance theorists in developing local public choice models (see, e.g. Buchanan, 1950; Tiebout, 1956). It is also enshrined in the standard accounts of the normative theory of fiscal federalism (see Oates, 1972; King, 1984). In this theory taxes assigned to local uses must be flat rate, proportional or benefit taxes (Foster et al., 1980; McLure, 1983). This is summed up well by Foster et al. (1980, p. 165):

> One of the criteria for a good tax to finance local expenditure is that it should be a local tax and that

there should be a close link between the expenditure undertaken locally and the tax collected locally. ... If local government were to charge for services a price equal to costs of production ... peoples' choices would be efficient in terms of resource allocation. From the standpoint of economic efficiency no more need be said (op. cit., p. 217)

From this perspective Jackman (1986) and Foster (1986) argue that both the present non-domestic rates and a UBT, which preserves the present level of non-domestic rate yields, violate the benefit principle at aggregate level since 51% of local taxes are paid by business which receives only aproximately 17% of local government expenditure benefits. In addition the UBT also violates the benefit principle in disconnecting the relationship between costs (which are uniform) and benefits (which will still vary between localities). Jackman (1986) therefore argues that there are two preferable approaches to reform: (i) design a local business tax on the benefit principle in which tax payments would be determined by the costs of services provided to business, or (ii) use of charges for local services in relation to level of use. The second approach is also supported by Foster (1986) and by some local authority commentators (e.g. Hepworth, 1986).

There is probably no dispute that benefit principle taxation could achieve many desirable features whether one takes a 'normative' or a 'partnership' perspective. The practical difficulty is that many services cannot be easily charged for, no satisfactory benefit tax is normally available (Mieskowski, 1976; Topham, 1983; Bennett and Krebs, 1987), and benefit taxation does nothing to tackle the problem of more effective linking of business to local government.

The second counter-theory to UBT is based firmly in the implementation of the 'partnership principle'. This is stated well by Wiseman (1964), Dafflon (1977) and Topham (1983): for a recent summary see Bennett (1987a, 1987b)). The partnership view states that any non-central action must be viewed in the context of the political and constitutional powers that form and maintain relations between business, people and government, and between central and local government. For any theory or policy to be meaningful it must accept as a starting point that local government exists in order to choose taxes and benefit strategies in accordance with its powers and preferences, which may well differ from those of central government. These cannot be criticised on the a priori grounds of normative theory. Haller (1968; quoted in Dafflon, 1977, p. 18), for example, states that 'it is misleading to label as 'inefficient' state policies which modify the policy that the central governments may want to implement, if these policies are proposed with knowledge of the relevant facts and originate simply in the different weights placed on specific issues by federal and state governments'. Again, Peacock (1972, p. 94) states that 'the "inefficiency" argument makes a confusion between political ends and fixed means'; he argues that a particular assignment of central-local taxes cannot of itself be said to be inefficient just because it conflicts with centralised criteria.

The 'partnership' perspective is based on a genuine concern by business that local authorities should have a good tax base so that business can gain the advantages of adequate infrastructure, environmental facilities, educational support, recreation and health facilities for its workforce. This approach is not strongly embedded, in Britain, into the positions of either business, which generally sees little benefit in local authority services (see Webb, 1986), or local government, which Hepworth (1986) argues to have been generally 'narrow and defensive' in this area. However, in other countries a much stronger attitude of partnership is present. In Germany, for example, the partnership approach is seen as a key to the strength of both business and local government; for example, Schoser (1986) states from an industry perspective that 'local authorities must be independent and not subject to the will of others'; and Zimmermann (1986) notes that 'business values the way in which local authorities care for them'. From this perspective a strong local revenue derived from business must be maintained for local government.

Against both the 'benefit' or 'partnership' principles the UBT proposal must be appraised negatively. Its only gain, in radically reducing distortions between assets and between locations, is won at the expense of eliminating effective relationships between businesses and local authorities, and by strongly eroding local autonomy. Clearly a preferable policy, depending upon the theoretical perspectives adopted, is implementation of reforms based upon either the 'benefit' or 'partnership' principles. Before moving to a set of proposals, however, it is first necessary to give a more rigorous appraisal of the 'problems' associated with the present non-domestic rates.

NON-DOMESTIC RATES: PRESENT CHARACTER AND 'PROBLEMS'

A first question to be answered is the importance of the rates as a component of business costs. The general answer to this question is that they are relatively low as a proportion of costs in manufacturing, but can be quite high for commerce. The Census of Production demonstrates that aggregate rate burdens rose from 1.4% to 1.9% of net output and from 3.1% to 4.0% of wages and salaries 1979-82. However, for commerce estimates of rate payments suggest burdens that are 2-3 times higher (Jackman and Ferry, 1978), or 4-5 times higher (Tyler, 1984). It is not unusual for rates to reach at least 30% of gross turnover levels in large commercial concerns. Thus although rate burdens are low in industry, they are much higher in commerce.

A further issue, however, is their variability between locations. Ranges of rate poundages in England and Wales since local government reorganisation in 1974 increased from 1:2.1 to 1:2.27 in 1985. This relatively modest change, however, conceals a situation in which the upwards skew of the distribution of rate poundages has rapidly increased, i.e. the number of local authorities levying rate poundages substantially above the mean has substantially increased. Indeed over the period 1981-6 the distribution has become trimodal: a marked mode at approximately average poundages, a second mode of 40-50 authorities at 20-30% above average, and a third mode of 10-20 authorities at 60-80% above average. Thus substantial differences have developed between groups of local authorities. This is partly related to urban structures, with central cities levying higher poundages than hinterlands (see Jackman and Ferry, 1978; Tyler, 1984; Bennett and Krebs, 1987), but is also related to local party political control: almost all of the highest rate poundages being in 'new left' localities. As a consequence marked differences in location costs arise for otherwise comparable industries.

We may conclude, therefore, that although rate burdens are in aggregate fairly small cost items, they are much higher in some sectors than others (especially commerce), they are one of the most variable costs between localities, and both level and variability have increased markedly over the 1974-85 period, particularly since 1978. However, despite their increasing effect, most commentators have concluded that rates have little effect on business decisions or investment intentions. Part of this negative conclusion is influenced by the conclusion of studies undertaken in the USA (see e.g., ACIR, 1967; 1981).

Because of the major differences in local tax systems, these have little relevance to Britain where few studies have analysed this question. Hence conclusions are based on little direct evidence. In a survey of 49 firms GLC (1983) found that only 10% cited lower rates as reasons for choosing a new location, although 12% of all firms (19% of small firms) did cite rates as one reason for relocating. The study by DTI (1985) did not survey rates specifically as a burden on business, but no respondent out of 200 wrote in rates as a response to questions of 'What is making business bad for you?', or 'Which central or local government requirements have burdened your business?' Instead, some of the major issues identified as burdens on business were VAT, employment protection, sick pay and central tax legislation; however, local authority planning, building and the local environment were identified as important issues respectively, by 20%, 7% and 6% of the firms.

Despite these negative findings, it is again the case that local studies in specific environments show considerable effects of rates on business decisions. Good examples are the local studies in Sheffield, Merseyside and Nottingham (Sheffield Chamber of Commerce, 1984; Merseyside Chamber of Commerce, 1986; East Midlands Employers' Association, 1984); or the decisions of the National Freight Consortium of Small Shopkeepers (reported in Bennett and Zimmermann, 1986, pp. 171-2). At regional level the CBI have documented businesses' perceptions of rates as a major effect on competitiveness, as well as current and future employment, in the North West and Yorkshire and Humberside (CBI, 1981, 1982, 1983). This has been argued to require control of the areas levying extreme rates (Birdseye and Webb, 1984; Webb, 1986). Some more limited evidence of the effect of rate burdens is also supplied by the effects of Enterprise Zones. The studies by RTP (1984) suggest that derating is the most important factor for businesses in setting up in an Enterprise Zone. Thus, as far as the limited evidence available can be believed, rates do not have a major and general effect on business decisions, but can be of major significance in the case of a restricted number of high tax locations.

A further question to be resolved is whom the influence of rates bears upon: what is their incidence. This question can be approached from two points of view: formal (or immediate) and final (or effective) incidence. Formal incidence concerns measurement of the effective tax rates on the taxed entity compared with other entities. This has been assessed for the non-domestic rates at aggregate level by King and Fullerton (1984) and Piggott and Whalley (1985); and at local level by Bennett (1986) and Bennett and Krebs (1987). The latter two studies find differences between localities of up to 21% in effective tax rates, with aggregate effective tax rates of non-domestic rates of 5-8%. Rate burdens are strongly distortionary not only between locations, but also between assets, sectors and sources of finance: burdens are heaviest for building assets in manufacturing industry, financed by debt and owned by tax exempt institutions; burdens are lightest for inventories in 'other' industry, financed by retentions, and owned by households.

Final fiscal incidence is notoriously difficult to estimate, but a number of recent studies for Britain have sought to resolve the question of the extent of shifting to other actors. (Note that possible capitalisation, sometimes incorrectly cited as a factor which eliminates local tax burdens altogether, is part of this shifting problem.) These studies have taken the pragmatic perspective advocated by Mieskowski (1976), Topham (1983) and Bennett and Krebs (1987), which have suggested that theoretical views on tax incidence have only limited relevance: in practice the extent of shifting depends on the specific nature of the tax system; how it impacts on each individual business, its market position and conditions for its factor supply and demand, and its extent of profit maximising or managerial behaviour. Hence we must rely on the empirical level to answer the incidence question.

For the non-domestic rates, studies by Damania (1986a) and Mair (1987) estimate possible price effects as fairly small, in the range 15-20%. This is confirmed by Bennett and Krebs (1987) using the differential incidence model approach suggested by Mieskowski (1972), who find that in most sectors price shifting reaches no more than 18%. Taking account also of possible effects of expenditure benefits, Bennett and Krebs demonstrate local actions to be almost totally negative for Britain; i.e., local general expenditures do not offset local tax rates, but instead give a further negative impact on profits burdens. All of these estimates are unsatisfactory to some extent, mainly because of the poor quality of available data to estimate reliable models. However, what they do indicate is that with a local tax which is clearly not based on the 'benefit' principle, unpredictable distortions to business decisions result between sectors, locations and assets.

Each of the preceding aspects is to some extent partial. The impact of local tax and expenditure decisions can also be assessed jointly as a 'macro' influence on the local economy as a whole. Only a few attempts have been made at such an assessment. The main group of studies is that by Cuthbertson et al. (1979, 1982) and Gripaios and Brooks (1982). They estimate a model of local employment dependent upon local authority expenditure taxes, density of manufacturing and service employment, market potential, population density, a measure of residential desirability, and a regional policy dummy variable. Their results, at county level in England and Wales in 1974, indicate positive effects of local authority expenditures on employment (excluding direct level authority employment) which is offset by only 60% reductions from tax effects. The net gain in services alone accounts for much of this net benefit (107%). They therefore conclude that £1m. of local authority expenditure could generate 2,500 additional jobs (including local authority employment). The model is extremely crude, and it is cross-sectional and makes no attempt to control for macro-economic conditions. However, Gripaios and Brooks (1982, p. 217) conclude that the results do 'emphasise the probable importance of local authority fiscal policy in the determination of employment'. These results are rather crude but they do have more credibility than the even cruder univariate relationships examined by Straw (1981, 1984), Hughes, (1981), Othick (1981), or Stonefrost (1983); or the statistically flawed study of Crawford, Fothergill and Monk (1985) (see Damania, 1986b) which all find little or no relation between local authority fiscal behaviour and jobs.

A major problem with all of these studies is that they are aggregate statistical generalisations: they do not take account of the features noted above, that rates are a problem focused on some sectors in a limited number of locations. To take full account of these features it would be necessary to undertake a much more detailed study of not only levels of tax rates, but their variable incidence across the industries concerned, and the specific benefits received, in each local economy. Unfortunately, no study has attempted this level of analysis, even for restricted case studies. A number of studies do examine the disposition of local industrial development initiatives, but they do not address the more general aspects of local fiscal burden or the incidence of non-specific local expenditures (see, for example, the studies by Evans and Eversley, 1980; Boddy, 1982; Young and Mason, 1983; North and Gough, 1983; Storey, 1983; Parkinson and Wilks, 1983; Young, 1986; Sellgren, 1981). One recent study does allow comparison of high-rated Sheffield with other areas for the hand tool industry (Bennett and Fearnehough, 1987). They find that local tax costs depress local profitability by at least 80%.

At present we have no totally satisfactory conclusions on the macro impact of local fiscal policy costs or benefits; however, we can conclude on the limited evidence available that in aggregate the general benefits of local expenditures policy do not greatly outweigh local tax costs; and in the specific case of high tax areas the benefits of local expenditures are redistributed into general expenditures which, because they do not directly benefit industry, instead further depress profitability, employment and the general image of the locality as a place for business to locate.

A PREFERABLE POLICY PACKAGE

In the light of the foregoing discussion the present form of the non-domestic rates can be argued to present only one major problem: that of excessive variability between areas and hence the Government's attempts to control 'local excesses'. The approximately twenty local authorities which form a distinct subset levying rate poundages, in 1986 30-80% above average creates very special burdens for business which are difficult for them to cope with unless the markets for the products of businesses located in these areas are very localised and non-competitive or non-local but monopolistic, making it possible to pass on rates in higher prices. If neither of these conditions apply, the rates bear on profits.

The causes of increased rates variability between areas can be attributed to two chief factors. First, the behaviour of central government has markedly reduced grant support to these localities; second, the behaviour of the local authorities themselves has sought radically to expand expenditure in line with local party political programmes. Some of central government's changes would have been similar if a Labour government had implemented its Green Paper proposals on Rate Support Grant reform (G.B. Government, 1977). Of course changes in RSG are consequent upon particular distribution criteria used in assessing GRE, which have not been as favourable to the inner city areas levying high tax rates as a Labour government would have been. Nevertheless, it can be argued that a large proportion of the effect of RSG changes on rate poundages are the consequences of transition to a grant system which seeks to assess need to spend against demographic and social data taking account of local tax base, rather than against past expenditure volume irrespective of local tax resources.

If, however, the 'problems' of non-domestic rates are derived in significant part from the 'excesses' of a limited number of local authorities, then one approach is to tackle them by more specific means than UBT. Rate capping and other limited reforms are means which are already available for central control as part of its 'fiduciary duty'. There is no reason to sacrifice the autonomy of the whole local financial system because of a very concentrated problem. However, central government also seeks a UBT to institute a control of total public expenditure, and because of the wide range of non-domestic tax bases which make it difficult to simplify its grant equalisation payments. Again, however, these are not good reasons to sacrifice the whole local government finance system.

A more radical approach derives from the previous discussion. At the theoretical level there is much to commend the use of charges as the main burden which local authorities impose on business. However, in addition to charges, which draw on the 'benefit' principle, an additional levy is required to guarantee that the 'partnership' principle is also strengthened at local level. To implement 'partnership' requires a local business tax, in addition to charges. The requirements for such a tax are that it should be on a broad tax base so that all business is captured; it should be as locationally specific as possible in order to avoid the difficulties of tax base attribution; it should be 'onerous' following the ability to pay principle (since the general cost of local services is borne by charges); firms in economically prosperous positions should be the main contributors to local economic development; no local discretion should be given over tax assessments; and all businesses in an area should face the same tax rates - this avoids the wasteful competition characteristic of the US; control on the total level of local tax burden should be available to prevent exploitation of 'locationally trapped' enterprises; and all revenue raised should be dedicated to the purposes of local economic development.

Ironically, as has been suggested elsewhere by the author (Bennett, 1987b) the best new tax which satisfies such a set of requirements is a reformed structure of non-domestic rates. This can be made a broad-based tax, it is locationally fixed, it can be related to ability to pay, and it can be integrated into a controlled interpretation of partnership. The reforms of non-domestic rates that are required are (i) introduction of all business into the tax base, i.e. eliminate derating of agriculture and other special bodies; (ii) eliminate 'formula' rating (mainly of nationalised industries, utilities, public sector facilities and mineral workings) and all forms of selective derating (e.g. in Scotland) in favour of a true NAV assessment based on either rental, profits or contractor's bases; (iii) place Scottish valuation on the same basis as England and Wales thus eliminating the present distortionary bias across the border (cf. CBI Scotland (1986)); (iv) maintain the present base of NAV: rental value can be argued to be a good measure of ability to pay as a measure of market demand for property and space; (v) but relate actual rate payments to level of profitability, thus exempting loss-making enterprises and (vi) implement revaluation of the tax base on a rolling basis every 3-5 years.

These reforms ensure the breadth of tax base, its locational specificity, and its relation to ability to pay. The ability to pay principle could be made to work in various ways, but one obvious formulation is to use the direct product of local rate poundage with NAV, as at present, but with scaling down of tax payments progressively to zero for low profit concerns. Multisite low profit enterprises would have this scaling implemented between localities using the ratio of total profits to total NAV. Note that these firms will not escape the contribution to those local services received on a pure cost basis through charges.

The issue of control of level of tax burden can be

addressed only by reform of the way in which local government represents the interests of business. It is clear from present experience that the 'consultation' with businesses imposed as an obligation on local authorities by the 1982 Local Government Finance Act does not work satisfactorily. Since it is suggested that all revenue raised from reformed non-domestic rates should be earmarked for local economic development, one means of achieving effective and controlled management is to separate decisions on its expenditure from that of the rest of the council's activities.

This suggests that a separate committee be established, small in size, with final executive powers not answerable to the general council of the local authority. There should be representation of local businesses who should form an absolute majority, as well as representation of local committees. Whilst the local council members could be appointed by the council, the local business representatives would have to be elected. The local chamber of commerce could be used as a vehicle to arrange such an election, although clearly the electorate should embrace all businesses, not just those which are members of the chamber. Such an executive committee could then translate in very effective fashion the needs of businesses for improvements of present facilities and infrastructure, as well as creating a strong investment fund, fuelled by non-domestic rates, which could be used for the generation of new business. In particular it would allow satisfaction of the criterion for reform called for by IOD (1986, p. 24): 'The best long term safeguard for business is close involvement with local authorities so that both recognise their interests are mutual and complementary'.

This proposal ensures accountability to business; increases, fosters and firmly lodges the concept of 'partnership' into local government activity; and it reinforces efforts to encourage economic regeneration by creating a new pool of earmarked resources. Combined with charging for the majority of services provided to businesses, it would combine the benefit and partnership principles; and since the non-domestic rates are retained in a form close to the present structure the whole package could be implemented with only modest legislative reforms.

CONCLUSION

This paper has sought to set the discussions of the 1986 Green Paper proposing a UBT into a wider context of theory of local business taxes. It has been argued on theoretical grounds that local taxes on business should either follow a 'benefit' or a 'partnership' principle. The paper has then appraised the nature of the 'problems', the solutions to which the UBT proposal is directed. The assessment of the 'problem' which has been given concludes that the central issue is one of the variability of effective tax rates between areas, particularly the deviation of approximately twenty local authorities from the general behaviour of the rest of local government. These local authorities are almost all guided by 'new left' local political parties. In addressing this problem it is argued that UBT is not the best approach. A modest proposal which merely tackles variability is to maintain rate capping. However, a proposal which allows central government to simplify its equalisation problem, and which also allows a much better approach of British local business taxation to theory, is proposed. This suggests charging for most services to local businesses on a cost-of-service basis. However, in addition a reform of non-domestic rates is also proposed. The receipts of reformed rates would then be used as a local economic development resource, allocated by an executive committee of the local authority with majority elected membership from local businessmen. This, it is suggested, can promote local policies in line with national markets and objectives, carefully tailored by business to its local investment needs. This presents possibilities for improvement not only of local government finance, but of the economic growth of the economy as a whole.

REFERENCES

ACIR (1967) State-local taxation and industrial location (US Advisory Commission on Intergovernmental Relations, Washington, D.C.)

ACIR (1981) Regional Growth - Interstate tax competition (U.S. Advisory Commission on Intergovernmental Relations, Washington, D.C.)

AMA (1986) The AMA's response to the Government's green paper, Paying for local government, Cmnd 9714

(Association of Metropolitan Authorities, London)

Auerbach, A.J. (1983) Taxation, corporate financial policy and the cost of capital, Journal of Economic Literature, 21, 905-40

Bailey, S.J. (1986) Rates reform - lessons from the Scottish experience, Local Government Studies, 12, 21-36

Bennett, R.J. (1986) The impact of non-domestic rates on profitability and investment, Fiscal Studies, 7, 34-50

------ (1987a) Tax assignment in multilevel systems of government, Government and Policy: Environment and Planning C, 5

------ (1987b) Local business taxes: theory and practice, Oxford Review of Economic Policy 3, 60-80

Bennett, R.J. and Fearnehough, M. (1987) The burden of the non-domestic rate on business Local Government Studies 13, 23-36

Bennett, R.J. and Krebs, G. (1987), Local business taxes in Britain and Germany (Nomos, Bamberg)

Bennett, R.J. and Zimmermann, H. (eds.) (1986) Local Business taxes in Britain and Germany: Conference Report (Anglo-German Foundation, London and Bonn)

Birdseye, P. and Webb, A.J. (1984) Why the rate burden on business is a cause for concern, National Westminster Bank Review, February, 2-15

Boddy, M. (1982) Local Government and industrial development, Occasional Paper No. 7 (School of Advanced Urban Studies, University of Bristol)

Boddy, M. and Fudge, C. (1983) Local Socialism (Macmillan, London)

Buchanan, J.M. (1950) Federalism and fiscal equity, American Economic Review, 40, 583-97

CBI (1981) CBI Rates survey highlights new threat to business, News Release 7/8/81 (CBI, London)

------ (1982) Rate increases will harm industry's competitiveness - CBI, News Release 20/10/82 (CBI, London)

------ (1983) Rates threat to business - survey results, News Release 26/1/83 (CBI, London)

------ (1986) CBI Response to 'Paying for Local Government' Cmnd 9714, (CBI, London)

------ Scotland (1986) The Contractor's principle of valuation for rating: a comparative study of rateable values and rates paid on properties in England and Scotland (CBI, Glasgow)

CIPFA (1986) Paying for Local Government: Beyond the

Green Paper - A Detailed Analysis (Chartered Institute of Public Finance and Accountancy, London)

Crawford, M. and Dawson, D. (1982) Are rates the right tax for local government? Lloyds Bank Review, 145, July, 15-35

Crawford, P., Fothergill, S. and Monk, S. (1985) The Effect of Business Rates on the Location of Employment, Department of Land Economy, University of Cambridge

Cuthbertson, K., Foreman-Peck, J. and Gripaios, P. (1979) Local authority fiscal policy and urban employment, Applied Economics, 11, 377-87

------ (1982) The effects of local authority fiscal decisions on population levels in urban areas, Regional Studies, 16, 165-71

Dafflon, B. (1977) Federal finance in theory and practice with special reference to Switzerland (Schriftenreihe Finanzwirtschaft und Finanzrecht reo. 21) (Paul Haupt, Bern)

Damania, D. (1986a) The incidence of the non-domestic property taxes (Ph.D. in preparation, University of Glasgow

------ (1986b) The impact of non-domestic property taxes on employment: a comment, Urban Studies, 413-18

DTI (1985) Burdens on Business: Report of a Scrutiny of Administrative and Legislative Requirements (Department of Trade and Industry, HMSO, London)

East Midlands Employers' Association (1984) Submission to Notts. County Council on the effects of local authority rates on the local engineering industry, 9/1/84 (EMEA, Oakham, Rutland)

Evans, A. and Eversley, D. (1980) The inner city: employment and industry (Heinemann, London)

Feldstein, M. (1978) Inflation, tax rules, and the long-term interest rate, Brookings Papers on Economic Activity, 1, 61-109

Foster, C. (1986) Conclusions, in R.J. Bennett and H. Zimmermann (eds.) Local business taxes in Britain and Germany: Conference Report (Anglo-German Foundation, London and Bonn)

Foster, C.D., Jackman, R. and Perlman, M. (1980) Local Government Finance in a unitary state (Allen and Unwin, London)

G.B. Government (1977) Local Government Finances. Green Paper Cmnd 6813 (HMSO, London)

------ (1982) Corporation Tax, Cmnd 8456 (HMSO, London)

------ (1986) Paying for local government, Cmnd 9714.
(HMSO, London)

GLC (1983) Plant relocation and closure in Greater London 1976-80 (Industry and Employment Committee, Report IEC890, Greater London Council)

Gripaios, P. and Brooks, N. (1982) The determination of employment in counties: some evidence of the importance of local authority fiscal policy and government regional policy in England and Wales, Applied Economics, 14, 211-18

Hale, R., Hepworth, N. and Stonefrost, M. (1985) Financing local government: A different approach (Chartered Institute of Public Finance and Accountancy, London)

Haller, H. (1968) Wandlungen in den Problemen föderativer Staatswirtschaften, Finanzarchiv, 249-70

Hedley, C. (1985) Commercial property and the rating system - a fair deal for all (Herring, Son and Daw, London)

Hepworth, M. (1986) Business taxes and local government in Britain, in R.J. Bennett and H. Zimmermann (eds.) Local Business Taxes in Britain and Germany: Conference Report (Anglo-German Foundation, London and Bonn)

Hill, B. (1986) Rating - uncertain prospects, Estates Gazette, 18 January, pp. 35-6

HM Treasury (1984) The Company tax measures: Appendix 10 in House of Commons, Fourth Report for the Treasury and Civil Service Committee: The 1984 Budget, HC (1983-84) 34 (HMSO, London)

Hughes, S- (1981) 'The mistaken belief that rates cost jobs', Municipal Review, October

IOD (1986) Paying for Local Government: Initial response to the Green Paper (Cmnd 9714) (Policy Unit, Institute of Directors, London)

Jackman, R.A. (1986) Accountability, the control of expenditure and the reform of local government finances in the United Kingdom. (Paper presented to International Institute of Public Finance, Athens)

Jackman, R.A. and Ferry, J. (1978) Results of CBI Survey on non-domestic rates, in R.A. Jackman (ed) The impact of rates on industry (Centre for Environmental Studies, London)

Jones, G., Stewart, J. and Travers, T. (1986) A reply to Jackman, Local Government Studies, 12, 59-64

King, D. (1984) Fiscal tiers: the economics of multi-level

government (Allen and Unwin, London)
King, M.A. (1977) Public Policy and the Corporation (Cambridge University Press, Cambridge)
King, M.A. and Fullerton, D. (1984) The Taxation of Income from Capital: A Comparative Study of the United States, United Kingdom, Sweden and West Germany (Chicago University Press, Chicago)
Lloyds Bank (1982) Down with the rates, Lloyds Bank Economic Bulletin, 39, March
Mair, D. (1986) Industrial derating: panacea or palliative? Scottish Journal of Political Economy, 33, 159-70
Mair, D. (1987) The incidence of the non-domestic rates: preliminary estimates, Government and Policy: Environment and Planning, C, 5
McLure, C.E. (1983) Tax assignment in federal countries (Centre for Research on Federal Financial Relations, Australian National University, Canberra)
Meade Committee (1978) The structure and reform of direct taxation: Report of a Committee chaired by Professor J.E. Meade (Allen and Unwin and Institute for Fiscal Studies, London)
Merseyside Chamber of Commerce (1986) Business Rates (Liverpool)
Mieskowski, P. (1972) The property tax: excise tax or profit tax?, Journal of Public Economics, 2, 73-96
------ (1976) The distributive effects of local taxes: some extensions. In R.E. Grieson (ed.) Public and Urban Economics (Lexington Books, Lexington, Massachusetts)
North, D. and Gough, J. (1983) The impact of local authorities on manufacturing firms: recent experience in London, in K. Young and C. Mason (eds) Urban Economic Development (Macmillan, London)
Oates, W.A. (1972) Fiscal Federalism (Harcourt, Brace Jovanovich, New York)
Othick, F. (1981) Exploring the myth that rates are a heavy burden on the business community, Local Government Review, 24 September
Parkinson, M. and Wilks, S. (1983) Managing urban decline - the case of the inner city partnerships, Local Government Studies, 9, 23-9
Peacock, A.T. (1972) Fiscal means and political ends, in M. Peston and B. Corry (eds) Essays in Honour of Lionel Robbins (Weidenfeld and Nicholson, London)
Piggott, J. and Whalley, J. (1985) UK tax policy and general equilibrium analysis (Cambridge University Press,

Cambridge)
Quirk, B. (1986) Paying for local government: Beyond the
    financial issues, Local Government Studies, 12, 3-11
RTP (1984) Monitoring Enterprise Zones - Year Three
    Report (Roger Tym and Partners, London)
Schoser, F. (1986) Business taxes and Industry in Germany,
    in R.J. Bennett and H. Zimmermann (eds) Local
    Business Taxes in Britain and Germany: Conference
    Report (Anglo-German Foundation, London and Bonn)
Sellgren, J. (1987) Local Economic Development Initiatives
    Local Government Studies, 13, 51-68
Sheffield Chamber of Commerce (1984) 1984 Chambers of
    Commerce/Engineering Employers' rates survey -
    preliminary results (Sheffield Chamber of Commerce,
    Sheffield)
Smith, S. and Squire, D. (1986) Who will be paying for local
    Government? (Institute for Fiscal Studies, London)
Stonefrost, M. (1983) The Impact of Rates on Commerce and
    Industry (Report to GLC Finance and General Purposes
    Committee)
Storey, D. (1983) Local employment initiatives in North East
    England: evaluation and assessment problems, in K.
    Young and C. Mason (eds) Urban Economic
    Development (Macmillan, London)
Straw, J. (1981) Rates and Jobs (House of Commons Library
    Research Staff)
------ (1984) Business Rates - Measuring their Burden
    (London: House of Commons Research Staff)
Tiebout, C.M. (1956) A pure theory of local expenditures,
    Journal of Political Economy, 64, 412-24
Topham, N. (1983) Local government economics, in R.
    Millward, D. Parker, L. Rosenthal, M.T. Sumner and N.
    Topham (eds) Public Sector Economics (Longham,
    London) pp. 129-98
Tyler, P. (1984) Geographical variations in industrial costs,
    Discussion Paper 12 (Department of Land Economy,
    University of Cambridge)
Webb, A.J. (1986) Business taxes: the views of British
    industry, in R.J. Bennett and H. Zimmermann (eds)
    Local Business Taxes in Britain and Germany:
    Conference Report (Anglo-German Foundation, London
    and Bonn)
Webster, K. (1982) Real concern for rates paid by industry?
    Local Government Chronicle, 17 September, p. R1010
Westminster City Council (1986) Paying for Local

Government - The Uniform Business Rate: Main Report (Coopers and Lybrand Associates, London)

Wiseman, J. (1964) The political economy of federalism: a survey and a proposal, mimeo: prepared for Canadian Royal Commission on Taxation

Young, K. (1986) Economic development in Britain: a vacuum in central-local relations, Government and Policy: Environment and Planning, C.4, 439-50

Young, K. and Mason, C. (eds) (1983) Urban Economic Development (Macmillan, London)

Zimmermann, H. (1986) Some possible effects of the Green Paper proposals for local business taxation, in R.J. Bennett and H. Zimmermann (eds), Local Business Taxes in Britain and Germany: Conference Report (Anglo-German Foundation, London, pp. 131-43

------ (1987) British and German local business taxes under criteria for a 'good' local tax, Government and Policy: Environment and Planning C: 5, 43-52

Chapter Ten

LOCAL GOVERNMENT FINANCE AND MACROECONOMIC POLICY

Richard Jackman

INTRODUCTION

> Because Governments are concerned with the overall management of the economy, they have to be concerned with the amount of local authority expenditure, borrowing and taxation (Department of the Environment, 1986, para 1.13)

In 1985, local authorities in the United Kingdom spent in total nearly £42 billion, which amounts to just over 25 per cent of all government expenditure and to about £750 per head of population. Their 'final' expenditure on goods and services amounted to just over 10 per cent of the gross national product. (1) Local government is therefore by any standards a major sector of the economy. The size of the sector, and the management of resources within it, are therefore inevitably important in terms of national economic well-being, or with the 'overall management of the economy', using that term in its broadest sense.

To accept that central government has a legitimate concern with the overall level of local government spending is not to imply a blanket justification for central intervention into local affairs. Local authorities are independently constituted political organisations empowered to make decisions both on the totality of their expenditure and on its allocation between services. While local authority spending decisions clearly matter, the key issue is whether the independent decisions of local authorities acting primarily in pursuit of local interests will at the same time be in the best interests of the nation as a whole. Is there a national interest in the level of local government spending different from the local interest, and if so why and of what form? If such a divergence is identified, what types of policy intervention might it justify and can such policies be made to work effectively and without adverse side-effects?

The first section of this chapter outlines the changing nature, as perceived by central government, of the local government spending problem over the last hundred years but more particularly over the last twenty to thirty years. This section argues that the nature of the local government expenditure problem has really always been the same - namely the tendency of local authorities to spend too much - though the manner in which this problem has been manifest and the way in which it has been analysed have changed in accordance with changing approaches to macroeconomic management and the control of public expenditure.

I then argue that the proposals in the recent Green Paper Paying for Local Government (Department of the Environment, 1986) seek to root out the fundamental cause of the tendency to overspend. Whatever the attractions of this approach in principle, there appears to be a substantial element of 'overkill' in the specific proposals which replace a financial regime which may in the past often have been too lax with one which is excessively restrictive.

Leaving this difficulty to one side, I next examine the implications of the Green Paper proposals for macroeconomic management. In particular, I suggest there is a strong case for excluding local expenditure financed locally from the public expenditure planning system and for replacing the present system of controls on capital spending by controls on new borrowing. Although neither of these proposals is actually made, or even discussed, in the Green Paper, both seem to be consistent with its structure of thought and indeed necessary for the exercise of the local accountability which it is the objective of the Green Paper to nurture.

THE CHANGING PERCEPTION

Central government's concern with local authority spending goes back at least a hundred years. As the functions and expenditure of local authorities increased in the latter part of the nineteenth century, so did payments of central government grant. By the end of the century all major local government services, including health, education, welfare, highways and the police, were supported by grant (Foster et al., 1980, p. 173).

Most grants at this time were proportional so the rapid growth in local spending led directly to an equally rapid growth in grant payments, which in turn placed an increasingly heavy burden on the central government budget. Seen from this perspective, it was natural that central government looked to solutions based on limiting the total grant outlay. The short-lived assigned revenue system, introduced in 1888, was seen primarily in these terms, as were the Treasury arguments for a block grant in the early decades of the present century (Foster et al., 1980, pp. 173-84).

These technical solutions were ineffective because in practice central government chose to support the growth of local services and had little alternative but to provide additional finance. The growth of expenditure and of grants continued unchecked by the various changes in structure. In contrast to more recent times, what is noticeable about this early period is that local authorities were seen as outside the government machine and their finances were a source of concern only to the extent that they impinged on central government finance. The level of local taxation in any place was a matter of local, but not of national, significance.

By the 1920s, however, levels of local taxation had become a matter of national concern. With the industrial depression, there was much concern about the burden of business rates and its impact on the competitiveness of manufacturing industry. At this time, the Labour Party was beginning to gain control of local government in many industrial towns, and many of the new socialist administrations were by no means averse from imposing higher rate bills on industry and commerce to pay for improved public services. The Local Government Act of 1929 provided for the (75 per cent) de-rating of industry, and was the first major piece of legislation designed to protect local ratepayers from their own local authorities (Mair, 1986).

Thus even before the advent of modern macroeconomic techniques of demand management, central government had shown itself concerned with local government current expenditure and with its finance. On the capital side, too, there were severe limitations on local authority borrowing, prescribing the type of assets for which borrowing was permitted and the period over which the loan was to be repaid. While the purpose of loan sanction was primarily prudential (Keith-Lucas and Richards, 1978, pp. 128 et seq.) it nonetheless constituted a significant constraint on local authority spending. Even so, it could reasonably be argued that, up until the time of the Second World War, there was no specific concern in central government with the aggregate level of local government spending as such (Young, 1985).

After the war, local government spending had to be fitted in to the Keynesian structure of demand management. The key concept here is the level of aggregate demand with the objective of policy to attain a level of aggregate demand neither too low (which would cause unemployment) or too high (which would cause inflation and balance of payments problems). The 'fiscal marksmanship' inherent in the Keynesian approach required central government to predict or control local government expenditure (as one component of demand) as accurately as it could. In practice, the approach led to a consolidation of central and local government in the public expenditure planning process. Thus the level of local government expenditure came to the forefront of attention, while payments of grant, being now merely transfers within the public sector, dropped out of the picture.

On the Keynesian approach the problem, as perceived by central government, became one of attempting to ensure that local government spending in aggregate grew along a path plotted out for it in the public expenditure planning exercise. Since central government had no powers to control local government spending, the situation could become rather vexed. By the mid 1970s, a 'high Treasury official' is quoted in the Report of the Layfield Committee as describing 'local government finance as it is at the moment as the 'Achilles' heel' of the Treasury's control over aggregate public spending' (Layfield, 1976, p. 307).

Even so, it might have been argued that the Treasury's concern with the level of local spending was unwarranted on a demand management perspective. Higher local spending financed by higher local taxes could be expected to be largely demand neutral in its effect, the expansionary effects of the expenditure being largely offset by the contradictory effect of the higher taxes. Higher expenditure financed by borrowing would have an expansionary effect on demand but the survival of the loan sanction arrangement gave the Treasury effective control (though not necessarily on a year-to-year basis) over local authority borrowing.

The Conservative government which took office in 1979 abandoned (at least in principle) the framework of Keynesian demand management in favour of a monetarist approach to economic policy in which the role of government was limited to constraining the growth rate of a particular measure of the stock of money. It was deemed essential for this purpose to control public borrowing. Even accepting this rather unorthodox interpretation of monetarism, it still followed that the control of public sector borrowing required only a control of local authority borrowing and not a control of local government spending or taxation (Jackman, 1982).

In retrospect it can perhaps be argued that these changing macroeconomic perspectives have served to confuse the issue by forcing the discussion into an inappropriate framework. The underlying problem is that local government spending has tended in general to be higher than central government thinks is warranted. Thus, even during the Keynesian era, the main reason for deviations of local government spending from the public expenditure plan was that local authorities chose to spend more than central government thought appropriate. The Rates White Paper of August 1983 (Department of the Environment, 1983) was however the first official document openly to make the point that the problem of local government spending as perceived by central government was that it was too high (see especially paras 1.6-1.8).

The weakness of the 1983 White Paper was that it offered no basis of legitimacy for central government imposing its views as to the right level of spending onto local authorities. What right has central government to impose its views, given that local authorities are elected for the purpose, inter alia, of determining local spending levels? The 1986 Green Paper faces up to this question. Its diagnosis and proposals are discussed in the next section.

LOCAL GOVERNMENT SPENDING AND THE MARGINAL PRINCIPLE

The key 'macroeconomic' question about local government spending is, therefore, on what principles its total volume should be determined. In the post-war period there have been two different principles operating simultaneously. One starts from the centre, from Parliamentary legislation and central government policy operating through estimates by central departments of the appropriate level of local expenditure necessary to deliver these services to the standards envisaged. The other starts at the local level, where local authorities are meant to set their budgets in response to the needs and preferences of the local communities to whom they are responsible.

Since the two principles are different and independent of one another, there is obviously no reason why they should lead to the same judgement as to what the appropriate level of local government expenditure should be. Thus, in much of the post-war period and perhaps in particular during the 1970s, there had been a search for a 'consensus'. Central government would take account of local representations in its expenditure planning process, while local authorities would take heed of central government exhortations in their spending decisions. The formation in 1976 of the Consultative Council on Local Government Finance was an official and public endorsement by central government of this approach.

This approach fell apart in 1979 because the new Conservative government wished to see much sharper cuts in local government spending than the local authorities themselves thought desirable. The central and the local approach to determining local expenditure were giving very different results, and it became impossible to reconcile the two. As Government ministers were to remark, the traditional consensus had broken down. It could be argued, though that the fault lay more in attempting to run the system on the basis of inconsistent principles than in the specific actions of particular local politicians at this time.

The breakdown of the consensus meant that central government could no longer hope to persuade local authorities voluntarily to adjust their spending levels away from what they thought best towards the level wanted by central government. So other weapons, most notably financial penalties in the grant system and, subsequently, rate-capping, were brought in. These policies were not, in practice, very successful: the grant penalties were designed in such a way that their effects tended to be perverse (Gibson, 1983; Smith and Stewart, 1985), while rate-capping has been evaded at least in the short run by financial

177

devices ('creative accounting') which have allowed authorities to spend substantially in excess of their constrained revenues.

There has thus been a tendency to see the reforms proposed in the 1986 Green Paper as a further attempt to tighten the financial stranglehold on local authorities in order to force down their spending. While at a crude operational level this characterisation may not be unreasonable, the actual form of the proposals in the Green Paper do derive from a rather more fundamental analysis of the problem. The Green Paper in a sense goes back to the two inconsistent principles set out at the beginning of this section, and attempts to unearth the source of the inconsistency. Why, it might be asked, should the representatives of the people in Parliament, as represented by the government of the day, take a systematically different view of the right level of local government expenditure from that of the representatives of those same people on local councils?

The fundamental structural difference identified in the Green Paper is one of finance. If central government wishes to increase its expenditure it has to raise the tax burden somewhere in the economy to finance it. Whilst it is true that some taxes are more painful and unpopular than others, all tax increases have costs and the awareness of such costs constitutes the budgetary discipline on central government. By contrast, if a local authority wishes to increase its expenditure, only a proportion of the cost falls locally. Some part of the expenditure is borne directly by central government insofar as it attracts additional grant or additional payments of rate rebates or allowances. (2) A further part, often the largest, falls on the non-domestic ratepayer. Much of this tax revenue is again incident outside the local authority: for example, on shareholders of firms, on consumers in the case of nationalised industries, public utilities or private firms which pass on rates in higher prices, or on central government in the case of public buildings such as hospitals or universities.

Thus, according to the Green Paper, the source of the systematic tendency for local authorities to spend more than central government thinks appropriate is that central government is conscious of the total cost of local government spending whereas individual local authorities are concerned only with that, relatively small, part of the cost which falls on local taxpayers. The solution therefore is to 'ensure that the full costs or benefits of any changes in a local authority's expenditure ... fall on its domestic taxpayers alone' (para 10.5). It is this principle, which has become known as the 'marginal' principle because of its focus on the funding of expenditure at the margin, which guides the overall fiscal design of the Green Paper's proposals.

The idea that the full cost of local spending decisions should be borne by those who benefit from the services provided, and who indirectly through the electoral process are responsible for the decisions that are made is described in the Green Paper as the principle of local accountability. But, from an economic point of view, the idea that local authorities be obliged to balance the full marginal social costs of the services they provide with the marginal benefits is the precise counterpart of the standard welfare economics criteria for efficient resource allocation. The marginal principle provides the incentive for individual local authorities, each concerned only with local interests, to reach decisions consistent with an efficient allocation of resources in the economy as a whole.

The marginal principle has been criticized on two main counts. First, that some of the benefits of local government spending accrue not to local households but to others, in particular local businesses, and it is wrong that households should have to pay the full costs of expenditure decisions when they do not receive the full benefits (Bramley, 1987; Jackman, 1987). Second, the application of the full cost principle to marginal rather than total expenditure creates potentially confusing 'gearing' effects. On the Green Paper's own figures, a typical authority wishing to raise its expenditure by, say, 10 per cent, would need to raise taxes on local households by 50 per cent. (3) High gearing is a worry because, to the extent that people think about local spending and taxes in proportional rather than absolute money terms, it weakens the perceived link between spending levels and levels of taxation and in this sense obscures accountability (Jones and Stewart, 1986). For the same reason it may lead to an excessive constraint on local spending, since a small proportional increase in expenditure will be associated with a large proportional increase in local taxation.

Fears that the Green Paper proposals will create excessive pressure for cutbacks in local government spending are reinforced by the parallel, though logically unrelated, proposal to replace domestic rates by the 'community charge' (which is essentially a poll tax). Because the community charge is thought to be more regressive than domestic rates (and clearly is so in the upper ranges of the income distribution), the burden of local taxation will be felt more acutely than is the burden of most central taxes. Again the pressure will be for cutting back local spending.

If the consequence of the Green Paper's proposals is that local authorities became excessively reluctant to raise local taxes, the relationship between central and local government would become the mirror-image of that which has prevailed in the past. Central government's main concern would be with underprovision and inadequate funding of local services. Its response would be to increase grants, but it would then find that local authorities might use their increased grant income to cut back local taxes rather than improve services. Clearly this would put pressure on central government to take direct control over local services. Alternatively, the system might move in the direction of that of the Netherlands, where local authorities are essentially wholly funded by central grant but retain what is little more than a token local tax yielding about 5 per cent of their revenues but allowing them some discretion on expenditure at the margin.

The package of specific proposals in the Green Paper thus seems to go a long way beyond the underlying rationale. The idea that localising the full costs of local spending decisions removes a fundamental cause of the difference in perceptions as to the appropriate level of local government spending between central government and the local authorities is an appealing one. But there seems a substantial element of 'overkill' in the specific proposals.

I next discuss the implications for macroeconomic policy on the assumption that the financial system proposed in the Green Paper can be expected to provide the 'right' degree of financial constraint on local spending decisions and thus removes the main motive for central government intervention.

REVENUE EXPENDITURE AND THE PUBLIC EXPENDITURE PLANNING SYSTEM

If the Green Paper proposals are successful in their

objective of removing the pressure for local government overspending, and with it the pressure on central government to intervene, the treatment of local authorities within the system of economic management could be radically reformed. I have argued that the only coherent justification for central intervention in local authority spending - at least with regard to revenue expenditure - is to counteract the tendency to overspend, and that narrower macroeconomic arguments to do with 'fine tuning' aggregate demand or with the size of the budget deficit are really lacking in any force whatsoever. It follows that, under the proposed system, local authority revenue expenditure as such need be of no concern to central government.

The Green Paper proposals would provide a basis for ending the recent convention of consolidating central and local government expenditures in public expenditure planning, and for returning to the traditional system in which central government's concern was with its own outlays. Local authorities could be treated like nationalised industries, the universities and other such organisations where the central government subvention rather than gross expenditure is relevant in public expenditure planning. In the context of the Green Paper proposals, what would be relevant for local authorities would be central government grant and the yield from the centrally determined non-domestic rates.

An objection of principle to such a proposal is that the standard definition of public expenditure includes all expenditure financed by taxation and borrowing and excludes expenditure financed from fees and charges. It follows from this definition that expenditure financed from local taxation might still have to be counted as public expenditure, and that local authorities differ from nationalised industries, universities, etc. in that they are empowered to levy taxes.

Against this objection, one might first make the point that definitions are not immutable and that concepts should be defined in a way that is compatible with efficient organisation. One may also argue, in terms of the economic issues involved, that the proposal in the Green Paper to replace domestic rates by the 'community charge' might in any event carry the logical implication that expenditure financed by the community charge, like other government expenditure financed by fees and charges, should fall outside the public expenditure definition. The Government stresses in the Green Paper that the 'community charge would mark a major change in the direction of local government finance back to the notion of charging for local authority services' (para 3.36, emphasis in original). If it is claimed that the community charge has the characteristics of a charge when it comes to issues of local accountability, it is hard to see why it should not also have the characteristics of a charge when it comes to the definition of public expenditure.

In administrative terms, it would have to be accepted that most of the existing machinery for estimating local government spending levels would need to be kept in place. The reason is that the size of the grant, and the importance of ensuring that it is distributed in an equitable way amongst local authorities, taking into account differences in their spending needs, would oblige central government to make detailed spending estimates. But once the estimates had been made and the grants determined, local authorities could make their own spending decisions free from further intervention from the centre. Central government would have the assurance that variations in local spending would not affect its own outlays or the level of business taxation.

The proposal to take local government spending out of the public expenditure planning system has been made part of more far-reaching proposals for the revival of local autonomy (Jones and Stewart, 1983). Their proposals, which involve a substantial reduction in the grant proportion and an abandonment of the objective of need equalisation in grant distribution, would allow central government to withdraw almost totally from making detailed local government expenditure estimates. These proposals raise the question whether there is a national interest in some degree of conformity in local authority services which raises political rather than macroeconomic issues. Clearly, the proposal to take government spending out of the public expenditure planning definition within the context of the implementation of the Green Paper proposals is less radical, but it could nonetheless constitute an important clarification of central and local government responsibilities and remove an unnecessary friction between the two levels of government.

CAPITAL EXPENDITURE AND BORROWING

Chapter 6 of the Green Paper is concerned with Capital

Expenditure. It differs from the other chapters in that it makes no reference to the fundamental reforms discussed elsewhere in the Green Paper but instead concerns itself exclusively with the weaknesses in the current system of capital controls. Yet, clearly, if one argues that the system proposed in the Green Paper removes the need for central government intervention, the rationale for controls over capital expenditure and borrowing is clearly called into question.

To put the point another way: if, in combination, the marginal principle and the community charge impose an appropriate awareness of the true economic cost of local expenditures on goods and services will they not also impose an appropriate awareness of the true costs of capital expenditure as measured by the interest payments on the borrowed money? And, if, in full awareness of the costs, particular local authorities choose to spend more or less than some given central assessment, why need this be of any greater macroeconomic concern to central government than would be a comparable over or underspend on current expenditure?

The Green Paper sets out the Government's objectives for a capital control system (para 6.8).

- It should provide effective Government influence over aggregate levels of local authority capital expenditure and borrowing.
- It should promote the Government's aim of reducing the size of the public sector by encouraging asset sales.
- It should provide a sound basis for local authorities to plan their capital programmes.

Of these three objectives, one might argue that two and a half could be achieved, under the proposed system, by the simple expedient of abolishing all capital controls. The constraints on revenue raising would provide an adequate limitation on overall capital expenditure and a strong financial inducement to the sale of surplus assets. It would also clearly provide the best possible basis for enabling local authorities to seek least cost techniques of service provision without the constraint of year-by-year capital allocations. Clearly the abolition of controls would also be consonant with the general free market ideology underlying the Green Paper's proposals.

The fact that the abolition of controls is not discussed

in the Green Paper is thus a bit odd. But had the issue been raised, it is clear that the main objection would have concerned borrowing. There are really two different issues here:

(i) individual local authorities may have an incentive to overspend if they can hide the cost of their spending decisions from current ratepayers or taxpayers.

(ii) aggregate overspending financed by borrowing is more disruptive in terms of the narrower demand management definition of macroeconomics than is overspending financed by revenue.

The first of these issues relates back to the original prudential argument for loan sanctions. Local authorities must not take actions today which impose an excessive burden of debt repayments on the taxpayers of the future. The standard procedure is to allow local authorities to borrow only for the purchase of capital assets, and to require the loans to be repaid over the useful lifetime of the assets (Hepworth, 1984, ch. 7). This procedure in principle synchronises the time stream of benefits from capital expenditure with the time stream of costs.

Although this conventional accounting principle may seem to make good sense, a little reflection shows that it is in fact seriously inadequate. First, in practice the distinction between capital and current expenditure seems based on largely arbitrary criteria that seem to have more to do with indivisibility of projects than with the time stream of benefits. For example, maintenance expenditure on buildings and roads counts as current although the benefits last over a period of years. The purchase of small items of equipment and of library books likewise counts as current irrespective of the expected life of the purchase. A large part of education expenditure can be regarded as investment in human capital yet again is treated as current expenditure. (4)

Likewise, while the user benefits from an asset may be spread over its lifetime, the political benefits may be concentrated at the time of purchase. A politician can claim credit for building council houses, but hardly from continuing to rent out a stock of houses built at some time in the past. Further, local employment opportunities, and the scale of activity of the local government's own employees, are increased by many capital spending projects at the same time they happen rather than when they produce benefits to the user.

Thus the political benefits of capital expenditure are immediate and visible while the costs are postponed and less visible. It could indeed be argued that the subsidisation and grant support of debt charges by central government has meant that in practice the cost of capital spending to a locality has been negligible or non-existent. At minimum, any reduction in controls on capital spending would have to be accompanied by a grant system which gave no general subsidy to debt repayments.

If one takes the view that the benefits of capital expenditure occur at the time the expenditure is undertaken, the logical consequence is not to place controls on capital expenditure but rather to limit borrowing, either to some fraction of the cost of the project, or to certain types of capital expenditure which offer clear future benefits. In terms of practical implementation, this proposal would again entail treating local authorities rather like nationalised industries, and giving them external borrowing limits (EBLs) linked to particular capital spending programmes.

The idea of replacing the present system of capital controls by one based on EBLs is discussed in the Green Paper (paras 6.25-6.31) and, though the idea is not dismissed, a number of objections are put forward. Most serious is the concern that, in essence, borrowing is the only way local authorities can deal with unavoidable and unexpected fluctuations in their income or expenditures, and if their overall borrowing was limited they might find themselves in a position where they could not meet their bills.

This problem arises because EBLs are defined consistently with national income accounting as changes in an authority's net indebtedness. This definition means, for example, that a local authority running down balances is counted as increasing its external borrowing. An alternative control target might be changes in gross indebtedness, or in new borrowing. With controls on new borrowing, a local authority could still hold and use balances and capital funds for dealing with unexpected contingencies and smoothing out year-to-year fluctuations in incomes or expenditures.

But if only new borrowing were controlled and local authorities were able to increase or run down their capital funds or balances without constraint, the government would have no control in the short run over a major element of local authority borrowing and therefore less control over the PSBR. In any particular year, the PSBR can be significantly altered by changes in local authority cash balances. This then raises the second of central government's possible concerns about borrowing, noted earlier in the section, namely the macroeconomic effects in the 'narrow' sense of the term.

Again, however, one must ask why should the government be concerned about year-to-year fluctuations in the PSBR? Clearly it is not attempting to 'fine tune' aggregate demand in the traditional Keynesian manner. It may have believed that year-to-year control of the PSBR was essential to the control of particular monetary aggregates, such as sterling M3, but that belief has been discredited by events and in any case sterling M3 is no longer a key variable in macroeconomic policy. Restraint of public borrowing is a necessary policy objective in the medium term for the reasons the Government stresses (to contain the growth of the national debt, to hold down interest rates, etc.), but these are medium term objectives. Fluctuation in local authority balances are of necessity temporary and, in general, self-correcting and cannot therefore imperil these medium term objectives.

To summarise this section, there are good prudential reasons for controlling the level of local authority borrowing. For operational reasons, such controls must be on new borrowing rather than total external borrowing. Controls on new borrowing cannot be guaranteed to deliver an exact year-by-year target for local authority borrowing, but will control local authority borrowing in the medium term, which is what is important for macroeconomic policy. Controls on new borrowing, in conjunction with Green Paper proposals on revenue, provide a sufficient constraint on the sources of funding of capital expenditure, so that controls on capital spending as such would be unnecessary.

CONCLUSION

The central proposal of the Green Paper - the marginal principle - can be seen as an essential finance prerequisite for the restoration of local autonomy. Without it, local authorities are able to raise taxation on people resident outside their boundaries who naturally turn to central government for protection. While this line of argument is advanced very clearly in the Green Paper (where it is characterised as 'enhancing local accountability'), its implications are not fully developed.

Most importantly, the purpose of the exercise should be to rid local government of central controls. In the past central controls have not only been often ineffective or counter-productive, but have undermined efficient decision-making in local government and weakened accountability by confusing the point of responsibility for individual decisions, as stressed by Layfield (1976). Yet the dismantling of controls is mentioned at no stage in the Green Paper, except for the rather muted suggestion (in para 5.28) that the rate-capping provisions (or their equivalent with the community charge) would no longer be required once the new system became fully effective. This suggestion has now been abandoned.

If the financial proposals set out in the Green Paper operate in the way that is claimed, attempts to control or influence local authorities' expenditure by administrative mechanisms can and should be abandoned. It is disappointing that the Green Paper does not have the courage of its convictions in proposing a dismantling of controls to accompany the new financial regime.

NOTES

1. Source of figures: United Kingdom National Accounts (Blue Book) 1986, Tables 1.1, 1.17, 8.1 and 9.1. Final expenditure excludes transfer payments to individuals which do not constitute part of the gross national product.

2. Until recently, most authorities effectively received matching grants (through the 'resources element' of the Rate Support Grant, or through Block Grant since 1981). With the advent of grant penalties in 1981, many authorities faced negative marginal grants because the more they spent the greater their grant penalty and hence the smaller the grant they received. On the other hand, the very sharp rise in unemployment since 1980 has meant that many more ratepayers, now about one-third of all households, are entitled to rate rebates or rate allowances.

3. For example, if its centrally assessed spending need were £100 per head, it might receive £80 per head in lump-sum grant (inclusive of its share of non-domestic

rates) and thus have to raise £20 per head in local taxes. A
10 per cent increase in expenditure, to £110 per head, would
attract no additional grant, so local taxes would have to be
raised to £30 a head, a 50 per cent increase.

4. In the last few years, a number of local
authorities have raised loans on the security of assets
bought out of revenue (ranging from vehicles to library
books). This is one of a number of practices known as
'creative accounting'.

REFERENCES

Bramley, G. (1987) 'Horizontal Disparities and Equalisation -
A Critique of 'Paying for Local Government', Local
Government Studies, January/February vol. 13 no. 1 pp.
69-89

Department of the Environment (1983) Rates (White Paper,
Cmnd 9008, HMSO, London)

------ (1986) Paying for Local Government (Green Paper,
Cmnd 9714, HMSO, London)

Foster, C.D., Jackman, R.A. and Perlman, M. (1980) Local
Government Finance in a Unitary State (Allen and
Unwin, London)

Gibson, J. (1983) 'Local 'Overspending': Why the Government
have themselves to blame', Public Money, December
vol. 3, no. 3 pp. 19-21

Hepworth, N.P. (1984) The Finance of Local Government
(7th edition, Allen and Unwin, London)

Jackman, R.A. (1982) 'Does Central Government Need to
Control the Total of Local Government Spending?',
Local Government Studies May/June vol. 8 no. 3 pp. 75-
90

------ (1987) 'Paying for Local Government: an appraisal of
the British Government's proposals for non-domestic
rates', Environment and Planning C: Government and
Policy, February vol. 5, pp. 89-98

Jones, G.W. and Stewart, J.D. (1983) The Case for Local
Government (Allen and Unwin, London)

------ (1986) 'Flaws in the Accountability Argument', Local
Government Chronicle 14 March p. 304

Keith-Lucas, B. and Richards, P.G. (1978) A History of
Local Government in the Twentieth Century (Allen and
Unwin, London)

Layfield, F. (1976) (Chairman) Report of the Committee of

Inquiry on Local Government Finance (Cmnd 6453, HMSO, London)

Mair, D. (1986) 'Industrial de-rating: panacea or palliative?' Scottish Journal of Political Economy, May vol. 33 no. 2 pp. 159-70

Smith, P. and Stewart, J. (1985) 'Local Authority Expenditure Targets' Local Government Studies July/ August vol. 11 no. 4. pp. 21-41

Young, K. (1985) 'Rereading the Municipal Progress - A Crisis Revisited' in Loughlin, M., Gelfand, D. and Young, K. (eds) Half a Century of Municipal Decline 1935-1985 (Allen and Unwin, London) pp. 1-25

Chapter Eleven

THE BRITISH REFORM IN ITS INTERNATIONAL CONTEXT

Ronan Paddison

INTRODUCTION

The introduction of the poll tax marks the most significant reform of the local tax base that has taken place since Britain became an industrial nation and, indeed, re-introduces a tax which was more characteristic of pre-capitalist Britain. The last time a poll tax was imposed in Britain was in 1698, but its imposition had been more frequent in earlier centuries, its one enduring quality being its unpopularity. In the late fourteenth century it had provided the spark for the Peasant's Revolt. Elsewhere, poll taxes have tended to belong to the feudal period and in contrast to their contemporary re-introduction were more often than not used as a measure for bolstering the central exchequer rather than providing for local revenue needs. In any case, with the onset of industrial society, on the one hand, and the gradual evolution of a system of local government charged with the provision of an expanding range of services, on the other, local taxation systems in Britain, as elsewhere, turned towards different kinds of bases, property in particular.

In a sense drawing out historical parallels in this fashion is misleading. As they were exacted in feudal Britain poll taxes were predicated on very different grounds from the reasoning which currently underlies their introduction. The state had a much more restricted function than was to become true following the emergence of industrial capitalism, while forms of local government were rudimentary and certainly not based on the principle of local democracy, a facet which, through the argument over accountability, has provided for its proponents one of the main reasons for the introduction of the community charge. But insofar as finding any British precedent for the poll tax necessitates such a long historical reach, drawing out the parallels is revealing if only to show to the radical nature of the current reform.

If domestic historical precedents are tenuous, are there any current international precedents which can illuminate the characteristics and rationale of a local poll tax? Discussion to date has centred around the uniqueness of the British proposals, an argument which will need to be qualified. Poll taxes are currently imposed elsewhere, though in a very limited number of countries, and never, as is the intention in Britain, as the sole local tax. The singularity of the British case poses an obvious analytical problem in seeking to put it within an international perspective; atypicality will tend to emphasise the points of difference rather than comparison. The central question needing to be addressed is the explanation of the atypicality of Britain: why within an advanced industrial nation with a developed system of local democratic government, responsible for an extensive array of investment and consumption expenditures (functions which, admittedly with variations however substantial, are shared with other countries in the OECD, for example), do the British reform proposals, both by their nature and in their implications, mark such a significant departure from elsewhere?

There is not the space in a single chapter to provide a full explanation. Rather some pointers as to the singularity of the British case are suggested. Ultimately, explanation emphasises political over economic reasoning. The British reform proposals give especial support to the general argument that restructuring local taxation systems owes as much, if not more, to considerations of political control (and, possibly, expediency) as it does to adopting economic rationale and ideals. In looking at these arguments we need to establish the uniqueness of the British case within an international context, both in terms of practice and theory.

INTERNATIONAL EXPERIENCE OF POLL TAXES

Uniqueness is an absolute. Thus, to be unique the introduction of a poll tax in Britain should not be matched by its imposition elsewhere. Obviously, expressed in such bold terms, the claim for uniqueness would be difficult to verify and, even were verification possible, puts the argument too simplistically. The problem of verification arises from the lack of a comprehensive compendium of local tax bases throughout the world. Studies by international agencies such as OECD are of limited coverage, whilst the IMF volumes on government statistics fail to report on the modes of local taxation comprehensively. However, it is apparent that some countries continue to employ local poll taxes, notably Japan, while others, notably Tanzania, have sought fit to re-introduce them.

Poll taxes, in the form of prefectural and municipal inhabitant taxes, form an important element of the Japanese local tax system. Japanese local government is a two-tiered structure, comprising prefectures, regional-level authorities, and municipalities, which are subdivided into several types basically in terms of their population size. Both types of local authority can use what, by British standards, is a long list of tax options: in the case of the prefectures this includes 10 'ordinary' taxes and 3 special purpose taxes, while in the municipalities the list is 10 and 6 respectively. (Some taxes are held in common in which case the municipality will tend to collect for the prefecture.) Three taxes dominate, the property tax charged by the municipalities, the enterprise or business tax charged by the prefecture and the inhabitants (poll) tax charged by both councils, but collected jointly by the municipality.

The local inhabitants tax is by no means an exact equivalent of the British proposal. One of the major differences is that it is levied not simply at a flat per capita rate, but also includes a graduated portion according to the income of the individual. The size of the tax rate in the flat per capita element varies according to the population size of the council, and a ceiling level on it is imposed by the central government. Similarly the graduated portion has an imposed ceiling so as not to exceed 1.5 times the 'standard tax rate' (Table 11.1). Some groups are exempt from paying the individual inhabitant tax, notably those receiving social security under the Social Aid Law. The 1986 Green Paper (Cmnd. 9714, page 132) notes that the inhabitants tax accounts for 48 per cent of local tax income.

In reality the Japanese poll tax is a form of crude local income tax with various exemptions and constraints and mirrors recent proposals, advocated by some Opposition

Table 11.1: Local inhabitant taxes - Japanese municipalities (1987)

(a) individual per capita rate (yen)

Population size of municipalities	Tax rate (per annum) Standard	Ceiling
Cities greater than or equal to 500,000	2,000	2,600
Cities 50,000 - 500,000	1,500	2,000
Other municipalities	1,000	1,400

(b) Individual income rate

Taxable income (1,000 yen)	Tax rate (per cent) Standard	Ceiling
less than 300	2	
300 - 450	3	
450 - 700	4	
700 - 1,000	5	
1,000 - 1,300	6	Standard
1,300 - 2,300	7	tax rate
2,300 - 3,700	8	x 1.5
3,700 - 5,700	9	
5,700 - 9,500	10	
9,500 - 19,000	11	
19,000 - 29,000	12	
29,000 - 49,000	13	
more than 49,000	14	

Source: Jichi Sogo (1982, 76-7).

Labour MPs, to have graduated income bands added to the community charge. Whilst it is not intended to extend the international comparison from the poll tax to the local income tax, it is clear from the 1986 Green Paper (Cmnd. 9714, page 132) that use of the latter is fairly widespread throughout developed countries. It is also quite likely that, once introduced, any future Labour Government would add such an income related element to a British poll tax.

Within a wholly different political and socio-economic context recent Tanzanian legislation has empowered urban councils to levy a poll tax. During British colonial rule poll taxes had been levied quite commonly in East Africa, though

Table 11.2: Development levy (poll tax) charges - Dar es Salaam (1985-6)

Household salary/wage per month (shillings)	Levy payable per year (shillings)
less than 2,000	150
2,001 - 4,000	300
4,001 - 6,000	400
6,001 - 7,000	500
7,001 - 8,000	600
8,001 - 9,000	700
9,001 - 10,000	800
10,001 - 11,000	900
more than 11,000	1,000

Source: Dar es Salaam, City Council, Circular 1985.

as often as not to bolster the central rather than the local fiscal base. Partly because of its associations with colonial rule, but also because of the general unpopularity of the tax, the Tanzanian legislation has labelled it as a 'development levy' (cf. 'community charge' in Britain) and its use by urban councils has been permissive, allowing them to supplement their principal source of local revenue, property rates. As the major urban authority, Dar es Salaam, began collecting the tax at a flat rate of 200 shillings per adult (1984-5), though in the following year it was levied as a graduated charge (Table 11.2). This again has the characteristics of a crude local income tax. The city council has experienced considerable opposition to the levy and in 1985-6 it was estimated that only 50 per cent of the levy was actually collected. Given the absence of any proper register of population - the last full census was taken in 1978 and the city council has been working on the basis of an estimated population of the urban area of between 1.5 and 1.8 million - the figure of 50 per cent is probably a considerable over-estimate.

The Japanese and the Tanzanian examples show that the British reform proposals will not be unique, but this scarcely detracts from the exceptional character of the British proposals. Apart from the obvious contrasts between the different local government systems, and the environments in which they operate, the fact remains that the British proposals represent the only case in which the poll tax is the sole form of taxation to be allocated to the local councils. Even in countries in which the poll tax has been given consideration as a new revenue source for local government it has rarely, if ever, been proposed as the sole tax. It has usually, if not always, been considered as a supplementary source of local tax income. Thus, in some of the Australian states, South Australia and New South Wales, the introduction of a poll tax, and its fiscal and administrative implications, have been aired in government enquiries, yet always in the sense of being a supplementary source of revenue to property rating. Furthermore, the British poll tax will be exceptional if there is no income grading and, without wishing to exaggerate its financial impact, it is highly unusual for a Western government to introduce such a blatantly regressive tax measure.

To summarise, then, the introduction of the community charge will not make the local taxation system in Britain unique insofar as in a small number of isolated instances other national systems do levy poll taxes. However, where they are levied they are of much more marginal significance than is envisaged for Britain, co-existing with other local tax options. What makes for the uniqueness of the British case is that, within an economically advanced nation in which local government has a strong tradition, the local taxation base is being restricted to a tax which is widely considered as regressive, administratively cumbersome and anachronistic.

INTERNATIONAL THEORY

(a) The fiscal crisis of the capitalist state

For much of the post-war period in Britain there had been a degree of consensus between the major political parties as to how the economy should be managed and the nature of the welfare state. Local government, through its expanding programme of service provision, played a more or less agreed role in which it enjoyed a degree of autonomy as to how services should be provided and how the local fiscal burden would be borne by different groups. Some authorities were able to use the opportunity to secure real improvements for their working-class populations at the expense of local business interests.

Initially, it might be tempting to argue that the

introduction of the poll tax reform should be seen within the wider conflict between capital and labour as it is mediated through the state, and in which the pendulum has swung towards capital. The argument that local authority financial decision-making was not accountable to the non-domestic ratepayer sector, industry and commerce, did provide one of the main reasons for the reform proposals. Non-domestic ratepayers accounted for over half the total rate income in England and as much as 64 per cent in Scotland (1984-5). The Green Paper argued, that on the grounds of both economic efficiency and local accountability, non-domestic rates are not a satisfactory tax impairing the competitiveness of businesses which have no local voting rights. Overall, it was argued, the effects of the high level of the non-domestic contribution was to obscure the true costs of service provision, and of marginal increases in spending, from domestic ratepayers.

While these arguments make a number of assumptions which are themselves debatable (see below) the salient point is that through central determination, it was anticipated that the level of contribution payable by the non-domestic sector will reduce the burden of local taxation for the capital sector. It is by no means the first measure since 1979 which has sought to wrest the relative autonomy local government had come to have from local business interests. Indeed, through either the direct intervention of the centre or the deliberate inclusion of local business interests, a succession of measures has eroded the autonomy of local government, ranging from the impact of the Manpower Services Commission or the removal of general housing subsidies (for example) and culminating in the mandatory provision included in the 1984 Rates Act for local authorities to consult with the non-domestic ratepayers prior to setting the rate. As an attempt to reduce the rate burden of industry and commerce the need to consult the non-domestic sector represented a step towards making local government more accountable, though the reform proposals mark a more concerted attempt to reduce overall the levels of local taxation through widening the net of accountability.

The reform of local government finance in Britain can be interpreted as a logical step in the progression of events characterising central-local relations since the late 1970s and to the aim by the centre to limit local spending. Politically, the issue of local finance has occupied a centre-stage position within the wider aims of reducing state intervention and of cutting public expenditure levels. From a comparative perspective Walsh (1988) provides the clue as to the singularity of the recent history of central-local fiscal relations by arguing that in Britain the fiscal crisis of the state has been 'devolved' to become focussed around the issue of local government finance. It is an argument worth examining in closer detail, though before doing so we need to outline briefly O'Connor's thesis.

Put at its simplest, the fiscal crisis of the state arises from its inability to support an ever expanding range of activities. According to O'Connor (1973) the foundations of the crisis arise from the necessity of the state to meet two basic, but contradictory functions, to facilitate private capital accumulation and to create the conditions for social and political order in which accumulation can take place. Increasingly as the process of capital accumulation develops, private and public economies become mutually dependent, state expenditures on both social capital and social expenses spending deepens. Within O'Connor's argument the inevitability of fiscal crisis arises from the widening gap between state expenditures and state revenues where, in effect, profits are privatised but the costs are socialised.

Tempting as the interpretation of reform proposals as being in favour of capital is, the problem with the argument is that business interests are divided in their support of the change, and particularly those changes envisaged for the non-domestic sector. Joining in the nearly universal opposition to the reform proposals, the Institute of Directors opposes the proposals because of the likely effects of the necessary revaluation of all business and commercial enterprises on the levels of the final imposed local business taxes. The likely increases will differ geographically; because of differences in current valuations and rate poundages, businesses in Northern England will pay less following the introduction of the new system, while those in the south stand to be disadvantaged. Representatives of capital in the north, then, such as the Chamber of Commerce in Newcastle-upon-Tyne, have come out in favour of the proposals, in contrast to their counterparts further south. Added to the confusion over the patterning of support, Conservative local authorities (while more sympathetic to the broad aims underlying the changes) have voiced opposition to the fixing by central government of the non-domestic rate poundage, wary of the power this gives to a future non-Tory government.

O'Connor's theory, while influential, has attracted considerable criticism (for a brief review see Newton and Karran, 1985), not least because of the lack of an international perspective. Scandinavia, with its high levels of taxation and of spending, particularly on social expenses functions, contrasts with the USA, the post-war experience of which O'Connor focussed on, and some of the other West European States, including Britain. Clearly, the structural gap, or the reality of fiscal crisis, varies between the industrial states, but the political reaction to it is also variable and it is this which begins to explain different international experience.

The explanation of these differences needs to take account of the complex nature of fiscal crises. Walsh (1988) argues for a multi-dimensional approach in which macro-theories, particularly Marxism and Liberalism, locate the origins of crisis relationships between state, economy and society and micro-theories attempt to explain the specific form(s) which crisis takes in alternative political systems, and which reflect different interests and institutions. While macro-theories help explain why crises occur, micro-theories will illuminate the reasons why crises assume particular forms.

With the emergence of the New Right in Britain liberalism has become the dominant ideology. Fiscal crisis has been interpreted in terms of an over-extended state, and as local government spending is part of overall public expenditure, so central government has sought to impose financial controls on the localities. The ability of the centre to act in this way in Britain is not new, but is an integral element of the institutions governing the British political system. From the limiting of local government to a single, restricted tax option to the detailed attempts at controlling local spending (in the 1980 and 1984 legislation, for example), there has been a long-standing crisis in British central-local fiscal relations. According to Walsh the dominance of the centre, which has been emphasised by its ability to weaken the oppositional institutions, including local government, has enabled central government 'to pass on fiscal difficulties to the local state, so that the crisis is then manifest as a crisis of central-local relations' (Walsh, 1988, p. 45).

In the United States recent developments in local

government finance have taken a different direction even though as in Britain liberalism has been the prevailing ideology in the 1980s and local government's fiscal base has been eroded (King, 1988). Cutbacks in federal financial assistance to local governments (as well as the States) have led, as in Britain, to reductions in service provision. But in contrast to Britain reduced intergovernmental funding has had the effect of forcing the municipalities to supplement their own tax bases, through the raising of special levies (the introduction of an income tax surcharge in New York in 1983, for example), some increased use of fees and charges (for example California) or the increasing of existing taxes (for example tourist taxes). American local government has been able to draw upon the greater discretion which they enjoy.

What the comparison with the United States highlights is that differences in political culture have a substantial effect on the form of local fiscal crisis. The American political system has a strongly decentralist tradition countering the 'natural' centralising forces within the federal structure. Local governments have more types of tax options which they can invoke, and though there are fiscal controls, exercised by state governments and the need to hold local referenda, local authorities have more tax-raising discretion than is the case in Britain. The lack of diversity in tax options, and the less emphatic tradition of local discretion means that in Britain there are fewer institutional safeguards to counter a centralising government. In several respects the poll tax reform both reflects and extends the strength of the argument.

That Britain is a relatively centralised state, which during the 1980s has become more so, is shown also by the small part the localities play within national political arenas. Comparison with France is revealing in this respect, where individual localities are able to exert considerably more influence at the centre than is true in Britain. The paradox is that both structurally and functionally local government in France is much weaker; there are some 36,000 communes, the principal unit of local government, while there are few functions which have exclusively been devolved to them. Yet, as Keating (1988) shows, the distribution of power in France is less a function of the structure and responsibilities of local authorities as it is of the relationships between different political actors, central and local. Through the cumul des mandats politicians, holding national and local political office simultaneously, help ensure that the interests of the locality are safeguarded or, at least, recognised. In effect, the centre has to bargain with territorial power-holders so that central government is in a much weaker position to unilaterally impose its will.

(b) Market place theory

The British reform represents an attempt to impose market place ideas on the operation of the local taxation system. By widening the net of ratepayers local government will need to be more responsive because of the power of the voting mechanism.

The Green Paper Paying for Local Government, laying the foundation for the poll tax reform represents a somewhat crude attempt at applying public choice theories to local finance. Public choice theorists, stimulated by Tiebout's classic paper (Tiebout, 1956), attempt to apply economic theory to democratic theory, the optimising behaviour of rational economic man will be matched by his political behaviour, voting choice and/or his choice of residential location among a mosaic of local governments being decided on the basis of economic self-interest. It is easy enough to show that the arguments are riddled with implausible or untested assumptions. Most critically it is by no means certain that economic and financial considerations are paramount to the local voter. As Midwinter and Mair (1987) illustrate in their hypothetical example of a young, unemployed non-householder assumed by the Green Paper to more likely to vote for the party advocating high-spending policies, on the grounds that (s)he is not a ratepayer, can be countered by the argument that the lower-spending party will be chosen because of the perceived effects this will have on attracting employment by reducing local taxation of businesses. In effect, both scenarios are speculative but equally plausible (or implausible!).

CONCLUSIONS

The introduction of the poll tax reform marks the singularity of the British case. Poll taxes are levied in a number of countries though these are so different by virtue of their political systems, level of economic development and social and cultural background, that meaningful comparison is at best tenuous. Further, the British reform proposals are unique in introducing a system of local finance in which the local tax option is restricted to the single measure of the poll tax, combined with a system of assigned revenues. It is also unique in being a flat rate with no income related element.

From a comparative perspective what is exceptional about the reform proposals is not only their nature but that the enabling legislation is being introduced in the face of widespread opposition. It says much of the ability of the centre to impose its will on the localities. The passage of the legislation and implementation of the reform, in England and Wales, .in particular, will also need to recognise the constraint which governments in the liberal democracies are always conscious of, the electoral cycle. Re-elected with a large, if somewhat reduced, majority the Conservative Government is anxious to implement its major manifesto commitments rapidly. Opinion polls taken shortly after the election show that voters become increasingly apprehensive about the proposals (Table 11.3). Within terms of the electoral cycle argument there is much to favour rapid introduction and implementation, from the Government's viewpoint. However, the complexities of its administrative installation, together with its regressive implications, point to the likelihood of a contentious Parliamentary scrutiny.

It is interesting to speculate whether the continued determination to implement the reform does not reflect the fact that with the British electoral system, the Conservatives are quietly confident that, unpopular as the measure may prove to be, they stand a more than even chance of being re-elected for a fourth term. (A majority of over 100 has been overturned only once since World War II). Put another way, quite apart from the other differences (of central-local relations, for instance), governments elected on PR or other 'more representative' systems, which includes the major West European democracies, could not contemplate such a reform. To do so would be to court electoral suicide.

Whatever the ideological and economic justification for reform it is clear that political factors have provided much of the stimulus for it. The singularity of the British case is not only that the fiscal crisis of the state has become translated into a crisis of the local state, but that the

201

Table 11.3: Gallup poll surveys on the community charge proposals (%)

Proposals are -	February 1986	July 1987
- good idea	45	28
- bad idea	39	54
- don't know	16	18

Under new system your household will be -	February 1986	July 1987
- better off	22	18
- worse off	33	42
- no difference	28	24
- don't know	17	16

Notes (1) Conducted among nationally represented quota samples.

Source: Daily Telegraph, July 27 1987.

distribution of power is such that the centre is able to impose reform in the face of concerted, but relatively weak, opposition.

Accepting that among the economically advanced liberal democracies the British reform proposals, both in their nature and the manner of their imposition, are exceptional, several reasons may help explain the singularity of the British case. These can be viewed as the interplay between two sets of factors, the one immediately relating to the particular ideology of the centre and the style of government, the other to more basic or underlying features, relating to the fiscal crisis of the state and the erosion of local autonomy.

Two features distinguished the emergence of the New Right as epitomised by Thatcherism; first, the virtues of the market in determining economic relations, implying a reduced role for the state and the replacement of consensual politics based on bargaining and, second, negotiation by a more confrontational style of convictional politics. Both are of critical importance in helping to explain the poll tax proposals.

The danger with interpreting Thatcherism as conviction

politics is that the reason for particular reforms being made becomes personalised. Just as it was tempting, but superficial, to argue that the abolition of the GLC was a personal attempt to extirpate Ken Livingstone, the same would apply to the current fiscal reforms. This is not to deny that for ideological as well as political reasons the Prime Minister has not invested heavily in supporting the reform proposals. Quite apart from the Tory backbench opposition the England and Wales legislation will receive once the Bill is introduced, rifts within the Cabinet have already been reported, the Scottish Secretary of State reportedly being opposed to the Community Charge in Scotland. The ability to control local expenditure more closely, though not admitted by government sources, and the extension of local accountability help explain the commitment to reform. There is certainly little or no international experience that points to the long-term viability of a local poll tax and the Government's commitment to it must be seen as an act of blind faith in its efficacy.

REFERENCES

Cmnd 9714 (1986) Paying for Local Government, HMSO, London

Jichi Sogo (1982) 'Local Public Finance in Japan', Tokyo: Jichi Sogo Centre

Keating, M. (1988) 'Local Government Reform and Finance in France', in Paddison, R. and Bailey, S.J. (eds), Local Government Finance: International Perspectives (Routledge, London)

King, D. (1988) 'Sources of Local Finance in the United States', in Paddison, R. and Bailey, S.J. (eds) Local Government Finance: International Perspectives (Routledge, London)

Midwinter, E. and Mair, C. (1987) Rates Reform (Mainstream Publishers, Edinburgh)

Newton, K. and Karran, T.J. (1985) The Politics of Local Expenditure (Macmillan, London)

O'Connor, J. (1973) The Fiscal Crisis of the State (St. Martin's Press, New York)

Tiebout, C. (1956) 'A Pure Theory of Local Expenditures', Journal of Political Economy, October

Walsh, K. (1988) 'Fiscal Crisis and Stress: Origin and

Implications', in Paddison, R. and Bailey, S.J. (eds) Local Government Finance: International Perspectives (Routledge, London)

Chapter Twelve

CONCLUSION

INTRODUCTION

The foregoing chapters have provided an in depth, multi-disciplinary analysis of the proposed reform of local government finance throughout Britain. The various authors have each examined the 1986 Green Paper proposals from a different viewpoint and so it remains for this concluding chapter to give a broad overview of their main findings, conclusions and recommendations.

The reader will undoubtedly be asking the following questions. First, is there still a need for autonomous local government in Britain or can such a geographically small country be governed from the centre? Second, is the rates issue a new problem requiring novel solutions or is it merely the latest eruption of a long-lived but muted controversy? Third, is a large part of the current problem simply due to the fact that local government has become too politicised, itself seeking confrontation with central government? Fourth, what are the legal safeguards and restraints pertaining to both central and local government, in other words who, if anyone, is breaking the rules? Fifth, is the 1986 Green Paper's analysis of the local government finance problem lucid and coherent or is it inconsistent and self-contradictory? Sixth, what were the views of the independent assessors, appointed by the Department of the Environment, and in particular did they all agree with the Green Paper's policy recommendations? Seventh, how will the abolition of the tax on domestic properties affect local housing markets? Eighth, will the new system of grants be better or fairer than the system so replaced? Ninth, do non-domestic rates really cause problems for industry and commerce and, if so, do the proposed reforms ameliorate them? Tenth, does central government really need to control local government spending under both the new system and its predecessor? Eleventh, have other countries used a poll tax or community charge and if so with what success?

Each of these questions has been addressed by the chapters in sequential order and the main findings are summarised below.

1. DOES MODERN BRITAIN STILL NEED LOCAL GOVERNMENT?

Ken Young's answer is an emphatic 'yes'. The case for local government (as distinct from local administration) rests on pluralism, participation and public choice. He notes that whilst no political party believes that the time for local government is past, nonetheless the cumulative impact of various recent measures is to change the nature of the polity. Those measures are based on the mistaken premise that the main function of local government is to provide services. Ken argues that 'local government is first of all a political institution and a vital part of the framework of democracy in Britain' (p. 8).

2. WHAT IS THE HISTORY OF THE RATES ISSUE?

Peter Richards' chapter reveals that the local property tax has long been vilified because of its high visibility. Its survival over the last 150 years or so has been largely due to its flexibility and the desire of past governments to follow the easier course of tinkering with partial derating rather than introducing more fundamental reforms. Furthermore, alternatives to the local property tax have themselves been seen as too problematic so that rates have generally been regarded as the lesser of several evils. Peter is sceptical of the efficacy of the community charge in this respect and notes the historical tendency towards increased dependence on grants from central government, a tradition that the new system will follow. 'Meanwhile the scale of local services and how they should be paid for will remain a fertile source for argument' (p. 40)

3. IS LOCAL GOVERNMENT TOO POLITICAL?

John Berridge takes a wider view of 'politicisation' than simply a 'party politics' perspective, noting that besides politicisation of party groups there can also be politicisation of issues or of institutions. The main causes of increased politicisation over the last several decades include the more effective organisation of local party groups, increased media coverage of local elections, the infiltration of extremist groups at national and local level, the emergence of high profile, controversial local politicians and attempts at increased control by central government over local authorities. Hence 'there are a number of different factors involved in the politicisation process, and ... to limit the analysis to partisan or party politicisation is not necessarily the most important, nor indeed the most fruitful approach' (p. 57).

4. WHAT ARE THE LEGAL SAFEGUARDS FOR LOCAL GOVERNMENT?

Christopher Himsworth seeks a legal basis for local government autonomy either directly within the realms of international law and/or constitutional law (or convention) or indirectly through legal limitations upon intervention by central government in local government affairs. Britain has refused to adhere to the 1985 European Charter for Local Self-Government; nor has it a written constitution, nor even constitutional convention, through which local autonomy could possibly be guaranteed. Hence the only degree of freedom retained by local government is achieved indirectly through the time taken for Ministers to push through Parliament the legislation necessary to give them more control. 'Governments have it within their legal power to give considerable spending freedom to local authorities but they also have the power, through their control of Parliament, to restrict that freedom. The concept of autonomy seems to be quickly emptied of meaning' (p. 67-8).

5. IS THE 1986 GREEN PAPER'S ANALYSIS VALID?

Clive Martlew and Steve Bailey begin by accepting the need for improved local accountability and pose the question as to whether or not the proposed reform will actually increase accountability as distinct from forcing expenditure reductions. They note that after reform, the increased reliance on both grants and revenues assigned from 'nationalised' non-domestic rates will hardly promote accountability. The same conclusion pertains to the community charge since non-householders (e.g. wives and adult offspring living at home) are aware of rate bills and the poll tax will be difficult to enforce. More generally the Green Paper ignores accountability at the service output (rather than tax input) stage and makes misleadingly poor use of its own data. 'Whilst agreeing with the foreword that 'local electors (should) know what the costs of their services are' and that 'effective local accountability must be the cornerstone of successful local government', the proposed reforms achieve neither precondition' (p. 89).

6. DID THE INDEPENDENT ASSESSORS AGREE WITH THE GREEN PAPER'S CONCLUSIONS?

Tom Wilson argues that financial self-sufficiency does not guarantee accountability. He welcomes the introduction of a neutral grant system whereby grant is fixed irrespective of local expenditure levels. Tom advocates a system where local authorities can vary their expenditure at the margin in accordance with local preferences but questions the adequacy of the community charge as the sole source of revenue at the margin. In particular he criticises this poll tax as anti-libertarian, being blatantly regressive and therefore resented, inappropriate for the financing of services with community-wide benefits, and erecting too forbidding a barrier against marginal increases in spending to the denial of local preferences. Hence the community charge would be a stepping stone to a local income tax which has its own defects and is not clearly preferable to the rating system. 'There seems no escape from the conclusions that another attempt will have to be made to review these issues and to make fresh recommendations' (p. 107).

7. HOW WILL THE REFORM AFFECT HOUSE PRICES?

Gordon Hughes notes that the crucial feature of the

reformed system will be the replacement of a substantial specific tax on housing (i.e. rates) by a lump sum tax on incomes (i.e. the community charge). This can be expected to generate large price and income effects which could provide the basis for a classic speculative bubble in house prices. This is more likely if there is a switch from renting to owner-occupation, an increase in household formation rates, and because more affluent urban areas will gain at the expense of poorer and rural areas. There will be a large increase in the potential demand for owner-occupied housing and the effect on house prices will depend jointly on the flexibility of local authorities in granting planning permission together with the response of the house building industry. The 1986 Green Paper predicted an average price rise of no more than 5% due to the reform of domestic rates. However, 'my calculations imply an overall price increase for England of three times that quoted in the Green Paper' (p. 119).

8. WILL THE NEW GRANT SYSTEM BE A BETTER ONE?

David King's analysis reveals that, whilst the new system is simpler, in some respects it is not as satisfactory as the one it will replace. In particular because community charge payers will have to fund 100% of any increase in spending which may also benefit industry and commerce, then efficiency will be impaired. Local domestic taxpayers will undervalue the total community-wide benefits of increased service provision and so there will be underprovision of services. Moreover, to the extent that there are differences between authorities in the composition of their populations, then the community charge cost of increased service provision will vary. This arises because only adult residents pay the community charge, so that authorities with relatively high proportions of children in total population will have relatively low taxable resources (i.e. adults). This will increase the community charge cost of higher expenditure levels relative to other authorities. Together with the effective conversion of non-domestic rates into a grant 'the Green Paper proposals are likely to lead to more central control of local authorities. In turn, it is likely that local spending patterns will converge more ... (and) ... these conclusions raise the question of whether there will be any point in continuing to have a system of local government at all' (p. 149).

9. HAVE LOCAL BUSINESSES BEEN OVER-TAXED BY LOCAL AUTHORITIES?

Bob Bennett's review of the evidence leads to the conclusion that rate burdens are fairly small cost items for business in general. Nonetheless, they do bear more heavily on commerce and are especially variable between localities, a variability which has increased markedly over the last decade. The result is unpredictable distortions between sectors, locations and assets which can only be revealed by local empirical studies rather than by aggregate statistical generalisations. The problems of the variability of local rate burdens can be tackled by more specific means than the outright 'nationalisation' of a uniform business rate under central government control. All central government has to do is to prevent the exploitation of business 'locationally trapped' in high spending local authorities. This could be achieved simply by rate capping but, in addition, non-domestic rates could be reformed (with rolling revaluations, ending of selective derating and relating rates to profits) and the proceeds used to promote local economic development. The main criticism of the uniform business rate 'is that it totally undermines any link of local authority and local business' (p. 152) and 'there is no reason to sacrifice the autonomy of the whole local financial system because of a very concentrated problem' (p. 162).

10. IS THERE A NEED FOR CENTRAL CONTROL OF LOCAL SPENDING?

Richard Jackman believes there is no such need for central control on purely economic grounds under either a Keynesian or a Monetarist perspective. The expansionary effects of increased local current spending on the real economy or on the money supply will be counterbalanced by the contradictory effect of higher local taxes. Similarly, the economic impact of increased capital expenditure is only important in so far as it is financed from borrowing rather than by taxation, asset sales or user charges. The only 'problem' of local government expenditure is that it has tended to be greater than the level deemed sufficient by central government. This is a political rather than strictly economic issue. If local domestic tax payers are willing to fund 100% of increased spending through the community charge under the new system, then there are no grounds for continued central control nor even for including local spending with the definition of public expenditure. Hence Richard recommends treating local government spending like that by nationalised industries where only central government subventions (rather than gross expenditure) are included within public expenditure totals and where there are limits only on external borrowing. 'It is disappointing that the Green Paper does not have the courage of its convictions in proposing a dismantling of controls to accompany the new financial regime' (p. 187).

11. DO OTHER COUNTRIES HAVE A POLL TAX?

Ronan Paddison finds use of local poll taxes in Japan and Tanzania. In both cases, however, the tax is at least partially graduated according to the income of the taxpayer with exemptions for low income groups in Japan. In both cases, therefore, the local poll tax is a form of crude local income tax. Nor are they the sole local tax in contrast to the British proposals. In other countries (e.g. Australia) a local poll tax has been considered and rejected, again usually only as a supplementary source of income in addition to the local property tax. Indeed in the United States of America, reduced intergovernmental funding has resulted in a wider (rather than narrower) local tax base. The different reactions of other countries to 'local fiscal crisis' reflects their differing political cultures (e.g. decentralist in the USA and politically interrelated in France). Poll taxes are generally regarded as regressive, administratively cumbersome and anachronistic. 'There is little or no international experience that points to the long-term viability of a local poll tax and the Government's commitment to it must be seen as an act of blind faith in its efficacy' (p. 203).

ONGOING DEVELOPMENTS

During the time this book of readings was being assembled, various developments have occurred, none of which affect the validity or relevance of the foregoing analyses but which should be noted for the sake of completeness.

The Abolition of Domestic Rates Etc. (Scotland) Act 1987 received Royal assent at the end of May and a similar poll tax bill was published for England and Wales in December, 1987. The plan is now to introduce the community charge in a single year. This will be 1989 for Scotland and 1990 for England and Wales. Various proposals for a phased introduction of the reforms (seen as necessary to cushion the impact of the changeover) have been abandoned, largely at the request of local authorities themselves. However, safety nets will be applied at the local authority level to avoid excessive changes in grant and assigned revenue entitlements during the first four years of the new system.

The imminence of the changeover for Scotland has emphasised the practical problems in assembling a community charge register. Besides the electoral and valuation rolls, other possible sources of information now being examined include the register of births and deaths, records of education authorities, of health boards, of national utilities such as gas, electricity and telephone companies, local newspapers, estate agent transactions, private trade organisations, as well as local authorities' own records on library memberships, concessionary bus fares, etc. This is no mean task! Each person will have a personal identifier, similar to that for driving licences, and which will effectively become a national identity system held on a local authority basis. There are obvious implications both for civil liberties and the scale of bureaucracy required to administer such a system. Furthermore, it has been claimed that the Government has made no allowance for evasion (RVA, 1987).

Abolition of domestic rates causes problems for English and Welsh water authorities. They could hardly continue to charge for water on the basis of the rateable value of properties and nation-wide water metering is unlikely before the turn of the century. Hence, in the meantime, some transitional arrangement will be required in the form of either a flat-rate charge on each household (administratively expensive and having many of the same problems as domestic rates) or a poll tax to charge all adults for water consumption. A water poll tax would be easy to collect if local authorities acted as collecting agents and collected it along with the community charge. However, it would increase the average poll tax bill by about a third in England and Wales. Scottish local authorities remain responsible for water and hence this is not a problem for them.

Other problems include the administration of rebates. Rent and rate rebates, administered through Housing Benefit, are compatible systems since both are property-based. The new community charge will be people-based and it will be difficult to operate both systems (rent and community charge rebates) together. Furthermore, doubt has been cast on plans to make the poor and unemployed pay their 20 per cent (annual average) share of the community charge by increasing their welfare benefits. The problem is that claimants will probably not save the extra (weekly) benefit to pay the (monthly) community charge, leading to politically embarrassing court cases, seizure of claimants' furniture and other possessions and even their imprisonment. Hence it is likely that the Department of Health and Social Security will have to adopt a system similar to the present one where rates are paid direct from the DHSS to local authorities. The DHSS does not relish the extra administrative burden and cost of the many more new local tax payers.

All these practical problems may be worth bearing if the community charge achieved the Government objectives of increased accountability. For this to be the case, annual changes in the community charge must vary in line with marginal changes in an individual local authority's expenditure. However, if the new system was currently in force, 'there would not have been one authority out of the 426 in England where the difference between the community charge per adult in 1986-87 and 1987-88 would have matched exactly the change in spending per adult' (Hale, 1987, p. 12). These results do not include the distorting effects of safety nets (which limit the extent of annual change) or of transitional arrangements. They reflect the inevitable and obvious fact that changes in an authority's community charge reflect not just changes in its spending but also changes in its receipt of central government grants and in assigned revenues. Grant receipts will vary due to changes in the adult population of both the individual authority and of all English authorities, changes in the authority's centrally addressed need to spend relative to all other authorities, and changes in the national totals of the standard grant, needs grants and unified business rate pool.

These results cast strong doubts on the 'increased local accountability' justification for the community charge. Furthermore, other research (Gibson, 1987; Harvey 1987) reveals that there will be such marked changes in the local tax burden (community charge versus rates) that the 'unacceptable' redistribution caused by the 1985 Scottish revaluation pales into insignificance. Ongoing changes in local tax bills from year to year as grants, expenditure levels, safety nets and transitional arrangements vary could be similarly disruptive. Furthermore, the distribution of the Uniform Business Rate (UBR) on a per capita basis will sharply increase the differences in local tax bills between authorities simply because the local discretionary tax base will be halved (IFS, 1987).

Not surprisingly, therefore, the Government has now proposed 'community charge capping' which will replace rate capping and act as a check on excessive demands on local taxpayers. Under this scheme the Government will be able to intervene during the financial year to require individual local authorities to reduce their community charge and/or impose conditions on the authority's expenditure or financial management. This will give the Government even more control than it has at present and directly contradicts the idea of increased local accountability. 'The notion that central governments can make judgements about local 'overspending' sits very uneasily with the rationale for decentralising redistributive functions to local government in the first place' (Helm and Smith, 1987, p. xix).

Similar disruptions in tax burdens for businesses will be caused by the combined effects of the 1990 revaluation and the UBR. Increases in the UBR will be limited to the rate of inflation and it is also intended to set a ceiling on the increase in businesses' rateable values resulting from the revaluation. This will phase in the effects of the changing tax base between revaluation years. It is seen as necessary for England and Wales given that the last revaluation was in 1973. However, notwithstanding these arrangements, a survey of the 10,000 members of the Forum of Private Business in September 1987 revealed that they would prefer a local business income tax as their first choice followed by a retention of the present system as their second choice. In 1981 42 per cent of members preferred a local income tax whilst now 64 per cent favour it. Only 5 per cent now favour the new uniform business rate system, undoubtedly because of the potentially large shift in tax burden upon its implementation and also the fact that it is not related to profits.

Whatever the transitional arrangements and modified detail 'the costs of adjustment will be large (and) it will be some years yet before the local expenditure system is easily explicable' (Livesey, 1987, p. 59).

RESEARCH POSSIBILITIES

Implementation of the new system will generate a large number of research possibilities and this section lists only a few of them. Political scientists will presumably be interested in researching the political processes underlying the passage of the poll tax legislation, the effects of pressure groups, the electoral implications, whether the new system does in fact prove to be more centralist or decentralist and so on. Public administrators will be interested in the practicalities of compiling the community charge register, its enforceability, the 'opting-out' effects on the electoral register, implications for the Data Protection Act, etc. The register itself will provide an invaluable information base of use to demographic researchers (Bailey, 1988a). Economists and economic geographers will be interested in monitoring the financial and geographical impacts on business and on household incomes caused by the local tax change. There will also be general interest in the operation of community charge capping (and in its legality), the impact of the new arrangements on types and classes of authority, as well as in the long-term implications for the viability of local government. The research possibilities on a single or multi-disciplinary basis are immense.

It is also possible to develop the premise in the Green Paper that user charges are a more direct way of improving local accountability. In 1976 the Layfield report had noted the implications of increased use of charges in terms of requiring a substantial redistribution of income and a radical change in the role of local authorities. Nonetheless, it may be possible to have a more gradual transition to increased use of charges for those services directed specifically at individuals or groups and where service standards are in excess of those provided for the community as a whole. However, 'there is a danger that the current emphasis on costs to the exclusion of benefits (since output is difficult to measure) will seriously undervalue local authority services. A 'hit or miss' approach to charging is inadequate (and) will be neither realistic nor effective' (Bailey, 1986, p. 418).

The dearth of experience with local government service charges in Britain necessitates looking further afield at experience in other countries. A recent study (Bailey, 1988b) examines innovative user charges levied by Canadian local governments. It finds much greater practical scope for charging than is generally recognised, without having serious adverse consequences for efficiency and equity.

AN OVERVIEW

Where relevant, each contributor to this book has expressed strong reservations about the policy recommendations put forward in the 1986 Green Paper. Whilst there is general agreement that the local government finance system has been in need of reform for some time now and, further, that the deficiencies identified by the Green Paper are valid criticisms, nonetheless the supposed 'solution' is unlikely to be a permanent one.

The various authors criticise the reform as being too narrowly focused on service delivery and financial matters to the exclusion of the political and democratic functions of local government. The simplified new grant system receives broad approval in that it provides the stability in intergovernmental transfers that has long been lacking and yet is necessary for efficient planning of local services. However, such benefits appear to be more than offset by the other reforms. The community charge is universally condemned as both inequitable and insufficient to fund discretionary expenditure. The standardisation of non-domestic rates is universally criticised as effectively taking a local tax away from local government and severing the link between local authorities and business.

The reader is left to question both whether such a radical reform is really necessary and whether it really will guarantee autonomy for local government. The reform has been described as 'overkill' elsewhere in this book and it certainly represents a radical change from the more pragmatic but limited reforms in the past. It is not self-evident that domestic rates must necessarily be abolished rather than being reformed and supplemented by one or more other local taxes. Certainly there is experience in other countries of fairly successful limited reform of this nature but none of sole reliance on a local poll tax.

Even accepting such a radical reform there appears little chance of reduced central government intervention, notwithstanding any radical improvements of local accountability. Local government has few if any legal safeguards concerning its autonomy. The increased politicisation of the central-local interface and the continuing belief by central government of the need to control public expenditure, offers little prospect for local authorities to be masters in their own house. Indeed other administrative measures are specifically designed to reduce local government responsibilities, including abolition of the Metropolitan Counties and the Greater London Council, the growth of non-elected bodies responsible for service delivery or urban development, the reduced powers of education authorities in technical or vocational training and in the running of schools, the privatisation of public sector housing management, of library services and so on.

Some of these measures have been implemented whilst others are only at the proposal stage. There may indeed be merits to these measures. The point to be made is that in combination with each other as well as with the reformed local government finance system they do serve to significantly reduce local autonomy and the prospects are for that reduction to continue indefinitely. The real policy question is one of the balance between local freedom and central control and that has not been resolved by the 1986 Green Paper.

Perhaps it would be naive to expect that question of balance to be resolved once-for-all. Earlier Labour and Conservative governments also failed to address that question, even after it was so strongly posed by the 1976 Layfield Report (Cmnd 6453). The choice outlined by that report was between a centralist and a localist solution. Continuing along the middle way was seen as leading ultimately to centralisation by default. The current reforms continue that pattern. To that extent they may almost be regarded as excusable.

If so, the attention refocuses on the community charge as the only radical change from that long lived process of centralisation. Will the poll tax work? The lesson of history is that it won't. The last attempt at introducing a poll tax in Britain took place in 1641. Even with some allowances for income and wealth it was only short lived because it raised relatively little revenue. 'The House of Commons had succeeded in raising a poll tax without raising a rebellion, but only at the price of turning the tax into a fiscal damp squib' (Russell, 1987, p. 11). Will history repeat itself?

REFERENCES

Bailey, S.J. (1986) Paying for Local Government: Charging for Services, Public Administration Vol. 64 no. 4 Winter pp. 401-19

------ (1988a) Information Requirements of the Community Charge BURISA Newsletter No. 83 April, pp. 10-13 British Urban and Regional Information Systems Association

------ (1988b) Practical Charging Policies for Local Government, Public Finance Foundation, London

Cmnd 6453 (1976) Local Governmnt Finance: Report of the Committee of Enquiry (Chairman Frank Layfield) HMSO

Gibson, J. (1987) The Poll Tax: Its Impact on the Residents of Durham INLOGOV Birmingham and County Hall Durham

Hale, R. (1987) Plotting the Poll Tax Public Finance and Accountancy 4 September pp. 12-13

Harvey, R. (1987) The Effect of the Poll Tax in Lewisham Public Finance and Accountancy 31 July pp. 15-16

Helm, D. and Smith, S. (1987) The Assessment: Decentralisation and the Economics of Local Government Oxford Review of Economic Policy Vol. 3 no. 2 Summer pp. i-xxi

IFS (1987) Local Taxes and Local Government Institute for Fiscal Studies London

Livesey, D.A. (1987) Central Control of Local Authority Expenditure Oxford Review of Economic Policy Vol. 3 no. 2 Summer pp. 44-59

Russell, C. (1987) England's Last Poll Tax History Today Vol. 37 October pp. 9-11

RVA (1987) Community Charge/Poll Tax: The Facts Rating and Valuation Association London

INDEX

CONTENTS OF COMPANION VOLUME, LOCAL GOVERNMENT FINANCE: INTERNATIONAL PERSPECTIVES, EDITED BY RONAN PADDISON AND STEPHEN BAILEY